A SILENT NIGHTMARE

The bottom line and the challenge of illicit drugs.

Sergio Ferragut

Photograph on back cover by Lourdes Maria Ferragut.

TABLE OF CONTENTS

"Prohibition goes beyond the bounds of reason in that it attempts to control a man's appetite by legislation and makes crimes out of things that are not crimes. A prohibition law strikes a blow at the very principles upon which our government was founded."

President Abraham Lincoln

Dedicated to my wife Marta and our children

Lourdes María,

Mónica,

José,

Sergio Jr.,

Karena,

Xavier, and

Montserrat

for their greater than life support.

AUTHOR'S NOTES AND ACKNOWLEDGEMENTS

"Drug books don't sell". Those were the words of Andrés Oppenheimer as we sat down over a cup of coffee at the Miami Herald's cafeteria and flipped through the pages of the first draft of A SILENT NIGHTMARE in early 2006. To his initial comment, he added some specific observations about the use of certain terminology and other valuable recommendations. It was a close encounter with the reality of writing and publishing. This brief interaction made a major contribution to how I proceeded with the project and for this I am extremely grateful to Andrés. My project was not about selling books though; it was more about delivering a message – in my opinion, an urgently needed one. Of course, the more books sold, the better the message gets around. After months of unsuccessfully looking for a literary agent to represent me and promote the book with publishers, I chose to go the self-publishing route. And, this is how I came to meet Lulu.com and how this first edition of A SILENT NIGHTMARE saw the light.

It was not easy to take time off from my management career to complete the research and write A SILENT NIGHTMARE, it involved stepping into completely new territory and facing unsuspected and formidable obstacles. Nevertheless, I was convinced the issue of illicit drugs was important enough for me to take a sabbatical to complete the research and write the book. Why me? Many friends have asked the question and there is no simple answer, I just had to do it. After many years of observing the ills brought about by drug trafficking, I could not comprehend why the authorities in the United States and other countries could not come up with an effective solution. Along the way, I came across the children of my friends, and the friends of my children falling under the clutches of drug addiction. As I got started on the project, I pulled together a conceptual framework with the different elements, which from my perspective, have helped to sustain the drug problem in America and all over the world.

The support of my wife Marta and our children made the book possible to begin with; Marta became the first reader and critic of the early work as chapter after chapter came into being. As the first full manuscript saw the light, many friends volunteered to read it and provided very valuable feedback, to all of them goes my gratitude. A formidable review work was done by Magdalena Llach, Mari Carmen Mariscal, and Jorge León, their specific feedback contributed greatly to the focusing of the book and the resulting end product. Of course, any remaining flaws are totally my responsibility. Not being a proficient MS-Office user, the support received from my son Sergio made it possible to translate ideas into a practical Word document as a prelude to publishing, many thanks to him also.

My gratitude also goes to the many authors and editorial houses that authorized the quoting of their work. Their previous research and publications contributed to the enrichment of A SILENT NIGHTMARE. It is my hope that adding this book to the many voices that have called for a change of paradigm on the issue of illicit drugs would contribute to finding a new path leading towards a more rational, coherent and humane drug policy. The issue of illicit drugs is not privy to the United States; it is a worldwide issue of concern to all countries. However, the current drug prohibition paradigm has been driven by the United States government since the beginning of the 20th century, and it is the U.S. government which is called upon to drive a new drug paradigm; perhaps one focusing on achieving a lesser evil rather than striving for an impossible dream. Many distinguished personalities, including the late Milton Friedman, Economics Nobel Prize winner, William F. Buckley, Jr., founder of the National Review, and Walter Cronkite, award-winning Journalist, have raised their voices calling for an overhaul of the current failed drug policy. Though not pretending to be in their league, I – a father of seven and a grandfather of many more children – add, through A SILENT NIGHT-

MARE, my humble contribution to this overdue need for a new direction in America's drug policy.

Sergio Ferragut
Reston, Virginia

PROLOGUE

With no victory in sight, plenty of collateral damage is the center-piece of the war on drugs after more than thirty years. At the dawn of the 21st century, illicit drugs touch, in different ways, a broad and diverse group of people in America. Occasional drug users, drug addicts, their parents and relatives, law enforcement agents, and government officials in all branches of government are touched by illicit drugs. This book focuses primarily on the problem of illicit drugs in the United States — though the problem extends far beyond its borders — and searches for an explanation to the persistent presence of drugs on the streets of U.S. cities. The supporting research includes published documents, books, and papers dealing with the subject matter. All this material proved invaluable in putting together a framework to cast light upon the issues. Nevertheless, not all relevant subjects are covered in print, and much of what is in print, though useful to the overall research effort, has limited forensic value. Hence, this work includes the author's empirical observations spanning more than thirty years. These observations reflect the author's involvement with Latin American banking, retailing, and information technology businesses. The observations, in conjunction with the research and an all-encompassing and integrated methodology, lead to a socio-economic-political framework; this framework incorporates drug relevant issues and how they drive and/or sustain the illicit-drug problem. The exposition explores new policy options for the current drug policy and presents a blueprint for a viable policy proposal under a different paradigm.

American children and young adults are a juicy target for those who make a living out of selling illicit drugs; their parents worry as drugs can have a devastating effect upon all of them. Law enforcement agents have always been, and continue to be, at the forefront of the struggle against the drug-trafficking organizations (DTOs). They have been given the charter to enforce the law and, overlooking the exceptions, have done a reasonable job under difficult circumstances. The DTOs have for many decades managed to build fortunes by selling illicit drugs on the streets of American cities. The plight of the occasional drug user trapped in U.S.

1

prisons by the implementation of extreme mandatory jail sentences, adds to the suffering of the drug addict, as the relatives of both stand by helplessly; all deserve a better chance to break away from their predicament. Government officials need to be better equipped to effectively address the demands of their jobs as they face the challenge posed by illicit drugs; they must be equipped with a viable drug policy, together with legislation and regulations which are enforceable.

As the reader steps into this exploratory journey, the multiplicity of drug-related challenges confronting society becomes evident. First and foremost, the nature of the problem and its different components is pinpointed. The proper definition of the problem is crucial before daring to put together a solution. If there is no widespread agreement on the existence and nature of the problem, there is no need to find a solution to it, for all practical purposes the problem goes unnoticed and unattended. If all the components of a problem are not recognized, only those that are accepted as being part of the problem will be addressed. Therefore, there is a need to identify the key issues behind the illicit-drug problem and figure out how they relate to each other. Looking at the complete drug picture provides a better vantage point; it helps to understand the interrelationship of the issues and to design a policy that will effectively address all of them as a unit. Each individual issue also improves its chances of finding a better solution.

What are the main issues surrounding illicit drugs? A systemic approach yields four fundamental issues: the use and abuse of illicit drugs, the illicit-drug trade, the war on drugs, and the laundering of drug money. These four categories are not isolated; they are intertwined and feed on each other. Throughout this presentation, relevant facts and the supporting arguments are brought out into the open. Also, a problem lasting for so many years, like illicit drugs, has given rise to many myths, and those need to be uncovered and resolved. In the end, to develop a new and viable policy, it is crucial to get to the bottom line. Identifying the bottom line involves figuring out what is truly relevant and at the kernel of the overall drug problem; it requires separating fact from fiction and focusing on root causes while putting aside apparent causes which are in fact just symptoms. History, as usual, stores significant lessons for those with a disposition to learn; a journey of discovery into the alcohol prohibition and repeal experience of the early 20th century yields invaluable lessons. Finally, the journey probes drug policy options and spells out the implications associated with each one of them.

Our primary focus is on the issue of drugs in the United States, but the world today is a global village. Even if desired, our neighbors cannot be ignored. There are international treaties covering illicit drugs on a worldwide scale, those cannot be pushed aside while only searching for an American solution. On the subject of illicit drugs, the world is the turf where the contest is taking place, it is not exclusively an American issue, and it involves many countries in places as far away as Afghanistan in Asia, or closer like Mexico and Colombia in Latin America. So, a unifying and well-articulated approach is called for to properly identify the issues and place them in the right perspective; it must be a global perspective. Throughout this process, potential solutions are unveiled, solutions which would otherwise stay away from the spotlight or be blurred by slanted points of view.

The exploration of the issues associated with **the use and abuse of drugs, the illicit-drug trade, the war on drugs, and the laundering of drug money**, including their inter-relationships, delivers **the bottom line** of the illicit-drug problem. To uncover the real bottom line of illicit drugs this presentation sifts through the maze of data to separate the root causes from secondary or symptomatic events, and introduces the concept of the lesser evil as a reasonable path to arrive at viable solutions. Thus, the bottom line highlights the facts as they are, unmasks the myths, and pinpoints the root causes of the illicit-drug problem. This presentation also explores **the lessons of history**; what is there in the not so distant past that may lead to a better understanding and a comprehensive solution to the drug problem? There are similarities between the criminalization of drugs today and the alcohol prohibition of the early 20th century in the U.S. There are also lessons in the expansion of opium use and addiction

3

during the 18th, 19th, and early 20th centuries under the auspices of the co-lonial powers of the time. This historical research contributes to the assessment of potential solutions to the drug problems of the 21st century. Society must make up its mind as to how best to solve the illicit-drug plague hanging over it. Do we require a zero tolerance approach? Would it be better to go along the path of consumption tolerance? What about laissez faire legalization? Or, is legalization and control a more effective path to follow? This presentation explores the four options and weighs the pros and cons of each one; they are the basic components of the **potential policy spectrum**.

The primary objective of this presentation is not to tell a new story, it is rather to place many stories in context, to apply a systemic analytical methodology to the issues involved and, with an all-encompassing perspective, deliver a blueprint for a viable policy proposal. America has been immersed in the struggle against illicit drugs for decades, but drug use and addiction continue to weigh heavily on the shoulders of our youth, crime associated with illicit drugs has increased dramatically, and the drug traffickers and their friends in the business world continue to grow richer. This partnership possesses ever-increasing economic power, and with such power it is exerting political pressure and gaining positions in legitimate U.S. businesses and in U.S. friendly countries, some of these countries and U.S. businesses are strategic for the security of the United States. Consequently, a new innovative drug policy is called for if America aspires to become a safer society, freer from drugs, in an environment respectful of its citizens' personal freedoms and civil liberties. Ultimately, little will happen without the active involvement of American parents. This presentation is for them, it is an undertaking that uncovers the drug facts — the myths, the root causes, and the many drug-related events — and brings them together with a unifying perspective to deliver the urgently needed hope that much can be achieved with a radically different drug policy under a new paradigm of legalization and control.

1

DRUG USE AND ABUSE

Less than 7.5 million Americans of the 110 million who have used drugs at least once during their lifetime were classified as abusers or drug dependent according to the 2004 National Survey on Drug Use and Health.

1.1 Drugs in the 21st Century

Drug use and abuse is a fact of life in the 21st century in America and in most countries around the world — this is certainly no reason for rejoicing. The sight of a person in the clutches of drugs is not a pretty one. A lot has been written on the subject of illicit drugs. Some material recounts real-life stories which demonstrate whatever progress, or lack of, the author believes is being made in the struggle against drugs. Some is written by dedicated law enforcement agents, immersed in the fight against drug traffickers, making the case for more severe measures and bigger budgets to combat drug crimes; some others may show the frustration of a mother who blames questionable law enforcement practices for the entrapment of her son. They all make valid points, though they do not seem to provide enough elements to point towards an effective solution to the drug problem. Unfortunately, the policy in effect for over three decades — under the paradigm of drug prohibition — has not kept drugs away from the reach of American children. Behind this grim reality lies the fact that the current drug policy has failed to look at all the facets of the drug problem with an integrated perspective. An integral and systemic analysis of the multiple drug-related issues has been lacking; hence, an absence of better proposals on how to address those issues. Society needs to make choices — some of them difficult — in order to minimize the overall threat to young people and to the safety of the community.

This chapter delves into the nature of illicit and licit drugs, what are they, what are the known facts, and what is the impact drugs have on human health? The subject of drug addiction is explored, what is known about it and what can be done and is being done to fight it from the corrective and preventive perspective. The treatment programs available and their success indicators are reviewed; the collateral damage inflicted on society by the use of illicit drugs are placed on the table for the reader to reflect upon. The understanding of the basic facts on drug use and abuse is one crucial element for comprehending the overall drug problem.

1.2 The Illicit-Drug Background

The United Nations [1] classifies illicit drugs into five groups, they are: opiates (heroin), cocaine, cannabis (marijuana), ecstasy, and amphetamine-type stimulants (ATS) other than ecstasy. These, or some sort of variation included within one of these categories, are the primary illicit drugs on the market today. This exposition relies on the technical definitions and assessments for each one of these drugs provided by the National Institute on Drug Abuse (NIDA), a dependency of the National Institutes of Health (NIH), which is part of the U.S. Department of Health and Human Services. The sources of information have been primarily NIDA's Research Report Series and NIDA's Info Facts publications. [2]

Heroin is classified as an illicit and highly addictive drug. It is considered the most rapidly acting of all opiates. Heroin is processed from morphine, a naturally occurring substance extracted from the seed-pod of certain varieties of poppy plants. Typically, it is sold as a white or brownish powder or as the black sticky substance known on the streets as "black tar heroin." Although purer heroin is becoming more common, most street heroin is "cut" with other drugs or with substances such as sugar, starch, powdered milk, or quinine. Because heroin abusers do not know the actual strength of the drug or its true contents, they are at serious risk of overdose or death. Heroin also poses special problems because of the transmission of HIV and other diseases that can occur from sharing needles or other injection equipment. The lack of quality control through a proper inspection process makes this and other illicit drugs more dangerous than if they were subject to adequate quality certification, as is the case with alcoholic beverages. Thus, the criminalization of heroin use introduces additional risks over and above those inherent to the drug itself.

NIDA researchers have confirmed that the three forms of heroin administration; smoking, sniffing, and intravenous injection are addictive. Injection continues to be the predominant method of heroin use among addicted use patterns. Sniffing/snorting heroin is now the most widely reported means of taking heroin among users admitted for drug treatment in a number of U.S. cities. With the shift in heroin abuse patterns comes an even more diverse group of users. The increase continues in new young users who, across the country, are being lured by inexpensive, high-purity heroin that can be sniffed or smoked instead of injected. Heroin has also been appearing in more affluent communities.

Mental function is clouded by heroin's effect on the central nervous system. Cardiac function slows. Breathing is also severely slowed, sometimes to the point of death. Heroin overdose is a particular risk on the street, where the amount and purity of the drug cannot be accurately known, there is no real quality control over the street product. One of the most detrimental long-term effects of heroin is addiction itself. Sharing of injection equipment or fluids can lead to some of the most severe consequences of heroin abuse infections with hepatitis B and C, HIV, and a host of other blood-borne viruses, which drug abusers can then pass on to their sexual partners and children. Injection drug use has been a factor in an estimated one-third of all HIV and more than half of all hepatitis C cases in the U.S. NIDA-funded research has found that drug abusers can change the behavior that put them at risk for contracting HIV through drug abuse treatment, prevention, and community-based outreach programs. They can eliminate drug use, drug-related risk behavior such as needle sharing, unsafe sexual practices and, in turn, the risk of exposure to HIV/AIDS and other infectious diseases. Drug abuse prevention and treatment are highly effective in preventing the spread of HIV.

Cocaine is an addictive stimulant that directly affects the brain. Cocaine became very popular during the 1980s and 1990s. However, it is not a new drug. In fact, it is one of the oldest drugs known to man. The pure chemical, cocaine hydrochloride, has been an abused substance for more than a hundred years, and coca leaves, the source of cocaine, have been ingested for thousands of years. It is an accepted and licit practice in Andean countries like Bolivia and Peru to consume coca leaf tea to effectively combat the ill effects of high Andean altitude. Pure cocaine was first extracted from the leaf of the coca bush, which grew primarily in Peru and Bolivia, in the mid-19th century. In the early 1900s, it became the main stimulant drug used in most of the tonics that were developed to treat a wide variety of illnesses. There are basically two chemical forms of cocaine: the hydrochloride salt and the "freebase." The hydrochloride salt, or powdered form of cocaine, dissolves in water and, when abused, can be taken intravenously or intranasally. Freebase refers to a compound that has not been neutralized by an acid to make the hydrochloride salt.

Crack is the street name given to a freebase form of cocaine that has been processed from the powdered cocaine hydrochloride form to a smokable substance. The term "crack" refers to the crackling sound heard when the mixture is smoked. Because crack is smoked, the user experiences a high in less than ten seconds. This rather immediate and euphoric effect is one of the reasons that crack became enormously popular in the mid 1980s. Another reason is that crack is inexpensive both to produce and to buy. Crack cocaine has been reported to be a serious problem in the United States since 2001. As is the case with heroin, drug traffickers do not show much concern for the safety of their customers; hence, the quality of the product, which goes through the cutting process incorporating additional substances, is never guaranteed. Such lack of quality is often the cause of serious health problems or even death. Again, as is the case with heroin, the criminalization of the use of cocaine and crack incorporates additional risks given the lack of proper quality control of the product in an illicit environment.

The principal routes of cocaine administration are oral, intranasal, intravenous, and inhalation. Snorting is the process of inhaling cocaine powder through the nostrils, where it is absorbed into the bloodstream through the nasal tissues. Injecting releases the drug directly into the bloodstream and heightens the intensity of its effects. Smoking involves the inhalation of cocaine vapor or smoke into the lungs, where absorption into the bloodstream is as rapid as by injection. The drug can also be rubbed onto mucous tissues. Cocaine use ranges from occasional use to repeated or compulsive use, with a variety of patterns between these extremes. Other than medical uses, there is no safe way to use cocaine. Any route of administration can lead to absorption of toxic amounts of cocaine, leading to acute cardiovascular or cerebrovascular emergencies that can result in sudden death. Repeated cocaine use by any route of administration can produce addiction and other adverse health consequences.

Cocaine is a powerfully addictive drug. Thus, an individual may have difficulty predicting or controlling the extent to which he or she will continue to want or use the drug. Cocaine's stimulant and addictive effects are thought to be primarily a result of its ability to inhibit the reabsorption of dopamine by nerve cells. Dopamine is released as part of the brain's reward system, and is either directly or indirectly involved in the addictive properties of every major drug of abuse. Use of cocaine in a binge, during which the drug is taken repeatedly and at increasingly high doses, leads to a state of increasing irritability, restlessness, and paranoia. This may result in a full-blown paranoid psychosis, in which the individual completely loses touch with reality and experiences auditory hallucinations.

There can be severe medical complications associated with cocaine use. Some of the most frequent complications are cardiovascular effects, including disturbances in heart rhythm and heart attacks; respiratory effects such as chest pain and respiratory failure; neurological effects, including strokes, seizures, and headaches; and gastrointestinal complications, including abdominal pain and nausea. Cocaine use has also been linked to many types of heart disease. Research has revealed a potentially dangerous interaction between cocaine and alcohol. Taken in combination, the two drugs are converted by the body to cocaethylene. Cocaethylene has a longer duration of action in the brain and is more toxic than either of the drugs alone. While more research needs to be done, it is noteworthy that the mixture of cocaine and alcohol is the most common two-drug combination that results in drug-related death.

Cocaine abusers, who inject, run the same risks regarding HIV/AIDS and hepatitis C infections as mentioned earlier for injected heroin use. Research has also shown that drug use can interfere with judgment about risk-taking behavior, and can potentially lead to reduced precautions regarding sexual behavior, the sharing of needles and injection paraphernalia, and the trading of sex for drugs, by both men and women. Additionally, hepatitis C has spread rapidly among injection drug users; Centers for Disease Control and Prevention (CDC) estimates indicate infection rates of 50 to 80% in this population. While currently available treatment is not effective for everyone and can have significant side effects, medical follow-up is essential for all those who are infected. At present, there is no vaccine for the hepatitis C virus. The virus is highly transmissible via injection, and hepatitis C virus testing is recommended for any individual who has ever injected drugs. Using sophisticated technologies, scientists are now finding that exposure to cocaine during fetal development may later lead to subtle, yet significant, deficits in some children, including deficits in some aspects of cognitive performance, information processing, and attention to tasks — abilities that are important for success in school.

Cannabis (Marijuana) — often called pot, grass, reefer, or weed — is a greenish-gray mixture of the dried, shredded leaves, stems, seeds, and flowers of Cannabis sativa, the hemp plant. Users have devised many different ways to smoke cannabis and often combine cannabis with another drug, such as crack cocaine. Cannabis is also used to brew tea and is sometimes mixed into foods. The amount of THC (delta-9-tetrahydrocannabinol) determines the potency and therefore the effects of cannabis. Between 1980 and 1997, the amount of THC in cannabis available in the United States rose dramatically. THC, the main active ingredient in cannabis, produces effects that can potentially be useful for treating a variety of medical conditions. It is the main ingredient in an oral medication that is currently used to treat nausea in cancer chemotherapy patients and to stimulate appetite in patients with wasting due to AIDS. Scientists are continuing to investigate other potential medical uses for cannabinoids. Research is underway to examine the effects of smoked cannabis and extracts of cannabis on appetite stimulation, certain types of pain, and spasticity due to multiple sclerosis. However, the inconsistency of THC dosage in different cannabis samples poses a major hindrance to valid trials and to the safe and effective use of the drug; this results from the lack of quality assurance of supplies in an illicit environment. Moreover, the adverse effects of cannabis smoke on the respiratory system will offset the helpfulness of smoked cannabis for a number of patients. Finally, little is known about the many chemicals besides THC that are in cannabis, or their possible deleterious impact on patients with medical conditions. The illicit nature of cannabis makes it additionally difficult to control the quality of the product that may be used in medical research. Also, given the fact that cannabis fields are often sprayed with herbicides, there is a risk that contaminated cannabis would find its way into the hands of the consumer; this creates additional health problems beyond whatever inherent risks might be associated with the drug itself. NIDA reports other cannabis related effects as follows:

- Scientists have learned a great deal about how THC acts in the brain to produce its many effects. When someone smokes cannabis, THC rapidly passes from the lungs into the bloodstream, which carries the chemical to organs throughout the body, including the brain. In the brain, THC connects to specific sites called cannabinoid receptors on nerve cells and thereby influences the activity of those cells. Some brain areas have many cannabinoid receptors; others have few or none. Many cannabinoid receptors are found in the parts of the brain that influence pleasure, memory, thought, concentration, sensory and time perception, and co-ordinate movement.

- The effects of cannabis begin immediately after the drug enters the brain and last from one to three hours. If cannabis is consumed in food or drink, the short-term effects begin more slowly, usually in thirty minutes to one hour, and last longer, for as long as four hours. Smoking cannabis deposits several times more THC into the blood than does eating or drinking the drug. As THC enters the brain, it causes a user to feel euphoric - or "high" - by acting on the brain's reward system, areas of the brain that respond to stimuli such as food and drink as well as most drugs of abuse. THC activates the reward system in the same way that nearly all drugs of abuse do, by stimulating brain cells to release the chemical dopamine.

- A cannabis user may experience pleasant sensations, colors and sounds may seem more intense, and time appears to pass very slowly. The user's mouth feels dry, and he or she may suddenly become very hungry and thirsty. His or her hands may tremble and become cold. The euphoria passes after a while, and then the user may feel sleepy or depressed. Occasionally, cannabis use produces anxiety, fear, distrust, or panic. Cannabis use impairs a person's ability to form memories, recall events, and shift attention from one thing to another.

- Some adverse health effects caused by cannabis may occur because THC impairs the immune system's ability to fight off infectious diseases and cancer. One study has indicated that a person's risk of heart attack during the first hour after smoking cannabis is four times his or her usual risk. The researchers suggest that a heart attack might occur, in part, because cannabis raises blood pressure and heart rate and reduces the oxygen-carrying capacity of the blood. Students who smoke cannabis get lower grades and are less likely to graduate from high school compared with their nonsmoking peers. Workers who smoke cannabis are more likely than their co-workers to have problems in their jobs. Several studies have associated workers' cannabis smoking with increased absences, tardiness, accidents, workers' compensation claims, and job turnover.

- Depression, anxiety, and personality disturbances are all associated with cannabis use. Research clearly demonstrates that cannabis use has the potential to cause problems in daily life or make a person's existing problems worse. Because cannabis compromises the ability to learn and remember information, the more a person uses cannabis, the more he or she is likely to fall behind in accumulating intellectual, job, or social skills. Someone who smokes cannabis once a day may be functioning at a progressively reduced intellectual level all of the time. More recently, the same researchers showed that a group of long-term heavy cannabis users' ability to recall words from a list was impaired one week following cessation of cannabis use, but returned to normal within four weeks. An implication of this finding is that even after long-term heavy cannabis use, if an individual quits using cannabis, some cognitive abilities may be recovered.

- Research has shown that babies born to women who used cannabis during their pregnancies display altered responses to visual stimuli, increased tremulousness, and a high-pitched cry, which may indicate problems with neurological development. During infancy and preschool years, cannabis-exposed children have been observed to have more behavioral problems and to perform tasks of visual perception, language comprehension, sustained attention, and memory more poorly than non-exposed children. In school, these children are more likely to exhibit deficits in decision-making skills, memory, and the ability to remain attentive and concentrated.

- Long-term cannabis use can lead to addiction for some people; that is, they use the drug compulsively even though it often interferes with family, school, work, and recreational activities. People trying to quit report irritability, difficulty sleeping, and anxiety. They also display increased aggression on psychological tests, peaking approximately one week after they last used the drug.

Ecstasy is an illicit drug that acts as both a stimulant and hallucinogen. It produces an energizing effect, as well as distortions in time and perception, and enhanced enjoyment from tactile experiences. Typically, ecstasy is taken orally, usually in a tablet or capsule, and its effects last for approximately three to six hours. The average reported dose is one to two tablets, with each tablet typically containing between 60 and 120 milligrams of ecstasy. It is not uncommon for users to take a second dose of the drug as the effects of the first dose begin to fade. **ATS** is an acronym for amphetamine-type substance and includes methamphetamines as well as amphetamines. Ecstasy is an especially popular variation of methamphetamine and reported separately by the United Nations Office on Drugs and Crime (UNODC) and NIDA. Ecstasy can affect the brain by altering the activity of chemical messengers, or neurotransmitters, which enable nerve cells in many regions of the brain to communicate with one another. Research in animals has shown that ecstasy in moderate to high doses can be toxic to nerve cells that contain serotonin and can cause long-lasting damage to them. Furthermore, ecstasy can interfere with the body's ability to control its temperature, which has on rare occasions led to severe medical consequences, including death. In addition, ecstasy causes the release of another neurotransmitter, norepinehrine, which is the likely cause of the increase in heart rate and blood pressure that often accompanies ecstasy use. Researchers have determined that many ecstasy tablets contain a number of other drugs or drug combinations that can be harmful as well. Adulterants found in ecstasy tablets purchased on the street include methamphetamine, caffeine, the over the counter cough suppressant dextromethorphan, the diet drug ephedrine, and cocaine. Moreover, as with many other drugs of abuse, ecstasy is rarely used alone. It is not uncommon for users to mix ecstasy with other substances such as alcohol and cannabis. Here again, the criminalization of the drug poses additional health issues because the quality of the product is not properly controlled; this undoubtedly leads to medical complications. It is difficult to determine the exact scope of the ecstasy problem because the drug is often used in combination with other substances and does not appear in some traditional data sources, such as treatment admission rates. Ecstasy does, however, appear to be a drug that has increased in popularity and become more widespread, particularly among people under the age of twenty-five.

Ecstasy has become a popular drug, in part because of the positive effects that a person experiences within an hour or so of taking a single dose. Those effects include feelings of mental stimulation, emotional warmth, empathy toward others, a general sense of well-being, and decreased anxiety. In addition, users report enhanced sensory perception as a hallmark of the ecstasy experience. Because of the drug's stimulant properties, when used in club or dance settings ecstasy can also enable users to dance for extended periods. However, there are some users who report undesirable effects immediately, including anxiety, agitation, and recklessness. As noted, ecstasy is not a benign drug. Ecstasy can produce a variety of adverse health effects, including nausea, chills, sweating, involuntary teeth clenching, muscle cramping, and blurred vision. Ecstasy overdose can also occur — the symptoms can include high blood pressure, faintness, panic attacks, and in severe cases a loss of consciousness and even seizures. Because of its stimulant properties and the environment in which it is often taken, ecstasy is associated with vigorous physical activity for extended periods. This can lead to one of the most significant, although rare, acute adverse effects — a marked rise in body temperature (hyperthermia). Treatment of hyperthermia requires prompt medical attention as it can rapidly lead to muscle breakdown, which can in turn result in kidney failure. In addition, dehydration, hypertension, and heart failure may occur in susceptible individuals. Ecstasy can also reduce the pumping efficiency of the heart, of particular concern during periods of increased physical activity, thereby further complicating these problems.

Over the course of the week following moderate use of the drug, many ecstasy users report feeling a range of emotions, including anxiety, restlessness, irritability, and sadness that in some individuals can be as severe as true clinical depression. Similarly, elevated anxiety, impulsiveness, and aggression, as well as sleep disturbances, lack of appetite and reduced interest in, and pleasure from, sex have been observed in regular ecstasy users. Some of these disturbances may not be directly attributable to ecstasy, but may be related to some of the other drugs often used in combination with ecstasy, such as cocaine or cannabis, or to potential adulterants found in ecstasy tablets. Studies have shown that some heavy ecstasy users experience long-lasting confusion, depression, and selective impairment of working memory and attention processes. Such memory impairments have been associated with a decrease in serotonin metabolites or other markers of serotonin function. Imaging studies in ecstasy users have shown changes in brain activity in regions involved in cognition, emotion, and motor function. However, improved imaging technologies and more research is needed to confirm these findings and to elucidate the exact nature of the effects of ecstasy on the human brain. It is also important to keep in mind that many users of ecstasy may unknowingly be taking other drugs that are sold as ecstasy, and/or they may intentionally use other drugs, such as cannabis, which could contribute to these behavioral effects. Additionally, most studies in people do not have behavioral measures for comparison from before the users began taking drugs, making it difficult to rule out pre-existing conditions. Factors such as gender, dosage, frequency and intensity of use, age at which use began, the use of other drugs, as well as genetic and environmental factors may all play a role in some of the cognitive deficits that result from ecstasy use and should be taken into consideration when studying the effects of ecstasy in humans.

Given that most ecstasy users are young and in their reproductive years, it is possible that some female users may be pregnant when they take ecstasy, either inadvertently or intentionally because of the misperception that it is a safe drug. The potential adverse effects of ecstasy on the developing fetus are of great concern. Behavioral studies in animals have found significant adverse effects in tests of learning and memory from exposure to ecstasy during a developmental period equivalent to the third trimester in humans. However, the effects of ecstasy on animals earlier in development are unclear; therefore, more research is needed to determine what the effects of ecstasy are on the developing human nervous system.

The drugs reviewed in this section, besides having the potential to be addictive in varying degrees, are illicit; the selling and use of these drugs is a crime in the United States and in most other countries. There is a legal framework for a multilateral drug control system under the auspices of the United Nations provided by three international drug conventions: The Single Convention on Narcotic Drugs of 1961, the Convention on Psychotropic Substances of 1971, and the United Nations Convention against Illicit Traffic in Narcotic Drugs and Psychotropic Substances of 1988. The United Nations Office on Drugs and Crime (UNODC) is the agency within the UN charged with the responsibility of overseeing the compliance of member nations with drug-related treaties and to compile statistics on drug issues worldwide. Illicit drugs are not an exclusive U.S. problem, they involve the whole world, and therefore any drug strategy must extend beyond the borders of the United States.

1.3 Illicit-Drug Use and Abuse

The data provided in the United Nations 2005 World Drug Report prepared by the UNODC shows the dimension of the drug problem on a global scale as of the year 2004. The UNODC estimates the total number of drug users in the world at 200 million, equivalent to 5% of the population aged from 15 to 64, of these 34.8 million, or 14.5% of the population aged 12 or older, are in the U.S. Cannabis is the most widely used substance (160.9 million people), followed by amphetamine-type stimulants or ATS (34.1 million, including 7.9 million for ecstasy). Some 13.7 million people use cocaine, and 15.9 million use opiates (heroin, morphine, opium, synthetic opiates), including 10.6 million who take heroin [3]. As mentioned earlier, these people are consuming illicit drugs which are not subject to any reliable quality control process; hence, they are taking risks

17

beyond the intrinsic risks associated with the drug itself; they may be introducing other substances into their bodies which are harmful to their health or may even cause death.

According to the 2004 National Survey on Drug Use and Health — NSDUH [4], illicit-drug users in the U.S. among persons aged 12 or older for all types of drugs were: 110.1 million had used drugs at least once in their lifetime, 34.8 million had used them during the past year, and 19.1 million had used them during the past month (including first-time users). Excluding cannabis, the figures are as follows: 70.7 million users sometime in their lifetime, 19.7 million during the past year, and 8.2 million in the past month. It is important to note the segregation of cannabis in the presentation of the study, which accounts for the largest number of users and is believed by many to be more benign.

Of the 10.6 million worldwide users of **heroin** estimated by the UNODC for the year 2004, 398,000 lived in the U.S. according to the 2004 NSDUH. The U.S. figure as reported in the 2004 NSDUH is low in light of the number of hardcore and occasional users reported by the Office of National Drug control Policy - ONDCP - in the 2000 report: What America's Users Spend on Illicit Drugs 1988--1998 [5]. The ONDCP number is 1,491 million (977,000 hard-core and 514,000 occasional users). Given the volume of heroin consumed that year, as we shall see in Chapter II, the ONDCP numbers seem more reasonable.

The UNODC reports 13.7 million **cocaine** users worldwide for 2004, of these about 5.6 million using cocaine within the last twelve months are in the U.S. The 2004 NSDUH estimated 2 million used it within the last month, including those being initiated in the use of the drug. The NSDUH also reports 34.1 million using the drug sometime in their lifetime in the U.S. Users of **crack cocaine** account for about 23% of cocaine users in the U.S.

The UNODC reports 160.9 million **cannabis (marijuana)** users worldwide for 2004; about 25.4 million of them are reported by the NSDUH in the U.S. Cannabis is the most commonly used illicit drug in the U.S. and in the world, more than 96.7 million Americans (40.2%)

aged 12 and older have used cannabis at least once in their lifetime according to the 2004 NSDUH. Of these, 25.5 million were reported using it within the last year and 14.6 million within the last month. The ONDCP reported 11 million cannabis users within the last month for 1998 in their 2000 report [6]. Later on in the presentation, the ONDCP figures on cannabis are challenged, not just their estimate of number of users, but also their estimated total value of the U.S. cannabis trade.

The UNODC reports 7.9 million **ecstasy** users and 26.2 million **ATS** — other than ecstasy — users worldwide in 2004. Of these, approximately 1.9 million users of ecstasy or 24% of the world users, and 2 million users of ATS or 7.6% of world users were in the U.S. Over 11.1 million persons aged 12 or older reported using ecstasy at least once in their lifetime according to the 2004 NSDUH, and over 23 million people were reported to have used ATS — other than ecstasy — sometime in their lifetime.

The data presented from UN, NIDA, and the 2004 NSDUH sources provide a precise picture of the widespread use of illicit drugs on a worldwide scale, and in the U.S. in particular. **Table 1.1** summarizes the number of worldwide and U.S. drug users for each one of the drugs discussed; it also shows the percentage of U.S. users for each one of them. It can be seen that the U.S. has an important consumer population for five drugs reviewed, though in no way does it represent the majority. It has indeed the largest population of cocaine consumers (40.9%). The documentation available in NIDA Research Reports reveals the addictive nature of these drugs under specific circumstances. Though not everybody who tries one of these drugs becomes addicted, persistent use may lead to addiction in all cases, according to NIDA. Addiction is in itself a health issue, but addiction is not a prerequisite of suffering from other health problems associated with drug use; HIV infection may come along during the first use of injected cocaine or heroin for instance. The matter of addiction treatment will be dealt with later on in the chapter. The contribution of NIDA to the understanding and treatment of illicit drugs is extremely valuable, and they must be commended for it. Their research

sheds light upon, and provides a better understanding of, the complex issues of illicit drugs, human health and drug addiction. As previously mentioned, the proper understanding of these issues is a must in order to effectively face the overall problem of illicit drugs.

Table 1.1 Users of Illicit Drugs in Millions (Estimates 2004)

Drug Type	Worldwide (a)	United States (b)	% in U.S.
Heroin	10.6	1.5(c)	14.1%
Cocaine	13.7	5.6	40.9%
Cannabis	160.9	25.4	15.8%
Ecstasy	7.9	1.9	24.0%
ATS (d)	26.2	2.0	7.6%
All drugs (e)	200.0	34.8	17.4%

(a) From the UN 2005 World Drug Report [1] Chapter 1.b
(b) From the U.S. 2004 National Survey on Drug Use and Health [4], Table 1.1A.
(c) From the ONDCP 2000 report What America's Users Spend on Illegal Drugs 1988-1998, Table 3.
(d) Amphetamine-type stimulants other than ecstasy.
(e) The total does not equal the sum of the individuals because of multiple-drugs users.

NIDA, under the leadership of Dr. Nora D. Volkow, M.D., has
placed great emphasis on research looking into the effects of young age
drug use on future addiction. To strengthen prevention and treatment of
drug abuse and addiction during the adolescent period, NIDA has implemented a three-pronged research strategy. It contains these components:

- The first component explores how developmental changes that
  occur in the adolescent brain may increase vulnerability to drugs,
  and how drugs in turn may subvert neurobiological maturation.
- The second component aims to increase the ability of people in
  charge of young people to dissuade teenagers from abusing drugs
  by focusing on the cognitive processes — learning, motivation,
  judgment, and decision making — that influence choices to abuse
  or avoid drugs. This component will address the question of why

some young people engage in drug abuse when they are thoroughly informed regarding its destructive potential. Is their risk assessment inaccurate, or do they comprehend the risks, but weigh them more lightly than abstaining adolescents do?

- The third component focuses on the period of emerging adulthood, which spans the years from 18 to 25. This is a time of continued brain development, but most of all of new personal and social choices and challenges, according to NIDA. These years are witness to the emergence of personal beliefs and values, exploration of career roles, transitions involving increased independence, and shifts in relationships with parents and peers. Overall rates of drug use peak and begin to subside during these years. Personal, social, and demographic factors such as education, employment, and home environment all appear to influence the patterns of abuse in this period.

NIDA's research places great emphasis on the search for knowledge that would lead to drug-use prevention amongst our young population. This is a good example of addressing the drug problem at the roots, and it is likely to deliver substantial and sound recommendations to parents, health specialists, and to society in general. This approach to drug use and abuse is crucial for an integral analysis of the overall illicit-drug problem.

1.4 Licit Drug Use and Abuse

As society raises concerns about illicit drugs, it is faced with similar, though not identical, issues associated with the licit drugs that are broadly consumed in the U.S. and in most countries. The cases in point are tobacco and alcohol, two licit-for-adults drugs widely used in modern society. This section explores their nature.

Tobacco is widely used in the U.S. even in the face of broad anti-smoking campaigns. The 2004 NSDUH reports 59.9 million people in the U.S. aged 12 and older, or 24.9% of this age group, as current cigarette smokers. This makes nicotine, the addictive component of tobacco, one of the most heavily used addictive drugs in the United States. When a person inhales cigarette smoke, the nicotine in the smoke is rapidly absorbed into the blood and starts affecting the brain within seven seconds. In the brain, nicotine activates the same reward system as other drugs of abuse such as cocaine or amphetamine, although to a lesser degree. Nicotine's action on this reward system is believed to be responsible for drug-induced feelings of pleasure and, over time, addiction. Nicotine also has the effect of increasing alertness and enhancing mental performance. In the cardiovascular system, nicotine increases heart rate and blood pressure and restricts blood flow to the heart muscle. The drug stimulates the release of the hormone epinephrine, which further stimulates the nervous system and is responsible for part of the "kick" from nicotine. It also promotes the release of the hormone beta-endorphin, which inhibits pain. People addicted to nicotine experience withdrawal when they stop smoking. This withdrawal involves symptoms such as anger, anxiety, depression, difficulty concentrating, increased appetite, and the craving for nicotine. Most of these symptoms subside within three to four weeks, except for the craving and hunger, which may persist for months.

Besides nicotine, cigarette smoke contains more than 4,000 substances, many of which may cause cancer or damage the lungs. Cigarette smoking is associated with coronary heart disease, stroke, ulcers, and an increased incidence of respiratory infections. Smoking is the major cause of lung cancer and is also associated with cancers of the larynx, esophagus, bladder, kidney, pancreas, stomach, and uterine cervix. Smoking is also the major cause of chronic bronchitis and emphysema. Women who smoke cigarettes have earlier menopause. Pregnant women who smoke run the increased risk of having stillborn or premature infants, or infants with low birth weight. Children of women who smoked while pregnant have an increased risk for developing conduct disorders. Cigar and pipe smokers and users of chewing tobacco and snuff can also become addicted to nicotine. Although cigar and pipe smokers have lower death rates than cigarette smokers, they are still susceptible to cancers of the oral cavity, larynx, and esophagus. Users of chewing tobacco and snuff have an elevated risk for oral cancer.

Alcohol is another licit drug reported by the National Institute on Alcohol Abuse and Alcoholism (NIAAA) as widely used in the U.S. today. A large portion of the adult population in the U.S. consumes alcohol legally; also, it is consumed by many young people below the legal drinking age. The 2004 NSDUH reports 120.9 million users of alcohol aged 12 or older, or 50.3% of this age group; 54.7 million are classified as binge alcohol users and 16.7 million as heavy alcohol users [7]. In addition, 10.3 million are classified as alcohol abusers and 8.4 million as alcohol dependent [7]. It is not the purpose of this exposition to promote the consumption of alcohol or any other potentially damaging drug, licit or illicit, and neither does it pretend to promote making the use of alcohol illicit amongst the adult population. Current legislation limiting the consumption of alcohol and other licit drugs, like tobacco, to the adult population finds its foundation on the broad research that has been conducted over the years regarding the damaging effects these drugs have on an immature brain. Therefore, being that alcoholism is an important health problem in the U.S. today, it must be highlighted to provide the proper perspective for understanding the multiple issues associated with drugs of abuse, licit and illicit.

Alcoholism, also known as alcohol dependency, is a disease that includes the following four symptoms:

- Craving which translates into a strong need, or urge, to drink,
- Loss of control, the alcoholic is not able to stop drinking once drinking has begun,
- Physical dependence, generating withdrawal symptoms, such as nausea, sweating, shakiness, and anxiety when the person stops drinking, and
- Tolerance, the person experiences a need to drink greater amounts of alcohol to get "high."

Alcoholism is a disease. The craving an alcoholic feels for alcohol can be as strong as the need for food or water. An alcoholic will continue

23

to drink despite serious family, health, or legal problems. Like many other diseases, alcoholism is chronic, meaning that it lasts for a person's entire lifetime; it usually follows a predictable course, and it has symptoms. The risk for developing alcoholism is influenced both by a person's genes and by his or her lifestyle. The genes a person inherits partially explain alcoholism, but lifestyle is also a major factor. Currently, researchers are working to discover the actual genes that put people at risk of alcoholism. Friends, the amount of stress in one's life, and how readily available alcohol is, are also factors that may increase a person's risk of alcoholism. Risk is not destiny though. Just because alcoholism tends to run in families does not mean that a child of an alcoholic parent will automatically become an alcoholic too. Some people develop alcoholism even though no one in their family has a drinking problem. By the same token, not all children of alcoholic families get into trouble with alcohol. Alcoholism cannot be cured at this time. Even if an alcoholic has not been drinking for a long time, he or she can still suffer a relapse. To guard against a relapse, an alcoholic must continue to avoid all alcoholic beverages. A recovering alcoholic knows he will be an alcoholic for the rest of his life, so he must learn to deal with this fact and stay away from drinking even the smallest amount of alcohol.

Any sensible policymaker knows that criminalizing the use of alcohol and tobacco, even though they are addictive and potentially damaging to human health, will not solve the abuse issues associated with these two drugs. In particular the experience with alcohol prohibition in the 1920s and early 1930s demonstrated the futility of trying to control alcohol consumption through coercion. American society learned much from this early 20th century experience.

1.5 Drug Treatment and Prevention

The treatment of drug addiction, whether licit or illicit drugs are involved, has made great progress in recent decades. The issue of prevention has also taken center stage and there are campaigns in place to prevent American youth from falling prey to drugs. However, drug addiction and hence its prevention is a rather complex subject, it involves many elements and is the responsibility of a variety of players. It is not the sole responsibility of society; it is first and foremost the responsibility of families and of parents in particular. The family continues to be the basic cell upon which our society is built; and as such, it has the primary responsibility to look after the well-being of the children, and that includes a multitude of things that, if properly cared for, will help keep the children from the allurement of drugs. Society has a role to play too, as there is much to be learned about the elements that may lead any particular individual to experiment with drugs, and even to become a drug addict. Table 1.2 reflects the levels of drug use, abuse and dependence as reflected in the 2004 NSDUH and the ONDCP 2000 Report.

Table 1.2 Substance Use, Abuse and Dependence in the United States (000s)

Drug Type	Users (1)	Abusers	Dependents	% Dependents +Abusers
Heroin (2)	1,491	-	977	65.5%
Cocaine (3)	5,658	396	1,175	27.8%
Cannabis (3)	25,451	1,799	2,670	17.6%
Ecstasy & ATS (3)	3,878	270	180	11.6%
Alcohol (3)	156,686	10,298	8,355	11.9%

(1) Past year users from the 2004 NSDUH for cocaine, cannabis, ecstasy & ATS, and alcohol, and hard-core plus occasional users for heroin from the ONDCP 2000 Report.

(2) Source: ONCDP 2000 Report "What America's Users Spend on Illegal Drugs 1988 -1998. Table 3. Reported hard-core users are included under "dependents" for heroin.

(3) Source: U.S. 2004 National Survey on Drug Use and Health. Tables 1.1A, 2.1A, 5.1A, and 5.13A.

NIDA reports a variety of effective **treatments for heroin addiction**. Treatment tends to be more effective when heroin abuse is identified early. These treatments vary depending on the individual, but methadone, a synthetic opiate that blocks the effects of heroin and eliminates withdrawal symptoms, has a proven record of success for people addicted to heroin. Other pharmaceutical approaches, like LAAM (levo-alpha-acetyl-methadol) and buprenorphine, and many behavioral therapies are also used for treating heroin addiction. Detoxification is the first step in the process of treating drug addiction. The primary objective of detoxification is to relieve withdrawal symptoms while patients adjust to a drug-free state. Not in itself a treatment for addiction, detoxification is a useful step only when it leads to long-term treatment that is either drug-free (residential or outpatient) or uses medications as part of the treatment. The best-documented drug-free treatments are the therapeutic community residential programs lasting at least three to six months.

Although behavioral therapies and pharmacological treatments can be extremely useful when employed alone, science has revealed that integrating them will ultimately be the most effective approach. There are many effective behavioral treatments available for heroin addiction. These can include residential and outpatient approaches. An important task is to match the best treatment approach to meet the particular needs of the patient. Moreover, several new behavioral therapies, such as contingency management therapy and cognitive-behavioral interventions, show particular promise as treatments for heroin addiction. Both behavioral and pharmacological treatments help to restore a degree of normalcy to brain function and behavior, with increased employment rates, lower risk of HIV and other diseases and criminal behavior.

There was an enormous increase in the number of people seeking **treatment for cocaine addiction** during the 1980s and 1990s according to NIDA. Treatment providers in most areas of the country, except in the west and southwest, report that cocaine is the most commonly cited drug of abuse among their clients. This matches the data provided in Table 1.1 above, which shows the number of cocaine users to be almost four times that of heroin users and three times that of ecstasy and of ATS users; it is still, however, much smaller than the number of cannabis users. The majority of individuals seeking treatment smoke crack, and are likely to be users of more than one substance. The widespread abuse of cocaine has stimulated extensive efforts to develop treatment programs for this type of drug abuse. Cocaine abuse and addiction is a complex problem involving biological changes in the brain as well as a myriad of social, familial, and environmental factors. Therefore, treatment of cocaine addiction is complex, and must address a variety of problems. Like any good treatment plan applicable to many drugs, cocaine treatment strategies need to assess the psychobiological, social, and pharmacological aspects of the patient's drug abuse. There are no medications currently available to specifically treat cocaine addiction. Because of mood changes experienced during the early stages of cocaine abstinence, antidepressant drugs have been shown to be of some benefit. In addition to the problems of treating addiction, cocaine overdose results in many deaths every year and medical treatments are being developed to deal with the acute emergencies resulting from excessive cocaine abuse.

Many behavioral treatments have been found to be effective for cocaine addiction, including both residential and outpatient approaches. Indeed, behavioral therapies are often the only available and effective treatment approaches to many drug problems, including cocaine addiction, for which there is, as yet, no viable medication. However, integration of both types of treatments may ultimately prove to be the most effective approach for treating addiction. It is important that patients receive services that match all of their treatment needs. For example, if a patient is unemployed, it may be helpful to provide vocational rehabilitation or career counseling. Similarly, if a patient has marital problems, it may be important to offer couples counseling. Cognitive-behavioral therapy, or "Relapse Prevention," is another approach. Cognitive-behavioral treatment, for example, is a focused approach to helping cocaine-addicted individuals abstain — and remain abstinent — from cocaine and other substances. The underlying assumption is that learning processes play an important role in the development and continuation of cocaine abuse and dependence. The same learning processes can be employed to help individuals reduce drug use and successfully cope with relapse. This approach attempts to help patients recognize, avoid, and cope; i.e., recognize the situations in which they are most likely to use cocaine, avoid these situations when appropriate, and cope more effectively with a range of problems and problematic behavior associated with drug abuse.

Long-term **cannabis** use can lead to **addiction** for some people; that is, they use the drug compulsively even though it often interferes with family, school, work, and recreational activities. Though only about 10% of cannabis users show signs of addiction (dependency in Table 1.2), along with craving and withdrawal symptoms can make it hard for long-term cannabis smokers to stop using the drug. People trying to quit report irritability, difficulty sleeping, and anxiety. They also display increased aggression on psychological tests, peaking approximately one week after they last used the drug, as stated earlier.

Treatment programs directed at cannabis abuse are rare, partly because many who use cannabis do so in conjunction with other drugs, such as cocaine and alcohol. However, with more people seeking help to control cannabis abuse, research has focused on ways of overcoming problems with the abuse of this drug. No medications are currently available to treat cannabis abuse. However, recent discoveries about the workings of THC receptors have raised the possibility that scientists may eventually develop a medication that will block THC's intoxicating effects. Such a medication might be used to prevent relapse to cannabis abuse by reducing or eliminating its appeal.

For some people, **ecstasy can be addictive**. Independently of the numbers shown in Table 1.2, where the population of abusers and dependents for ecstasy and ATS in less than 12% as reported in the 2004 NSDUH, NIDA reports a survey of young adult and adolescent ecstasy users found that 43% of those who reported ecstasy use met the accepted diagnostic criteria for dependence, as evidenced by continued use despite knowledge of physical or psychological harm, withdrawal effects, and tolerance (or diminished response), and 34% met the criteria for drug abuse. Almost 60% of people who use ecstasy report withdrawal symptoms, including fatigue, loss of appetite, depressed feelings, and trouble concentrating. Ecstasy affects many of the same neurotransmitter systems in the brain that are targeted by other addictive drugs. Experiments have shown that animals prefer ecstasy, much like they do cocaine, over other pleasurable stimuli, another hallmark of most addictive drugs. As social context and networks seem to be an important component of ecstasy use, the use of peer led advocacy and drug prevention programs may be a promising approach to reducing ecstasy use among adolescents and young adults. High schools and colleges can serve as important venues for delivering messages about the effects of ecstasy use. Providing accurate scientific information regarding the effects of ecstasy is important if we hope to reduce the damaging effects of this drug. Education is one of the most important tools for use in preventing ecstasy abuse.

There are no specific treatments for ecstasy abuse. The most effective treatments for drug abuse and addiction are cognitive behavioral interventions that are designed to help modify the patient's thinking, expectancies, and behavior, and to increase skills in coping with life's stresses. Drug abuse recovery support groups may be effective in combination with behavioral interventions to support long-term, drug-free recovery. There are currently no pharmacological treatments for dependence on ecstasy. Antidepressant medications might be helpful in combating the depressive symptoms frequently seen in ecstasy users who have recently become abstinent.

Like addiction to heroin or cocaine, **addiction to nicotine is a chronic**, relapsing disorder. A cigarette smoker may require several attempts over many years before they are able to permanently give up smoking. Less than 10% of unaided quit attempts lead to successful long-term abstinence. However, studies have shown significantly greater cessation rates for smokers receiving interventions compared to control groups who do not receive the interventions. Interventions that involve both medications and behavioral treatments appear to show the most promise. The primary medication therapy currently used to treat nicotine addiction is nicotine replacement therapy, which supplies enough nicotine to the body to prevent withdrawal symptoms, but not enough to provide the quick jolt caused by inhaling the smoke from a cigarette. Four types of nicotine replacement products are currently available. Nicotine gum and nicotine skin patches are available over the counter. Nicotine nasal spray and nicotine inhalers are available by prescription. On average, all types of nicotine replacement products are more or less equally effective, roughly doubling the chances of successfully quitting.

Alcoholism can be treated. **Alcoholism treatment** programs use both counseling and medications to help a person stop drinking. Most alcoholics need help to recover from their disease. With support and treatment, many people are able to stop drinking and rebuild their lives. A range of medications is used to treat alcoholism. Benzodiazepines (Valium® or Librium®) are sometimes used during the first days after a person stops drinking to help him or her safely withdraw from alcohol. These medications are not used beyond the first few days, however, because they may be highly addictive themselves. Other medications help people remain sober. One medication used for this purpose is naltrexone (ReVia™). When combined with counseling, naltrexone can reduce the craving for alcohol and help prevent a person from returning, or relapsing, towards heavy drinking. Another medication, disulfiram (Antabuse®), discourages drinking by making the person feel sick if he or she drinks alcohol. Though several medications help treat alcoholism, there is no "magic bullet." In other words, no single medication is available that works in every case and/or in every person. Developing new and more effective medications to treat alcoholism remains a high priority for researchers. Alcoholism treatment works for many people, but just like any chronic disease, there are varying levels of success when it comes to treatment. Some people stop drinking and remain sober, others have long periods of sobriety with bouts of relapse, and still others cannot stop drinking for any length of time. With treatment, one thing is clear, however: the longer a person abstains from alcohol, the more likely he or she will be able to stay sober.

In summary, tobacco and alcohol abuse has placed a heavy burden on society. The health issues associated with lung cancer and other tobacco-induced diseases and alcoholism place a financial burden on families and on society as a whole. Nevertheless, the cigarette smoker is doing so while exercising his individual rights and free will. So long as his/her actions do not have a negative impact on other individuals he/she is free to smoke the cigarette of choice, a cigar, a pipe, or even chew tobacco. In recent years society has increasingly recognized the rights of the non-smoker and placed limitations on the places and conditions under which a smoker can light up. Today, no airline allows smoking on board airplanes as a sign of respect for the health of non-smokers. Restaurants, if smoking is allowed at all, segregate smokers from non-smokers. Public facilities either have special sections reserved for smokers, or prohibit smoking altogether. Therefore, society has chosen to preserve the rights of the non-smoker. At the same time, the right to smoke, even if just in the privacy of the home, is also being protected. These are trademarks of the American democratic society; the safeguarding of individual rights is a guiding principle, the smoker is entitled to smoke as long as he/she does not infringe on the rights of non-smokers.

A similar situation applies to alcohol, but with a twist. Adult alcohol consumption is legal in the U.S. even if it may lead some people to alcoholism. Ever since the lifting of alcohol prohibition in the U.S. in 1933, the sale and consumption of alcohol has been regulated by each individual state. Alcohol consumption in the U.S. is restricted to people twenty-one years old or older and, depending on the state or county, the sale of alcoholic beverages may be restricted to certain locations and schedules. Otherwise, alcohol has been a legal substance for the consumption by the adult population for almost a century in the U.S. Still, the consumption of alcohol carries certain perils to the community not present in the smoking of tobacco. Because of the effect alcohol may have on the person consuming it to excess, an individual performing certain functions under the influence of alcohol may not be in full control of his reflexes and may be prone to cause an accident, or not respond adequately in the face of an accident caused by someone else. Strong legislation and regulations are today in place to address the dangers to the community that may result from driving an automobile under the influence (DUI) of alcohol. American democratic society has implemented the necessary rules to respond to the two-pronged need to respect individual rights while at the same time protecting the safety of the community. Those who choose to violate the rules face severe sanctions.

Education seems to be the best tool at hand to prevent the use of drugs of all kinds by young people. Recent scientific studies have brought to light that the teenage brain has not completed the maturing process yet; these reports claim that it is not until the mid-twenties that the brain completes the maturation process. The implication of this finding is that young people, including young adults, are more prone to making rash decisions and more vulnerable to peer pressure. Hence the greater importance of education when dealing with drug issues in today's social environment. The role of education cannot be underestimated if society is going to effectively cope with the problem of drug addiction — be it licit or illicit drugs.

1.6 Collateral Damage

Addiction to drugs inflicts severe damage to individuals and society. Individual lives are wasted and whole families are destroyed when drug addiction takes hold of a family member. This has been the primary banner of the current drug policy, which leans heavily on law enforcement through coercion and punishment. The emphasis on law enforcement has survived for many decades, even as the official statistics reflect that not all drug use leads to drug addiction, as illustrated in Table 1.2 earlier. This table shows relatively low rates of addiction with respect to users of the drug during the past year; much lower rates of addiction are revealed with respect to the population that used the drug sometime during their lifetime [8]. The conclusion that drug use does not necessarily lead to drug addiction is not presented to promote drug use, but to establish the relative damage drugs may inflict on society and its individual members. From a moralistic perspective, it may be argued that any damage is significant and enough justification for the current drug policy. Nevertheless, drug use and abuse is not the only issue associated with the drug problem — it does not stand alone. Drug use and abuse is one of the key issues driving and/or sustaining the drug problem, it is intertwined with the drug trade, the war on drugs, and drug money laundering. The four of them feed on each other and none can survive without the other three. Hence, all four must be addressed in concert if society is to find a viable and effective solution.

Besides, the use and abuse of drugs, licit and illicit, brings about a lot of collateral damage; the impact of this damage is no less severe on individuals and/or society than the direct damage inflicted by drug addiction. Some aspects of this damage is highlighted below:

- **HIV/AIDS infection** can result from the unsanitary injection use of heroin and cocaine. It is responsible for one-third of the HIV cases in the U.S. today. This certainly has a detrimental impact on society as a whole, imposing an economic burden on the health system of the country and resulting in the loss of workers productivity. The life of individuals with the HIV virus or AIDS changes dramatically; it is a chronic disease, even though there are treatments today capable of prolonging the life of those infected. However, medical science has not yet found a cure for it. The criminalization of drug use weighs heavily on this damage to society.

- **Hepatitis C infection** is another disease that can be transmitted by the use of injected drugs. Seventy five percent of all hepatitis C cases in the U.S. are caused by the unsanitary injection of illicit drugs. There is currently no cure for hepatitis C, it is a chronic disease and there are treatments to prolong life. As in the case of HIV/AIDS, this also places an economic burden on the health system of the country and results in loss of workers productivity. It has a severe impact on the life of the infected patient and that of their family. The criminalization of drug use is highly responsible for this damage to society.

- **Pregnancy complications** can arise in women using drugs; they are exposed to premature birth of the child or even the loss of the child as a result of their addiction to heroin. In addition, deficient development of the fetus may result from the use of other drugs. Children of addicted mothers may be born with a drug dependency, though this can be quickly treated in the nursery right after birth. Nothing good happens to a child whose mother consumed drugs, licit or illicit, during her pregnancy.

- **The nationwide yearly economic cost** from alcohol and drug abuse is estimated to be in the order of $245.7 billion; of this cost, $97.9 billion is due to illicit-drug abuse and other drugs taken for non-medical reasons. This estimate includes substance abuse treatment and prevention costs as well as other healthcare costs, costs associated with reduced job opportunity or lost earnings, and other costs to society such as crime and social welfare.
- **Community safety** can be placed at risk by drug use. Automobile accidents caused by drivers under the influence (DUI) of alcohol or other drugs are the cause of thousands of deaths in the U.S. In addition, many crimes are committed by addicts in search of money to support their addiction.

The above is a sample of the collateral damage that results from the use and abuse of drugs. As progress is made in this exposition, through the analysis of the multiple drug-related issues, the subject of collateral damage will be brought forward. As we shall demonstrate throughout this presentation, collateral damage has become the centerpiece of the drug problem, and society needs to fully understand it in order to devise a comprehensive and effective drug policy.

Direct and collateral damage resulting from the use and abuse of drugs has become a veritable nightmare for many Americans. Those who find themselves under the hold of drug addiction experience living hell, in most cases even their unaided desires to break away end up in profound frustration — they can not liberate themselves from the nightmare. Their relatives — parents, children, spouses, and others — do not get a break either; they share the hell with the addict. The nightmare did not materialize overnight; it crept into their lives little by little, in the silence of their otherwise peaceful existence. Perhaps, when they were looking in a different direction, somebody approached their loved one and induced him/her to try drugs. That was the beginning of the nightmare — in silence, unnoticed. Because even if not all drug users become addicts, those that do find themselves on a one-way express direct to hell, with little or no chance of a timely exit.

2

THE ILLICIT-DRUG TRADE

At $125 billion – as estimated by the United Nations Office on Drugs and Crime – the U.S. illicit-drug market is almost twice as large as the $65 billion acknowledged by the U.S. government. This discrepancy casts doubts on the motivations of the USG for continuing the current drug policy.

2.1 The Business of Illicit Drugs

It is broadly believed that the illicit-drug trade is a $400-billion business. This revenue size attests to the big business nature of illicit drugs. The 2004 Fortune 500 list of America's largest corporations reveals that illicit-drug revenue is equivalent to the revenue of the twenty largest U.S. commercial banks, including Citibank and Bank of America. The figure is 45% greater than the combined revenues of the nine top computers and office equipment companies, including IBM and Hewlett-Packard. It is also 45% above the combined revenues of the nineteen largest food and drug store chains, including Kroger, Albertson's and Walgreen. It is also equivalent to the combined revenues of the four largest general merchandisers, including Wal-Mart Stores, Target, Sears Roebuck, and J.C. Penney. And it is 9% greater than the combined revenues of General Motors Corporation and Ford Motor Company. Illicit drugs are in the same revenue league as some of the major industries in the U.S. — illicit drugs are big business. Because it is an illicit business, it is not easy to come up with reliable figures and the numbers that bounce back and forth in government reports result from estimates obtained using different methodologies. The $400-billion figure is not as precise as that of the Fortune 500 companies.

Drug traffickers do not pay taxes, meaning legitimate taxes, so there are no accurate aggregate records of the overall industry size. Instead of paying taxes, drug traffickers do pay bribes to obtain the cooperation of law enforcement and government officials willing to look the other way and not interfere with the smooth movement of their products and cash.

As in any legitimate business, the illicit-drug industry involves many different, interconnected activities or processes. The business starts with the cultivation of the crops to obtain the raw materials required, it involves the procurement of the essential or precursor chemical agents required for their transformation, and that is followed by the product manufacturing itself. Once the manufactured product is packaged, it is transported in its wholesale presentation to the finished product laboratories, where it is converted and/or repackaged into the finished product for delivery to the retail network and into the hands, and the brains, of the consumer. Because it is a clandestine industry, the above process faces many unusual obstacles along the way, difficulties not commonly encountered by legitimate businesses. Understanding the sheer size of the business is crucial to comprehending the other issues surrounding the drug trade. This business is not a Mom and Pop operation — it is indeed huge [1].

2.2 Sizing the Illicit-Drug Business

Estimating the size of the illicit-drug business is not trivial; there are no reliable sources. Governments and international agencies like the United Nations depend on estimates based on different methodologies. Table 2.1 below shows the estimates for expenditure on illicit drugs in the U.S. from 1990 through to 2000 published by the ONDCP in 2000: What America's Users Spend on Illegal Drugs: 1988-2000 [2]. According to these estimates, the illicit-drug business in the U.S. was in the order of $62.9 billion at the beginning of the 21st century. The study also reflects a reduction from $77.9 billion in 1990. The ONDCP 2000 report used data from 1998 and projected years 1999 and 2000; later on, this presentation uses the year 1998 for comparisons. Our presentation mixes data from the UN and the ONDCP in order to highlight trends in the amount of heroin and cocaine consumed from 1990 through to 2000. Table 2.2 below illustrates prices for cocaine and heroin in the U.S. as reported by the UN in the 2005 World Drug Report [3]. There are no similar price figures reported for this time period for the other drugs in Table 2.1.

Table 2.1 – ONDCP Estimated Total U.S. Expenditure on Illicit Drugs, 1990-2000
(Billion current dollars)

Drug Type	1990	1991	1992	1993	1994	1995	1996	1997	1998	1999	2000
Cocaine	49.2	46.0	42.5	40.7	38.4	40.2	39.8	41.2	39.0	37.1	36.1
Heroin	14.1	11.5	9.4	9.0	9.5	10.5	11.3	12.0	11.6	12.0	11.9
Meth	2.1	1.8	2.0	2.4	3.0	2.6	2.3	2.0	2.2	2.2	2.2
Cannabis	10.8	10.7	10.8	9.9	10.4	8.7	8.7	9.9	10.7	10.2	10.4
Other Drugs	1.8	1.9	1.3	1.3	2.4	2.5	2.6	2.5	2.3	2.3	2.3
Total	77.9	71.9	65.9	63.5	63.6	64.5	64.6	67.5	65.8	63.8	62.9

Table 2.2 Prices for Cocaine and Heroin in the U.S. as Reported in the UN 2005 World Drug Report
(U.S. average retail price per gram in current dollars)

Drug Type	1990	1991	1992	1993	1994	1995	1996	1997	1998	1999	2000
Cocaine	184	177	170	147	137	131	126	127	124	118	129
Heroin	281	279	268	268	204	196	170	151	162	137	126

Table 2.2 shows prices of cocaine and heroin — the drugs accounting for 76% of the 2000 expenditure according to the ONDCP report — dropping since 1990. By the year 2000, the price of cocaine had dropped by 30% and that of heroin by 51%. This resulted from an increase in the

supply of these two drugs, and the increased supply took place in the midst of very intense activity against drug trafficking. Table 2.3 reflects the volumes of cocaine and heroin consumed in the U.S. from 1990 through to 2000 and is directly derived from Tables 2.1 and 2.2. It shows that cocaine consumption increased by almost 9%, while heroin consumption increased by 46% between 1990 and 2000. These figures reflect a growing drug business during the 1990s. Even if cocaine and heroin revenue decreased in the U.S. during the 1990s, the reduction is accounted for by lower drug prices in the face of an increase in the availability of these drugs during those years.

Table 2.3 Quantity of Cocaine and Heroin Consumed in U.S. from 1990 to 2000 (Metric Tons)

Drug Type	1990	1991	1992	1993	1994	1995	1996	1997	1998	1999(a)	2000(a)
Cocaine	267	260	250	277	280	307	315	324	314	299	291
Heroin	50	41	35	34	47	53	66	80	72	74	73

(a) Volumes for 1999 and 2000 calculated with 1998 price given that ONDCP estimate was done in 1998.

In the 2005 World Drug Report, the UN, for the first time since it began publishing the report, presented a detailed estimate of the global illicit-drug market. Even if this estimate is still subject to error given the clandestine nature of the industry, it does present a much clearer picture of the overall market [4]. Table 2.4 reflects the UN estimates regarding the global drug revenues at the producer, wholesale, and retail levels for 2003. The total retail value of $322 billion reported is in the same order of magnitude of the widely publicized $400 billion figure mentioned earlier. [5]

Table 2.4 Global Revenues of Illicit-Drug Market in 2003
(Billion dollars)

Drug Type	Retail Level	Wholesale Level	Producer Level
Heroin	64.8	20.6	1.2
Cocaine	70.5	18.8	0.5
Cannabis Herb	113.1	29.7	8.8
Cannabis Resin	28.8	10.4	0.7
ATS	28.3	6.8	0.6
Ecstasy	16.1	7.7	1.0
Total Illicit Drugs	321.8	94.0	12.8

To highlight the relevance of these figures, the UN compares them to the worldwide wholesale value of other commodities in 2003. This comparison is shown in Table 2.5. The wholesale value of all illicit drugs is in the same order of magnitude as the sum of all cereals and meat exports. It is also 74% greater than the aggregate exports of tobacco products, wine, beer, coffee and tea. From whatever perspective it is looked at, the illicit-drug business is huge.

**Table 2.5 Value of Illicit Drugs at Wholesale and Export Value of
Selected Agricultural Commodities in 2003
(Billion dollars)**

Commodity	Export Value
Illicit drugs	94.0
Meat	52.5
All cereals	40.7
Tobacco products	21.6
Wine	17.3
Wheat	16.0
Chocolate products	9.9
Beer	6.7
Coffee	5.7
Tea	2.6

According to the ONDCP, the U.S. market for illicit drugs added up to $65.8 billion in 1998. However, a close analysis of the UN 2005 World Drug Report yields a different figure for retail revenues in the U.S. Table 2.6 reveals these numbers and compares them with the equivalent ONDCP numbers for 1998. The difference reflected in the UN 2003 versus the ONDCP 2000 estimates is not likely to result from an increase in market size between 2003 and 2000, but it is suspected by many as a deliberate effort by U.S. anti-drug authorities to play down the market forces driving the industry in the U.S. Cannabis, as well as ecstasy and ATS have important domestic sources of supply which may suggest a bias toward underestimating the value of domestic supplies in the ONDCP 2000 report. If the UN based estimates are accurate, and there is no reason to believe they are not, then the U.S. illicit-drug market is almost twice as large as many U.S. authorities claim it to be. In recent years, U.S. authorities have openly spoken of a market in the $65 billion [7] range, slightly over half of what the UN figures yield. This discrepancy is kept in focus as the presentation continues.

Table 2.6 Retail Revenues of U.S. Illicit-Drug Market in 2003 and 1998 (Billion Dollars)

Drug Type	UN 2003 Estimate [6]	ONDCP 1998 Estimate	% 2003/1998
Heroin	7.8	11.6	-33%
Cocaine	38.9	39.0	0%
Cannabis	54.7	10.7	+411%
ATS/methamphetamine	15.7	2.2	+614%
Ecstasy/other drugs	7.7	2.3	+235%
Total Illicit Drugs	124.8	65.8	+90%

Heroin. The worldwide potential production of heroin for 2004 was 565 metric tons. Afghanistan was the main opium producing country that year, accounting for about 85% of global production. This is a huge increase from the Taliban regime days when heroin from Afghanistan hit a record low of 185 metric tons in 2001, or 12% of global production. How much heroin ends up in the hands of American users? The UN reports the U.S. price of heroin at $116 per gram for 2003 and estimated expenditure of $7.8 billion for that year; these numbers yield 67 metric tons of heroin consumed in the U.S. in 2003. This number is close to the 73 metric tons estimated in Table 2.3 for 2000 and yields that the U.S. consumed approximately 14% of the world production of heroin in 2003 — global heroin production was 477 metric tons in 2003 — while accounting for 14.1% of world heroin users as illustrated in Table 1.1 in Chapter I. Though heroin is considered one of the most dangerous and addictive drugs, its impact on the U.S. is not as important as in other parts of the world. This can be explained by the distance between the U.S. and the main producing countries in Asia. Even though Colombia and Mexico are also producing heroin, their combined production would have delivered a maximum of 16 metric tons, barely enough to account for 24% of U.S. consumption. The drug cartels may find it more expedient to supply cocaine, a drug with which they have a lot of expertise. It must be kept in mind though, that market forces and innovation may change this preference in the future.

Cocaine. The worldwide production of cocaine for 2004 was 937 metric tons, up from 784 metric tons in 2003, a 30% increase in spite of action taken to reduce the cultivation of the coca bush in Bolivia, Colombia, and Peru; the only three producing countries in the world. The cocaine business continues to be very big regardless of the efforts to curtail the growing of the coca bush in these three countries.

How much cocaine ends up in the hands of American users? Chapter I revealed that almost 41% of cocaine users live in the U.S. The UN estimates yield a U.S. consumption of cocaine of $38.9 billion for 2003, which at the reported price of $75 per gram yields a total consumption of 519 metric tons of cocaine in the U.S. in 2003. The UN also reports a purity level of 70%; hence this tonnage is equivalent to 363 metric tons of pure cocaine, or equivalent to 46% of the 784 metric tons produced that year. These figures indicate that 41% of the world's cocaine users — the American users — consumed 46% of the cocaine produced in 2003.

Cannabis. Table 2.6 reflects a huge discrepancy between the UN estimated value for cannabis consumption in the U.S. in 2003 and the value estimated by the ONDCP in 1998, and there is sufficient data to believe that the UN figures are closer to reality. According to the UN,[8] 14.3% of the world production of cannabis is consumed in the U.S.; this figure is close to the 15.8% U.S. cannabis users' share of global users reported in Table 1.1. The U.S. users account for 48.4% of the global retail value of cannabis given the higher price for cannabis in the U.S. market, equivalent to $54.7 billion. The discrepancy between U.S. and UN estimates may reflect a deliberate effort on the part of U.S. government authorities to underestimate domestically produced drugs like cannabis; in the case of cannabis the underestimation ratio is a one to five. Cannabis is used by 161 million people worldwide; this is 80% of the worldwide population of 200 million illicit-drug users. Given the widespread use of cannabis, the bulkier nature of the drug itself, which makes concealed transportation more difficult compared to heroin and cocaine, and the relative ease of cultivation, it is no wonder that a significant share of the cannabis consumed in many countries is domestically grown. Besides, the cultivation of cannabis does not have the same requirements of soil and climate as the opium poppy and the coca bush. Cannabis production is truly a global enterprise. Some reports estimate that up to two-thirds of the cannabis herb consumed in the U.S. is domestically produced; the imports essentially come two-thirds from Mexico and one-third from Canada.

ATS. Table 2.6 reflects a huge discrepancy between the UN estimated value for ATS consumption in the U.S. in 2003 and the value estimated by the ONDCP in 1998. According to the UN, [9] 31.6% of the world production of ATS is consumed in the U.S.; this figure shows a big gap from the 7.6% U.S. share of the global ATS user population reported in Table 1.1. The UN numbers yield an estimated yearly consumption of ATS per user of 52 grams in the U.S. The U.S. users account for 55.5% of the global retail value for ATS given the higher price for ATS in the U.S. market. In the case of ATS, an increase in U.S. consumption has been reported in recent years, which may account for all or some of the discrepancy shown in Table 2.6. On the other hand, U.S. government authorities have not recognized this discrepancy publicly, which may cast some doubt on their motivation to underestimate domestically produced drugs like ATS; in the case of ATS the differential UN and ONDCP numbers deflects a one to seven underestimation ratio. ATS is used by 26.2 million people worldwide; this is 13.1% of the worldwide population of 200 million illicit-drug users. The use of ATS and other synthetic drugs has become more popular in recent years and their manufacturing process is relatively simple compared with heroin and cocaine, as it does not involve the planting and harvesting of a crop; the drug is manufactured from precursor chemicals. All the ATS consumed in the U.S. is produced in North America according to the UN and it is very likely that a significant portion is produced in the U.S. itself because of the ease of setting up an ATS laboratory. Significant domestic sourcing is something ATS has in common with cannabis.

Ecstasy. As mentioned for cannabis and ATS, Table 2.6 also reflects a significant discrepancy between the UN estimated value of the ecstasy business in the U.S. in 2003 and the value estimated by the ONDCP in 1998. According to the UN, [10] 47.8% of the world retail ecstasy busi-

45

ness is generated in the U.S., reflecting the consumption of 38.4% of the global ecstasy production. The UN numbers yield an estimated yearly consumption of ecstasy per user of 17 grams in the U.S. In the case of ecstasy — similar to ATS — an increase in U.S. consumption has been reported in recent years, which may account for all or some of the discrepancy shown in Table 2.6. Following the same pattern shown for cannabis and ATS, the U.S. government authorities have not publicly recognized this discrepancy, which again may cast some doubts on their motivation to underestimate a drug like ecstasy which has a big potential for domestic production [11]. Ecstasy is used by 7.9 million people worldwide; this is less than 4% of the worldwide population of 200 million illicit-drug users. It is among the synthetic drugs that have become more popular in recent years and its manufacturing process is relatively simple compared with crop-based drugs; as in the case of ATS, the drug is manufactured from precursor chemicals. The potential for significant domestic sourcing is something ecstasy has in common with cannabis and ATS.

   In summary, our research yields relevant information regarding the size and composition of the global illicit-drug business and U.S. participation in this business. Table 2.7 illustrates the composition of the global and U.S. illicit-drug business side by side, and Table 2.8 shows the global production in metric tons and the portion consumed in the U.S. market, as well as the average per capita consumption for each drug in the U.S. Some important conclusions follow:

- The global market size for illicit drugs is estimated at $321.8 billion; very close to the figure of $400 billion, for many years the widely used number to size this market. This market value is higher than the GDP of 88% of the countries in the world, that is, higher than the GDP of 163 out of the 184 countries for which the World Bank has GDP data.
- The U.S. market, at $125 billion, is almost twice as large as the widely publicized figure of $65 billion. This discrepancy is accounted for primarily by cannabis, ATS, and ecstasy, three drugs

with a large component of domestic production in the U.S. — cannabis and ATS — or the potential for doing so — ecstasy.

- U.S. government authorities have not come forward with the $125 billion figure and continue to refer to the $65 billion figure in public forums. This posture casts doubts on the effectiveness of USG to pursue the current policy and/or its motivations for continuing with the current drug policy.

- Even though the U.S. accounts for only 17.4% of the 200 million global illicit-drug users (see Table 1.1), it accounts for 38.8% of the business because of the higher drug prices prevalent in the U.S. This makes the U.S. the largest single illicit-drug market in the world. This is nothing to be proud of, but a crude fact which places additional responsibilities on American authorities and policymakers. The U.S., because of its unquestionable leadership position in the community of nations, its role as the leading illicit-drug market, and the role it played in the promotion of current worldwide illicit-drug treaties, should take the lead in the search for a more effective drug policy.

**Table 2.7 Composition of the Global and U.S. Illicit-Drug 2003 Business
(Billion Dollars Retail)**

Drug Type	Global	U.S.	% U.S./Global
Heroin	64.8	7.8	12.0
Cocaine	70.5	38.9	55.2
Cannabis	113.1	54.7	48.4
ATS	28.3	15.7	55.5
Ecstasy	16.1	7.7	47.8
Total Illicit Drugs	321.6	124.8	38.8

Table 2.8 Global and U.S. Illicit-Drug 2003 Business – Quantity

Drug Type	Global MT	U.S. MT	% U.S./Global	Yearly Gm/U.S. User
Heroin	477	67	14.0	44.7
Cocaine	784#	363*	46.0	64.8
Cannabis	33,552	4,798	14.3	188.9
ATS	326	103	31.6	51.7
Ecstasy	86	30	34.9	15.7

\# From the 2006 UN World Drug Report.
* This volume, 363 metric tons, yields the 519 metric tons at 70% purity level reported by the UN. The 519 MT at $75 per gram yields the $38.9 billion business in Table 2.7.

2.3 The Cultivation-Production-Distribution Cycle

The processes required to produce each one of the drugs under analysis in this presentation are unique in the sense that they are initiated from different raw materials and different points of origin; nevertheless, they are similar in terms of the logistics and merchandising methods involved. **Heroin** is an end product obtained from opiates that are extracted from the opium poppy. The opium poppy is primarily cultivated in Asia, most of it in Afghanistan, and some has been grown in Colombia and Mexico in recent years. Cocaine is obtained from the coca bush leaf, which only grows in Colombia, Peru, and Bolivia in South America. Cannabis is grown in 142 countries. Cannabis can be grown in the open air or in covered or even underground facilities with artificial lighting. Ecstasy and ATS are produced in laboratories from precursor chemicals that are available for other legitimate purposes; therefore, all it takes is a laboratory facility and the availability of those chemicals to produce these two drug types.

Why would farmers get involved with the cultivation of the opium poppy, the coca bush, or the cannabis plant given their illicit nature? The answer is simple: there is a huge economic incentive to produce any of these crops that far exceeds what they can obtain from traditional food crops. It is simple economics; the farmer will lean toward the cultivation of whatever crop yields the greatest economic benefit, even if such crops are illegal. The potential rewards handsomely compensate for taking the additional risks.

During the 1990s Afghanistan established itself as the largest provider of illicit opium and its derivative, heroin, in the world. After the decline of opium production during the Taliban regime and following the invasion of the country by the U.S. led NATO forces in 2001, opium poppy cultivation reached an all time high of 327,500 acres in 2004. Ninety-two percent of opium poppy cultivation took place in fertile irrigated land, and it could be found in all thirty-two provinces of the country. This rapid expansion of opium poppy cultivation came at the expense of cereal cultivation, mostly wheat, which declined significantly in 2004. In that year 356,000 Afghan families were involved in opium poppy cultivation, this represented about 2.3 million people, 10% of the total population and 12% to 14% of the rural population of Afghanistan. The yearly gross income from opium poppy cultivation per family was estimated at around $1,700 in 2004 and the gross income per acre was $1,840. This figure reflects a decline of 64% from the previous year, but is still almost twelve times higher than the gross income a farmer gets from one acre of wheat ($156). The 2004 farm-gate value of the opium harvest was estimated at around $600 million. This farm-gate value is equivalent to 13% of GDP and three times the size of the Government's total domestic revenues. Because of falling opium prices, the overall farm-gate value of opium production was 41% lower than in 2003 and 50% lower than in 2002.

Colombia, Peru, and Bolivia are the only countries cultivating the coca bush from which the coca leaf is obtained for the manufacture of **cocaine**. Colombia accounted for 200,000 acres of coca bush cultivation, making it the most important producer of coca leaf in 2004. It was followed by Peru with 125,750 acres under coca bush cultivation, and Bolivia with 69,250 acres. Even though Colombia experienced decreases in coca bush cultivation during the four previous years, caused by the Colombian Government's eradication campaign, it still accounted for 68% of global coca production in 2004. It produced 640 metric tons of coca in 2004 with a total farm-gate value of $510 million. While Colombia stabilized its coca bush cultivation, Peru and Bolivia increased theirs, offsetting the small de-cline experienced by Colombia and resulting in an overall increase in co-caine supply of about 20% from 2003. While Colombia accounted for 51% of the coca bush cultivation area, Peru accounted for 32% and Bolivia for 17%. As is the case with opium poppy cultivation in Afghanistan, the cul-tivation of the coca bush in Colombia, Peru, and Bolivia is much more profitable to the farmer than traditional food crops; hence, their willingness to assume the associated risks.

Cannabis has a much simpler cultivation and preparation process, so much so that 142 countries are involved in this illicit activity. A signifi-cant proportion of cannabis crops are destined for domestic consumption in the country of origin; this is certainly the case in the U.S., where some ana-lysts estimate that two-thirds of the cannabis consumed is grown domesti-cally, as mentioned earlier. As is the case with the opium poppy and the coca bush, the economic incentives make it tempting for the farmers to plant cannabis over traditional food crops. The economic rewards outweigh the inherent risks.

After the harvesting of the raw materials, the opium latex, the coca base, and the cannabis plant undergo a transformation process to become a consumable opiate, including heroin, cocaine, crack cocaine, smokable cannabis or cannabis resin. All these presentations are properly packaged to make the journey to their destination markets. Packaging for transporta-tion has become very sophisticated over the years. These products have to be properly concealed to avoid interception by law enforcement officers in the country of origin, in transit, or at destination. The final manufacturing of the drug typically takes place in the country of origin or a nearby coun-try; for example, Peruvian coca leafs or base may be used to manufacture cocaine in Colombia. Proper packaging is done at the manufacturing labo-ratories, as mentioned, to allow for concealment during transportation. Transportation takes place in many different and innovative ways, some of them exposing the person carrying the drug to very high personal risks. Take for example the cocaine leaving Colombia directly for the U.S. mar-ket; it is a flight of a few thousand miles and a few hours. Some people make those flights loaded with capsules of cocaine in their stomach to be released upon arrival at their U.S. destination. The 2004 movie *Maria Full of Grace* depicts in great detail how this transportation scheme — using human mules, as they are colloquially called — is executed by highly sophisticated and unscrupulous drug trafficking networks. However, most of the cocaine that enters the U.S. does not come in on a direct flight from Colombia, it is estimated that up to 90% of the cocaine entering the U.S. today goes through the Central America-Mexico corridor. It is here that Mexico comes in to play an important role in the illicit-drug business. Mexico shares a 2,000-mile border with the US, and this vast border translates into opportunities for drug traffickers. Later on, the section "Profiles of Drug Providing Countries" expands on this subject. The drug is sent from Colombia through Central America and on to Mexico either by ship or plane, drug traffickers have been known to fly Boeing 727s fully loaded with cocaine into clandestine landing strips in Mexico. From there the drug is transferred to trucks in order to cross the US-Mexican border by land. The transportation process has to evade the many authorities along the way that could interfere with the delivery objectives. Some shipments are intercepted on route as a result of the intensified efforts by the authorities in many countries to stem the flow of illicit drugs; many more go through to their final destination in the retail distribution networks. As mentioned earlier, Mexico is also a drug manufacturer; some of the cannabis grown, ATS, and the heroin produced in Mexico is exported to the U.S.

After the drugs are successfully introduced into the destination markets, they go into the retail network for delivery to the consumer. The retail network goes all the way down to the neighborhood drug dealer. It is at this stage of the cycle that the local drug peddler enters the schools and playgrounds in search of potential young customers. In addition, the upscale market is serviced by these individuals, providing the drugs to the occasional user and the addict as well. There are hundreds of thousands of individuals involved in the retail drug business in the U.S. alone. As the drug moves along towards the consumer, there is an increase in the risks involved and, in economic terms, value is added to the product; as the drug

51

gets closer to the reach of the consumer it becomes more valuable, having successfully overcome the many obstacles along the way. A kilogram of cocaine does not have the same value in Colombia, Mexico, and the U.S. In 2003 the wholesale value was $1,550, $7,880, and $21,500 per kilo in each of these locations; the retail value in the U.S. was $74,600. This rapid increase in value is in direct proportion to the proximity of the consumer. Table 2.9 illustrates the evolution of the value of the drug as it approaches the consumer from the farm gate to the retail transaction in the U.S.

Table 2.9 Farm-gate, Wholesale and Retail Prices of Illicit Drugs (Dollars per Kilogram in 2003)

Drug Type	Equivalent Farm-gate	Wholesale	Retail
Heroin	2,830[b]	60,000[a]	115,800[a]
Cocaine	780[b]	21,500[a]	74,600[a]
Cannabis	936[b]	2,035[a]	11,400[a]
ATS	3,028[b] [c]	31,000[b]	153,000[b]
Ecstasy	24,483[b] [c]	103,000[b]	260,000[b]

(a) From Chapter 7 of UNODC 2005 World Drug Report.
(b) From Chapter 2 of UNODC 2005 World Drug Report.
(c) Laboratory prices for ATS and ecstasy.

Table 2.9 displays the equivalent farm-gate prices of the heroin, cocaine and cannabis end products and not the actual price paid for the raw materials; that is, the amount of money shown in the table is what the farmer receives for the amount of raw material required to produce a kilogram of the finished drug in the case of these three drugs. The big increment from the farm-gate price to the wholesale price attests to the complexity and the risks involved in the manufacturing and transportation of the drugs, and to the relatively small benefits received by the farmers involved in this illicit activity. The cannabis farm-gate price shown is the one reported for North America, and, as mentioned earlier, two-thirds of the U.S. consumption is very likely produced domestically. For ATS and ecstasy there is no cultivation process as the drugs are manufactured from legitimate precursor chemicals. The wholesale prices in Table 2.9 are an indication of the value added to the product through the manufacturing and wholesale distribution process, this value covers the intrinsic risks associated with these activities. The farmer's share of the heroin business is only 2.4% of the total revenue generated if we take the U.S. prices from Table 2.9 as the reference point. The retail network takes 48.2% of the business, and the manufacturing-distribution cartels take 49.4%. In the cocaine business the farmer takes only a 1% share, the retail network keeps the 71.2%, and the manufacturing-distribution cartels account for 27.8%. Some of the drug trafficking organizations (DTOs) have developed their own retail networks in the U.S. and they are sharing in the profits from the retail business. The farmer's share of the cannabis business is 8.2%, the wholesaler gets 9.6%, and the retailing network gets 82.2%. In the case of ATS and ecstasy, the retail network also gets the bigger chunk of the overall pie. This large increase between the wholesale and the retail price is an indication of the relative importance of the retailing networks and reflects the additional risks entailed in bringing the drug to the consumer.

The sharing of rewards among different players in the cultivation-production-distribution cycle reflects, as in any other business, the complexities associated with the activities involved. These complexities have more to do with the risks involved in each stage than with any technical issues, and the risks are linked to the illicit nature of the business. What would be the price of drugs if they were not illicit and there was not any "illegality risk" in taking the product to market? If the retail price of cocaine were ten times the farm-gate price in a legal environment, the retail price would be $7,800 per kilo, or almost 90% below the reported retail price in 2003 in the U.S. How would this drug market behave? The answer to this question becomes crucial in any consistent search for a more effective drug policy.

2.4 The Evolution of the Drug Business in the Last Three Decades

The Drug Intelligence Brief: The evolution of the drug threat from the 1980s through 2002[12] prepared by the DEA Intelligence Division in

May 2002 presents a law enforcement perspective on illicit drugs; it is the source of much of the information in this section. This information is relevant to the understanding of the DTOs' capabilities to mutate and adapt to new environments. As it turns out, after more than thirty years of law enforcement actively confronting DTOs in many countries, illicit drugs continue to be available to an eager mass of consumers. Even worse, drug dealers have even established a presence on the doorsteps of elementary schools, ready to deliver the product to new customers. Throughout this process multibillion-dollar fortunes have been made by DTOs and their associates.

The DEA is aware of the fact that the illicit-drug trade in the United States is influenced by a variety of elements; including consumer demand, sources of supply, the organizational strengths and adaptability of criminal groups, and the ability of law enforcement to disrupt or dismantle drug distribution systems. They claim to understand that current intelligence must be brought together with a historical perspective to effectively evaluate the dynamics of the illicit-drug trade and identify the most significant drug threats to the U.S.

The DEA identified the most significant changes in the drug threat over the twenty years prior to the report preparation, as reflected in the National Narcotics Intelligence Consumers Committee Report (NNICC) over the years. The NNICC report provided a historical foundation for a current drug threat assessment, and offered a perspective on the dynamics that will affect the drug threats facing the United States in the near future. It also provided a summary of the most significant factors shaping the distribution of illicit drugs. As to be expected, such assessment was conducted within the framework of law enforcement as called for by drug policies and legislation in effect and the specific charter given to the DEA.

The 1980s: Smuggling and market transformation. The intelligence brief reported that the U.S. experienced the rampant growth of cocaine trafficking and abuse as the single most important transformation of the U.S. illicit-drug market in the 1980s. There was a consumer perception that cocaine was a benign stimulant; because of this perception cocaine

54

trafficking and abuse introduced radical changes in the illicit-drug environment. Cocaine availability replaced synthetic drugs. In addition, the introduction of crack cocaine increased demand. During this period Bolivia and Peru were the largest coca and cocaine base producers, but Colombian traffickers dominated the final production of cocaine hydrochloride. Colombian sources supplied at least 50% of the cocaine smuggled to the United States, with Colombian distribution organizations firmly entrenched in South Florida. The Caribbean was the primary cocaine smuggling corridor, utilizing maritime and air smuggling routes through The Bahamas.

Southwest Asia was the primary source of heroin to the United States, supplying approximately 60% of the U.S. heroin market. Pakistan was the largest and most accessible heroin producer in the region. Opium poppy cultivation in Afghanistan was severely disrupted as a result of the fighting between Soviet forces and the Mujahedeen; however, because interdiction efforts in the country were primarily directed at controlling the flow of weapons to Afghan guerillas, heroin exports continued, though at a reduced level. Some Mexican heroin also found its way to the western part of the U.S. during this time period.

Colombia was the primary source of foreign-produced cannabis in the United States during this period, supplying approximately 80% of the cannabis smuggled into the U.S. Mexico and Jamaica supplied the balance of the foreign-produced cannabis. Domestic production supplied less than 10% of the market. Most of the cannabis smuggled from Colombia used maritime routes through the Caribbean.

The production and trafficking of synthetic drugs was not significant in the 1980s. Domestic clandestine laboratories supplied nearly all of the available synthetic drugs in the U.S., with the exception of diverted pharmaceuticals. Although the majority of clandestine laboratories in the U.S. produced methamphetamine, PCP was the only clandestinely produced drug that was identified as a significant problem in the Drug Abuse Warning Network (DAWN) Emergency Room data. Outlawed motorcycle gangs (OMGs) dominated the production and trafficking of methamphetamine, as well as cannabis distribution.

The DEA reports that the 1980s witnessed substantial changes in the law enforcement and security resources directed against drug trafficking. The resources of the Central Intelligence Agency were brought into the counter-narcotics mission by executive order in 1982. In 1986, National Security Decision Directive 221 articulated the policy that, "The international drug trade threatens the security of the United States by potentially destabilizing democratic allies." U.S. military assets were formally directed to provide support to the counter-narcotic mission under the National Defense Authorization Act of 1989. The decade closed with the Anti-Drug Abuse Act of 1988, which authorized the Director of the Office of National Drug Control Policy (ONDCP) to designate regions of the United States as "high intensity drug trafficking areas" (HIDTAs). The diversity of the drug trafficking threat was reflected in the geographic diversity of the initial five HIDTAs: the cities of New York, Los Angeles, Miami, and Houston, as well as the southwest border — all counties along the United States – Mexico border from San Diego to Brownsville, Texas. The 1980s witnessed the intensification of the struggle against the DTOs and the transformation of the DTOs into more violent organizations.

The 1990s: Shifting supplies. The DEA reported Mexico emerging during the 1990s as the most significant transshipment corridor for illicit drugs smuggled into the U.S. Although cocaine continued to move through the Caribbean, increased radar surveillance deterred the use of aircraft flights directly to the U.S. Traffickers thwarted the increased surveillance by combining drug airdrops with high-speed boats operating beyond the range of the new systems. The increased law enforcement and military presence in the Caribbean forced traffickers to explore more elaborate smuggling options. As a result, Colombian DTOs in their search for new routes recruited the services of Mexican and Dominican DTOs to introduce cocaine shipments into the U.S. By the mid-1990s, Colombian organizations started paying Mexican transportation organizations with portions of the smuggled cocaine load, with up to half of the load provided to the transporters. This arrangement reduced the need for large financial transactions, and firmly established Mexico-based DTOs as significant illicit-drug wholesalers in the U.S. The Central American corridor was increasingly used for air and overland cocaine shipments to Mexico. Aircraft, large and small, were used to move cocaine from Colombia to Northern Mexico.

Drug-related violence spread and continued to threaten governance by legitimate governments in South America. Over 150 groups loosely organized in cartels operating out of Medellín and Bogota dominated the cocaine trade. Colombian insurgent groups such as the Revolutionary Armed Forces of Colombia (FARC) and the Army of National Liberation (ELN) also profited from the cocaine trade by levying taxes and collecting protection money for safeguarding crops, laboratories, and storage facilities; payment was occasionally received in weapons. The activities of the insurgents often got intermingled with that of the DTOs.

The disruption of Southeast Asian (SEA) heroin supplies in the late 1980s led to the expansion of opium poppy cultivation and heroin production in Colombia in the early 1990s. The Colombians filled the void left by the decrease of SEA heroin to the East Coast markets. During the mid-to-late 1990s, Colombian heroin traffickers easily undermined the SEA heroin market with a readily available supply of high-quality, low-priced white heroin. They also undercut their competitors' price and used established and effective drug distribution networks to facilitate supply. Since Colombian heroin, often sold on the street with a purity of 90%, can be snorted like cocaine, it avoided the stigma of needle usage; thus, Colombian traffickers had a built-in marketing advantage over traffickers from Southeast or Southwest Asia. Throughout the 1990s, Mexico-supplied heroin continued to dominate user preferences in the Western U.S.

By 1990, Mexico was reported as the largest supplier of cannabis to the U.S. According to the National Household Survey, the number of then current cannabis users (any use within the past thirty days) decreased from 22.5 million in 1979 to 10.2 million in 1990. Despite decreased demand, the profit margin for cannabis not only fueled Mexican trafficking organizations, but also led to an increase in domestic cannabis cultivation — particularly indoor-grown operations producing high-potency cannabis.

Synthetic drugs, especially methamphetamine, continued to be produced domestically primarily. In the early 1990s, high-purity "ice" methamphetamine (80%-90% pure methamphetamine with a crystalline appearance) appeared on the West Coast. In addition to domestic production, primarily in California, ice was supplied from laboratories in South Korea and the Philippines. Outlawed motorcycle gangs (OMGs) dominated the production of methamphetamine through the early 1990s. In the mid-1990s, however, Mexican DTOs started large-scale production and trafficking of methamphetamine. The introduction of high-quality, low-priced methamphetamine undercut the monopoly once held by outlawed bikers. Some OMGs reportedly relied upon Mexico-based sources of supply for their methamphetamine, preferring to avoid the risks associated with the manufacture of the drug. A sharp decrease in the purity of Mexican methamphetamine at the end of the 1990s reportedly pushed OMGs back into drug production. In the late 1980s and early 1990s, ecstasy gained popularity among young, middle-class college students in limited areas of the U.S. Ecstasy use and availability greatly escalated in 1997, when clandestine laboratories, operating in Europe, began exporting significant quantities to distributors in the U.S.

Threat assessment - 2002. By 2002, the DEA reported cocaine as the primary illicit drug of concern based upon abuse indicators, the violence associated with the trade, and/or the volume of trafficking. Heroin remained readily available in major metropolitan areas, but at a much lower level than cocaine. Despite the availability of high-purity white heroin, which can be snorted, abuse appears to have stabilized in recent years. Methamphetamine trafficking and abuse was on the rise, and cocaine remained the drug of choice in many regions of the country.

Current drug threat. As of late 2005, the southwest border remained the most vulnerable region of the U.S. for border security, followed by the Gulf Coast. Different assessments report 60% to 90% of the cocaine entering the U.S. comes through the southwest border. Traffickers have not changed smuggling methods or routes following the September 11, 2001, terrorist attacks. Although the transportation centers are likely to be located near the border, the command and control centers could operate from nearly any location in the U.S. Mobile communications and Internet encryption allow DTOs to operate from remote locations.

Availability of drugs. Cocaine and heroin production are limited not only by the same factors that affect any agricultural product, but also by the traffickers' abilities to either control production regions or to thwart government crop eradication efforts. Supplies of synthetic drugs, such as ATS and ecstasy, are not limited by these same factors. The traffickers' capability to quickly move production sites of synthetic drugs presents a significant challenge to law enforcement authorities. Besides, a significant percentage of synthetic drugs are manufactured domestically and subject to shorter and less hazardous transportation issues.

Heroin. Even if the DEA emphasizes the supply of heroin from Mexico and Colombia, highlighting the availability of high purity, fit to snort, heroin from these sources, the UN numbers reflect that all Colombian and Mexican production of heroin would only account for 24% [13] of total U.S. consumption. Therefore, the source of most of the heroin available in the U.S. is Asia, most likely Afghanistan. The U.S. supply of heroin is believed to be stable and, as mentioned earlier, in the order of 67 metric tons per year, equivalent to 14% of potential global production capacity.

Cocaine. Currently, Colombian DTOs rely more and more upon the eastern Pacific Ocean as a trafficking route to move cocaine into the United States. Some estimates place 72% of the cocaine shipped to the U.S. as moving through the Central America-Mexico corridor. Despite the shift of smuggling operations to the eastern Pacific, the Caribbean corridor remains a crucial smuggling avenue for Colombian cocaine traffickers. Puerto Rico, the Dominican Republic, and Haiti are the predominant transshipment points for Colombian cocaine transiting the Caribbean. Colombian trafficking organizations reportedly continue to control wholesale level cocaine distribution throughout the heavily populated northeastern United States and along the eastern seaboard. There are indications that other drug trafficking organizations, especially Mexican and Dominican groups, are playing a larger role in the distribution of cocaine in collaboration with the Colombians. Mexican drug trafficking organizations are increasingly responsible for the transportation of cocaine from the southwest border to the New York market. Mexico-based trafficking now controls the distribution of multi-ton quantities of cocaine in many U.S. cities according to the DEA.

Cannabis. The DEA reports that cannabis trafficking is prevalent across the nation, with both domestic and foreign sources of supply. They point to lax public attitudes regarding cannabis' effects, the high seizure threshold required for federal prosecution, and various state legalization efforts undermining public support of law enforcement endeavors. In particular, there is a strong movement in favor of legalizing the medical use of cannabis. The DEA reports that some Mexican DTOs use cannabis as a "cash crop"; the proceeds being used to cover the expenses associated with the trafficking of other drugs. As mentioned earlier in this chapter, U.S. authorities seem to de-emphasize the importance of the cannabis trade in the U.S. According to the UN, an estimated 4,798 metric tons of cannabis with a retail value of $54.7 billion were consumed in the U.S. in 2003, while the ONDCP estimated cannabis consumption at less than 1,000 metric tons, valued at $10.4 billion, in 2000. U.S. law enforcement appears to play down the importance of cannabis in the U.S. illicit-drug market. Some foreign analysts [14], like Mexican political analyst Jorge Fernandez-Menendez, claim that the high percentage of U.S. domestic production of cannabis may have something to do with this contradiction. Briefly, cannabis supplies are quite stable and the vicissitudes of a long journey to get to market are reduced by domestic producers in charge of two-thirds of the supply.

ATS from either foreign or domestic sources is widely available in most U.S. cities. According to the DEA, large-scale methamphetamine laboratories, located primarily in the western United States, and to a lesser extent in Mexico, provide the majority of the drug. The smaller clandestine laboratories pose a significant public health and safety threat as they carry greater quality risks. The majority of these small toxic laboratories are not connected to large-scale drug trafficking organizations. "Super labs" (laboratories capable of producing in excess of ten pounds of methamphetamine in one twenty-four-hour production cycle), however, are generally funded and supplied by larger DTOs. An increase in the number of super labs in the Midwest suggests an increased demand for methamphetamine. The increased availability of methamphetamine in urban environments, especially the indications that the drug is occasionally sold in conjunction with, or in place of, club drugs such as ecstasy, may usher in a new generation and class of drug abuser. As mentioned earlier, the data available from the UN yields a consumption of ATS of 103 metric tons valued at $15.7 billion, by far a greater figure than previously reported by the ONDCP in 2000. As in the case of cannabis, most of the available supplies are domestically produced, and apart from the general comments reflected in the DEA Drug Intelligence Brief, U.S. authorities have not come forward with recognition of the important relative role played by domestically produced ATS in the overall U.S. illicit-drug market.

Ecstasy is reported by the DEA as a significant threat. The increase in domestic ecstasy production, although still limited by stringent precursor chemical controls, further illustrates the profitability of this drug. Although the majority of ecstasy production takes place in Western and Central Europe, the transferability of the laboratories adds a dynamic to the drug trade that is difficult to address with much precision. Laboratories can be relocated to any nation in the European Union, Eastern Europe, or the former Soviet Union, as long as precursor chemicals can be obtained and transported. The U.S. consumed thirty-three metric tons of ecstasy, valued at $7.7 billion, in 2003 according to the UN. This number is over three times the size of the market as estimated by the ONDCP in 2000. Today ecstasy plays a significant role in the illicit-drug landscape and shows an upward trend, but its role is being de-emphasized by U.S. authorities, as is the case with cannabis and ATS.

Post 9/11 a new set of variables came into the U.S. law enforcement arena. There was a reallocation of resources from counter-narcotics to counterterrorism; this reduced the available enforcement assets focusing on DTOs' activities and goes in detriment of the DEA's stated goals.

The DEA report provides a reasonable description of the evolution of the drug business for almost thirty years. However, nowhere does it say that the struggle against illicit drugs is delivering the desired fruits. On the other hand, it clearly explains the capability of drug traffickers to *"continue to identify and exploit vulnerabilities in order to maintain a steady supply of drugs to the illicit-drug market in the US"*. What the report does not say is that the drug business, like any other business, is ruled by the law of supply and demand, and that as long as there is demand for drugs, there will be drug entrepreneurs willing to take whatever risks are necessary to satisfy that demand. Of course, they will do it provided the rewards for delivering the service compensate the concomitant risks. A $125-billion-per-year reward is certainly juicy enough for the DTOs to invest in state of the art technology and sophisticated equipment to minimize their risks and assure the arrival of their products to the U.S. consumer. The DTOs use extensive marketing and promotional methods to expand their business. Over the last thirty years illicit drugs have been reaching more children in America, this population segment is seen by the DTOs as an excellent entry point for the market development of their products. Experimenting with drugs among children is not the result of some ingrained trait in young people; it seems to be the result of a number of factors, including family structure, peer pressure, new values, and other societal pressures. However, at the same time, drugs have to be available for children to acquire them; this is the role of the DTOs and their retailing arm, the local drug dealer. They will always be there ready to deliver the product to any youngster as long as there is an economic incentive for them to do so. And the incentives are there, there are fortunes to be made from drug dealing and drug distribution as illustrated earlier.

2.5 Profiles of Drug Providing Countries

The world is a village, what happens in the streets of New York is not strictly a local issue; it may be linked to events on the other side of the world. Take for instance a photographic camera being sold at a shop in Manhattan, it is quite possible that the camera was manufactured in Japan, but it may incorporate a microprocessor produced in Singapore, based on a design made in Portland, Oregon. Today's world economy is global, corporations function on a global scale with worldwide strategies. This is how the legitimate business world works, but it is also the way DTOs operate. The same technology and business resources available to legitimate businesses are within the reach of DTOs. The illicit-drug business is an international enterprise addressing the needs of customers in every country on the face of the Earth. Heroin and cocaine manufacture and/or distribution are linked to the economy and the livelihood of specific countries. Some of these countries are U.S. allies, so there is a genuine concern in America for their well-being. There are three countries that specifically fit this mold; they are Afghanistan in Asia, Colombia in South America, and Mexico in North America. They are not the only countries fitting the profile, but each one is certainly a good example of how DTOs, in their global endeavors, impact specific communities.

Afghanistan's contemporary history is characterized by war and civil strife, with only brief periods of relative calm and stability. The Soviet Union invaded in 1979 with the excuse of protecting a pro-Soviet Afghan government under siege by local Mujahedeen forces. Afghanistan became the Soviet Union's equivalent of the U.S.'s Vietnam. The soviets were forced to withdraw ten years later by anti-communist Mujahedeen forces supplied and trained by the U.S., Saudi Arabia, and Pakistan among others. Fighting subsequently continued among the various Mujahedeen factions, giving rise to a widespread strife amongst warlords that hatched the Taliban in the early 1990s. The Taliban regime was able to seize most of the country, aside from Northern Alliance strongholds primarily in the northeast, until the U.S. led NATO military action in search of Osama Ben Laden and al-Qaeda bases led to the collapse of the group. Hamid Karzai was appointed Chairman of the Afghan Interim Authority on December 22, 2001 and was later elected president of the country.

Afghanistan is an extremely poor, landlocked country, highly dependent on farming and raising livestock (sheep and goats). It has a population of twenty-four million and a total land area of 256,000 square miles, slightly smaller than the state of Texas. The country shares borders with China (47 miles) and Pakistan (1,518 miles) to the east and southeast, with Iran (585 miles) to the west, and with Tajikistan (753 miles), Turkmenistan (465 miles) and Uzbekistan (85 miles) to the north. Economic considerations have taken back stage to political and military upheavals during two decades of war. During that conflict one-third of the population fled the country, with Pakistan and Iran sheltering a combined peak of more than six million refugees. Gross domestic product has fallen substantially over the past twenty years because of the loss of labor and capital and the disruption of trade and transport; severe drought added to the nation's difficulties between 1998 and 2001. The majority of the population continues to suffer from insufficient food, clothing, housing, and medical care, problems exacerbated by military operations and political uncertainties. Inflation remains a serious problem. In this scenario, the UN reports an active involvement of Afghanistan in the illicit cultivation of the opium poppy and the production of opium from 1990 through to 2004. During the 1990s the country increased the production of opium and its share of the world opium market; in 2001, under the Taliban, there was a drastic drop in opium production to be followed by a spectacular recovery in the following years after the U.S. led NATO invasion. In 2004 Afghanistan supplied 88.5% of the opium available in the world market compared to less than 12% in 2001 under the Taliban.

Because of geopolitical considerations, the U.S. has a very strong interest in Afghanistan. The country harbored Osama Ben Laden and his al-Qaeda terrorist organization during the days of the Taliban and today the mountains of Afghanistan may still be providing a safe heaven for fugitive terrorist. The increased drug trade since the collapse of the Taliban regime has become a source of funds for Al Qaeda and their allies, the Taliban, which happen to be regaining ground in the country. The alliance between drug traffickers and terrorist organizations is a natural consequence of entities finding common ground in the illicit habitat. Opium production is a key component of Afghanistan's economy. The country is strategic for U.S. national security, while at the same time supplies the world with almost 90% of the world's illicit heroin, and diverts some of this revenue to towards financing al-Qaeda. This is not a very encouraging setup. Heroin is illicit, which in turn makes prices skyrocket, the high prices provide an incentive for drug entrepreneurs to go into the heroin business currently concentrated in the country harboring the world's most wanted international terrorist. This terrorist and his associates are profiting from the illicit-drug trade to finance their terrorist activities; these activities have radically changed the way Americans live in the 21st century. Everybody, except the traffickers and the terrorists, seems to be on the losing side of the equation. There is more illicit heroin available in the world today — over three times more — than fifteen years ago, heroin money is helping finance the terrorist who attacked New York on September 11, 2001, and five years after the defeat of the Taliban, Osama Ben Laden is still a fugitive and al-Qaeda continues to threaten the security of the U.S. For the U.S. and its allies, it is a lose-lose proposition — Afghanistan is not a safe place and the Taliban is recovering influence in the country, and there is more heroin from Afghanistan going around the world. However, what would happen if heroin use were suddenly decriminalized? Would the price of heroin drop enough as to dry up the rivers of cash going into the traffickers' hands, the hands of their associates in al-Qaeda and the Taliban?

Colombia, with a territory of 444,887 square miles, is located in northern South America, bordering the Caribbean Sea between Panama and Venezuela, and bordering the eastern Pacific Ocean, between Ecuador and Panama. It has land borders with Brazil (1,027 miles) to the southeast, with Ecuador (369 miles) and Peru (935 miles) to the south, with Venezuela (1,281 miles) to the east, and with Panama (141 miles) to the west. It has a population of more than forty-one million and a GDP in the order of $255 billion, translating into a GDP per capita of $6,300. It is a country rich in natural resources, but because of internal strife lasting almost half a century and the burden imposed by DTOs, the country has become a very insecure place to live in or visit and has not made much progress in terms of economic development. At one point, it ranked number one in the world for the number of kidnappings for ransom, running into the thousands every year. Besides being the main supplier of cocaine to the world, Colombia also cultivates opium poppies and cannabis. The heroin production has remained relatively stable in recent years, ranging between seven and eight metric tons; it is a significant supplier of heroin to the U.S. market. However, the main line of illicit drugs is cocaine. Colombia became the leading supplier of cocaine in the world in 1990 and has remained so to this day. The shift in the production of cocaine from Peru and Bolivia to Colombia was driven by the eradication campaigns conducted by the governments of Peru and Bolivia starting in the mid 1990s. As the eradication campaigns — induced by the U.S. Government — made progress, the DTOs shifted their activity to Colombia or new DTOs, seeing the opportunities, got started in the business. In Colombia the DTOs found fertile ground. In the early 1990s Colombia was already immersed in a civil strife led by leftist guerrilla groups, primarily the Revolutionary Armed Forces of Colombia (FARC) and the National Liberation Army (ELN). These guerrilla groups were later followed by illegal self-defense paramilitary groups, the Autodefensas Unidas de Colombia (AUC), created under the excuse of protecting the population from the leftist guerrillas. In the end, both the leftist guerrillas and the self-defense units became involved with the drug trade themselves. The combination of illegal armies with the financial resources provided by the drug trade has become one of Colombia's most important security and stability issues. Press reports in early 2005 link the FARC with illegal activities in other Latin American countries, including the kidnapping and murder of the daughter of a former president of Paraguay and a plot to assassinate the president of Honduras. These are clear signs of a terrorist organization spilling over into other countries fueled by the financial resources provided by illicit drugs.

A report prepared by the DEA Intelligence Division [15] in March 2002 provides an excellent perspective of the evolution of the drug trade in Colombia since the early 1990s through to December 2001. The DEA has been active in Colombia for many years, providing assistance to the Colombian authorities in their struggle against Colombian DTOs. Colombian drug traffickers have dominated the cocaine production since 1998; even in

2004, after an intensive eradication campaign by the Government of Colombia (GOC) spanning for a number of years, Colombian DTOs accounted for 68% of global cocaine production. Over the past fifteen years Colombia has experienced the decentralization and fragmentation of the cocaine trafficking organizations. This is interpreted by some analysts as reducing their ability to influence the Colombian political process; nevertheless, it has done little to thwart the cocaine business itself. The Medellín Cartel broke up with the death of its leader, Pablo Escobar, in December 1993. This gave prominence to the Cali Cartel for a while until the capture of the Rodriguez-Orejuela brothers in 1995, the death of Jose Santacruz-Londono in March 1996, and the surrender of Helmer "Pacho" Herrera in September 1996. These events accelerated the decentralization of the drug trade. Experienced traffickers who had been active for years, but worked in the shadows of the Medellín or Cali drug lords, increased their roles in the cocaine trade, as did independent Peruvian trafficking groups. The DEA reported:

"Decentralization of the cocaine trade, however, is not a phenomenon limited only to Colombia. In recent years, independent Peruvian trafficking groups have increasingly produced cocaine HCl."

In other words, decentralization only changed the way of doing business, but did not significantly reduce the ability of Colombian and Peruvian DTOs to stay in business. As mentioned earlier, in 2004 the reduction of coca leaf production in Colombia was offset by increases in Peru and Bolivia. The overall business shifted a bit to adjust to new environmental conditions. Under these new conditions Colombian drug traffickers looked for ways to diminish their risks, particularly the risk of deportation to the U.S. In this context they engaged the services of Mexican DTOs to handle a significant portion of the cocaine transportation to the U.S. In tandem, they began payment-in-product to their Mexican associates. This was the beginning of a significant change in the drug trading patterns. As reported by the DEA:

"Since the mid-1990s, some Mexican drug transportation groups have received up to 50% of the Colombian cocaine they move to the

United States as payment for a successful smuggling operation. The major Mexican drug trafficking groups increasingly have capitalized on this 'payment-in-product' arrangement to expand their own wholesale cocaine distribution networks in the United States. In fact, Mexican trafficking groups now dominate the wholesale distribution of cocaine in the United States' West and Midwest. Colombian traffickers, however, continue to control the supply of cocaine at its source and dominate the wholesale cocaine markets in the eastern United States and in Europe."

During this time period Colombian DTOs developed an interest in the European market potential, driven primarily by the higher wholesale prices for cocaine which resulted in higher profits. As reported by the DEA:

"The Iberian Peninsula continues to be the principal gateway for cocaine entering Europe, given its cultural, linguistic, and ethnic ties to South American countries. Accordingly, Colombian trafficking groups appear more active in Spain than in any other European country. Colombian trafficking groups have also established drug trafficking operations in the Netherlands, another important European gateway country for cocaine."

Even as Mexican DTOs began to play an important role in the cocaine business in the US, the Colombian DTOs continued to control the production and were able to expand their business into Europe. They also managed to maintain a hold on certain markets in the U.S. As reported by the DEA:

"Colombian traffickers in the United States are focused on the wholesale cocaine market and are not involved in drug trafficking at the retail level. Diverse assortments of criminals from varying ethnic groups are responsible for most of the domestic street trade in cocaine and crack cocaine."

The above sheds much light onto the operation of the Colombian DTOs. They have been able to stay in business by expanding into the European market and retaining some of the smuggling routes into the U.S., always concentrating on the production and wholesale distribution segment of the business. In the midst of this new trend by Colombian DTOs, the

DEA continues to fight the illicit-drug trade in the U.S. and beyond its borders. There are many achievements in the annals of the DEA, as well as many heroic actions on the part of its agents, and the agency must be commended for this. They have been given a charter, and over the years they have achieved significant successes. Unfortunately, as it transpires in their own report, the DTOs are alive and kicking today after three decades of increasing activity by the DEA. Their own conclusion best summarizes the end result of three decades of intense activity:

"Despite the fragmentation of the cocaine trade, the DEA anticipates that Colombian cocaine trafficking organizations will remain the dominant players in the international cocaine trade well into the 21st century. Colombian traffickers are increasingly more self-sufficient in cocaine base production; have a firm grip on Caribbean smuggling routes; and dominate the wholesale cocaine markets in the eastern United States and in Europe."

Mexico shares a 2,000-mile border to the north with the U.S. To the south it has a 156-mile border with Belize and a 600-mile border with Guatemala, two Central American countries. The country itself is part of North America, bordering the Caribbean Sea and the Gulf of Mexico, between Belize and the US; it borders the eastern Pacific Ocean between Guatemala and the U.S. It has more than 5,800 miles of coastline. In 2003, the country had a population of more than 104 million and a GDP in the order of $942 billion, yielding a GDP per capita of $9,000. A significant proportion of the population (40%) is below the poverty level according to Mexican standards, which happen to be significantly below U.S. poverty standards. In this geopolitical and economic environment, Mexico is immersed in the illicit-drug trade. It is involved in the illicit cultivation of the opium poppy and heroin production, cannabis cultivation, and some production of ATS. It is believed that the Mexican government eradication efforts have been fundamental in keeping illicit crop levels low. Still Mexico is a significant supplier of heroin and the largest foreign supplier of cannabis and ATS to the U.S. market. However, the most significant illicit-drug activity is as the primary transshipment country for U.S.-bound cocaine from South America. Major drug syndicates control the majority of drug trafficking throughout the country.

A DEA Mexico Country Brief [16] published in January 2001 provides a Mexican profile vis-à-vis the illicit-drug trade. The geographic location of Mexico, sharing a border with the U.S. and in close proximity to the only cocaine producing region of the planet, makes it a natural candidate for providing illicit drugs to the most important drug market on Earth — the U.S. Consequently, powerful and highly effective Mexican organizations have sprung up during the past thirty years which control drug production and trafficking in and through Mexico; they are also very effective in the laundering of drug revenue. Since 1930, and until the election of President Fox in 2000, Mexico had been essentially under one-party rule, the Institutional Revolutionary Party (PRI). This political climate was very conducive to the flourishing of corruption in all branches of government. In this fertile ground, Colombian DTOs came together with fledgling Mexican drug traffickers. The net result has been the development of some of the most powerful DTOs on the American continent — the Mexican DTOs. These organizations, propelled by the practice of getting payment-in-product for cocaine transshipment services from the Colombian drug traffickers, quickly established themselves as a key player in the cocaine business in the U.S. In addition, they continued with the substantial export to the U.S. of Mexican produced heroin, cannabis, and ATS. Because of the sheer size of the Mexican economy, the country also provides the economic environment that facilitates the laundering of drug proceeds. According to the DEA report:

"Drugs are smuggled into and through Mexico via every commercial and noncommercial transportation means available, including smuggling across the land border with Guatemala; concealing shipments in containerized maritime or air cargo; maritime smuggling using fishing vessels, go-fast boats, and mother-ships; smuggling by private aircraft to clandestine airstrips; and air drops to go-fast boats off Mexican coasts. Drugs then are moved to northern Mexico border areas for stockpiling and entry into the United States. Drugs are smuggled across the southwest border by every means imaginable including in commercial and private vehicles, by body carry, in aircraft, on rafts, on horseback, and through tunnels." [17]

Mexico is currently the transit point for at least 60%, and perhaps as much as 90%, of the cocaine entering the U.S., the southwestern border being the primary entry point for cocaine since the late 1980s. Mexican DTOs use the most advanced logistics, telecommunications, and information technologies to support their smuggling activities. As a matter of fact, their abundant financial resources place them well ahead of Mexican Law enforcement authorities and allow them to effectively compete with the resources available to the DEA and other U.S. law enforcement agencies. Comparing the average wholesale price of a kilogram of cocaine in Mexico ($7,880) to the price in the U.S. ($21,500) [18], the value added though the smuggling of cocaine into the U.S. by the Mexican DTOs stands out; it increases more than 170%. As reported by the DEA:

"Mexican organizations now have a major share of the wholesale cocaine market in the United States, directly controlling the wholesale distribution of cocaine throughout the western and mid-western portions of the United States. Chicago and Los Angeles are the primary command and control centers for Mexican drug trafficking organizations in the United States. In addition, over the past several years, Mexican groups have worked towards establishing themselves in the eastern United States as transporters for Colombian organizations. In some cases, Mexican transportation organizations are now transporting shipments from Mexico all the way to New York. The most prominent Mexican drug transportation and distribution organizations that impact the United States are the Arellano-Felix organization (AFO), the Armando Valencia organization, and remnants of the Carrillo-Fuentes organization (CFO). Following the death of its leader, Amado Carrillo-Fuentes in 1997, the CFO split into separate factions headed by Amado's brother, Vicente Carrillo-Fuentes, Juan Esparragosa-Moreno, Ismael Zambada-Garcia, and Alcides Ramon-Magana." [19]

The UN estimates that Mexico produces about eight metric tons of heroin per year; this is somewhat below 2% of global heroin production.

71

The DEA reports that most of this is shipped to the U.S. market, and that while Mexican heroin traditionally dominates the western half of the United States, it has recently appeared on rare occasions in the northeast and Atlanta, Georgia. Mexico's privileged geographical situation has also led couriers to smuggle South American heroin to the United States via Mexico.

Mexico is the primary foreign supplier of cannabis to the United States, accounting for about two-thirds of all imported cannabis; this it is believed adds up to about 22% of U.S. cannabis consumption. Our research indicates that 4,798 metric tons of cannabis is consumed in the U.S. every year (see Table 2.8), though U.S. authorities, as mentioned earlier, have underestimated domestic consumption by a factor of five to one, suggesting it is in the order of 1,000 metric tons according to ONDCP figures. The DEA reports:

"Since 1999, net production of marijuana (in Mexico) has remained relatively stable, as eradication efforts have kept pace with a slight increase in cultivation levels from 1999 to 2002. An estimated 7,900 metric tons of marijuana were produced in 2002, compared to 7,400 metric tons in 2001 and 7,000 metric tons in 2000." [20]

This level of Mexican production is enough to supply the estimated market demand in the U.S., and far exceeds the U.S. official estimates of cannabis consumption, a situation which makes the position of U.S. drug authorities highly suspect. Besides, it is widely believed that two-thirds of the cannabis consumed in the U.S. is domestically produced. Even in the early 1990s Harrison, Lana D., Michael Backenheimer and James A. Inciardi (1995) in their essay "Cannabis use in the United States: Implications for policy." reported 50% of domestic cannabis production, and referred to DEA estimates for domestic cannabis production in the range of 2,595 to 3,095 metric tons in 1992. [21]

More recently, on April 30, 2003, during the Third Annual Arizona Drug Court Conference, in his speech, Errol J. Chavez, Special Agent in Charge Drug Enforcement Administration, Phoenix Division, stated:

"Reporting from law enforcement and public health agencies indicates marijuana availability changed little over the past year. Available data suggest that marijuana production is high both in the United States and in foreign source areas." [23]

Though in more recent DEA reports, the estimates for domestic cannabis production are not mentioned, it remains true by their own admission that they are "high." Our presentation continues with the assumption that two-thirds of the cannabis consumed in the U.S. is domestically produced. The contradiction between UN supported data and the position of U.S. authorities makes any serious analyst wonder about the effectiveness of U.S. drug policy and/or the motivation for keeping the current drug policy alive. As a side note, if more liberal estimates of cannabis consumption and domestic production are incorporated, the illicit U.S. drug trade would be close to $180 billion and not the $125 billion used in this presentation.

The DEA estimates that Mexican trafficking groups control 70 to 90% of the supply of methamphetamine (ATS) in the United States. Outlawed motorcycle gangs and small independent producers are still active in domestic methamphetamine production, but not on the same scale as the Mexican traffickers. Due to Mexico's economic environment, many of the chemicals necessary for the clandestine manufacture of illicit drugs are available in Mexico. Precursor and essential chemicals are imported from the United States, Europe, and Asia for use in the pharmaceutical and chemical industries and are diverted to clandestine laboratories. Mexico is also an important transshipment country for essential chemicals used in the manufacture of cocaine and heroin. These chemicals are diverted to clandestine laboratories throughout Latin America. The diversion of chemicals is facilitated by both legitimate and nonexistent Mexican firms misrepresented as consignees of chemical shipments that exceed legitimate national needs according to DEA reports.

2.6 International Terrorism and the Illicit-Drug Trade

After September 11, 2001 the U.S. has intensified the focus on the terrorist threat that ended the peaceful and serene life of America and most of the world. U.S. immediate security became the center of attention of the authorities; since then, significant resources have been allocated to the war on terror. In the meantime, DTOs continued to engage in the business of smuggling illicit drugs into the U.S. DTOs operating in and from Afghanistan, Colombia, and Mexico, among others, have continued to smuggle heroin, cocaine, cannabis, ATS, and ecstasy into the U.S. to supplement the domestic sources of some of these drugs. Though in recent reports the DEA associates domestic production of cannabis and ATS to Mexican DTOs operating within the U.S., this assertion has further implications, as we shall see when the subject of the war on drugs and money laundering are covered later on in the presentation. Coincidentally, Afghanistan is also the country were the most wanted terrorist in the U.S., Osama Ben Laden, has been hiding even after the defeat in 2001 of the Taliban regime by NATO forces. Colombia happens to have organizations labeled as terrorists by the Colombian and U.S. governments, like the FARC and the AUC, which are intimately associated with the illicit-drug trade; and finally Mexico, a very strong trading partner of the U.S., may be vulnerable to becoming a source of terrorist penetration as it is already the originator of most of the illegal immigration entering the U.S. These facts unveil an unquestionable and dangerous link between illicit drugs and international terrorism. The DEA highlighted this reality in a Drug Intelligence Brief [23] published in September 2002.

Illicit trafficking is not necessarily specialized; it often deals with more than one commodity. As Moises Naim points out in his book *ILLICIT: How smugglers, traffickers, and copycats are hijacking the global economy* [24], traffickers can be found to deal with multiple illicit products. It is possible, according to Naim, to find a criminal network simultaneously involved in arms and human traffic, besides illicit drugs. In addition, organizations specializing in money laundering can offer their services to all kinds of illicit traffickers, including terrorists. Globalization has had a phenomenal impact on modern society; today's world is a village. Legitimate and criminal entrepreneurs have access to the tools of globalization, exploiting advances in technology, finance, communications, and transportation in pursuit of their endeavors, some legitimate while others illicit. In this setting, terrorists can find a propitious atmosphere in which to pursue their destructive objectives. The DEA reports:

"Since September 11th, 2001, the public's image of terrorism is magnified. Not only is the proliferation of illicit drugs perceived as a danger, but also the proceeds from drugs are among the sources for funding for other criminal activities, including terrorism." [(23)]

The definition of a narco-terrorist organization may vary according to the source of the definition; besides, in the current context of world events, today's terrorist to some may be considered a freedom fighter by others. Are narco-terrorists drug traffickers who use terrorism to further their business agenda, as may have been the case of infamous drug lord Pablo Escobar in Colombia in the 1980s and early 1990s? Or are narco-terrorists, above all, terrorists who use drug money to finance their cause? Whether they are one or the other, both definitions embody the problem at hand: drug proceeds can be used, and are being used, to further terrorist causes. The $125 billion generated by illicit drugs in the U.S. is to some extent contributing to financing terrorist organizations. Whether the financing goes to the recovering Taliban or al-Qaeda in Afghanistan, to the FARC or AUC in Colombia, or to some little known fledgling terrorist group at America's footsteps in Mexico, does not make much of a difference. All these groups identify the U.S. as their enemy and consider it an important target. Besides, it would be naïve to rule out cooperation amongst different terrorist organizations in a globalized world; it may prove unwise to rule out alliances of terrorist groups with different agendas.

In the above context, the DEA sees a direct link between the anti-terrorist and the anti-drug trafficking activities conducted by the U.S. Government and international agencies. And they report:

"Nations throughout the world are aligning to combat this scourge on international society. The War on Terror and the War on Drugs are linked, with agencies throughout the United States and internationally working together as a force-multiplier in an effort to dismantle narco-

terrorist organizations. Efforts to stop the funding of these groups have focused on drugs and the drug money used to perpetuate violence throughout the world. International cooperative efforts between law enforcement authorities and intelligence organizations are crucial to eliminating terrorist funding, reducing the drug flow, and preventing another September 11th."
(23)

This emphasis reflects the law enforcement charter handed down to the DEA; they are in the business of implementing a drug policy and enforcing the laws associated with it. It is unquestionable that proceeds from illicit drugs are a welcome resource in terrorist organizations; they are one more way of financing their pursuits. The generation of huge amounts of money from the illicit-drug trade, used to finance terrorist activities, is a crucial issue challenging civilized society. The DEA maintains there is a link between the War on Terror and the War on Drugs, and there is, but there may be more ways than the DEA way to thwart the flow of drug money into the hands of terrorists.

The illicit-drug trade is a business, albeit illegal, which generates $322 billion of yearly revenue. The nature of the business itself, with high profit margins, has not deterred the drug entrepreneurs from taking big risks to satisfy the demands of the market. It does not matter what law enforcement agencies across the planet do to interfere with their business, these entrepreneurs will find a way to overcome whatever obstacles are put in their way. If their leaders are captured and imprisoned, they are quickly replaced by new leaders, but the drug flow does not stop; production may be reduced in any given supplying country to be expeditiously replaced by newfound supplies from a different country. Here, as in any other business, the law of supply and demand is at play; if there is demand for a given product, say illicit drugs, there will always be sufficient individuals, entrepreneurs, willing to supply the product to satisfy that demand, provided the price is right.

2.7 Collateral Damage

In summary, there is a global illicit-drug trade valued at $322 billion, of which $125 billion are generated in the U.S. Over the past thirty years, this illicit business nurtured the growth of powerful DTOs that have gained economic and political power in countries allied with the U.S. At the same time these DTOs are cooperating with known terrorist organizations that are sworn enemies of the U.S. This web of players and events generates negative direct impacts on society, they include: making millionaires and billionaires of common criminals, delivering mind-altering substances into the hands of millions of children, and the financing of terrorist groups. However, there is also some collateral damage worth mentioning.

Peasants in producing countries are lured into producing drug-related crops and away from food crops. The attraction of bigger profits leads peasants in Afghanistan and other countries to cultivate the opium poppies, peasants in Colombia, Peru, and Bolivia to cultivate the coca bush, and peasants in 142 countries to cultivate cannabis. The illicit-drug trade places a high price on these three crops and, moved by the profit incentive, the peasants abandon traditional food crops. These people are in the lower echelons of their societies and the newfound crops bring them the hope of moving up a few notches and finding what to them seems to be a better life. The drug business has placed them in harm's way, risking their very own freedom and security while they take their focus away from traditional food crops. Life has been turned upside down for droves of peasants at the bottom end of the illicit-drug business.

Corruption is devouring the moral fiber of society. The illicit-drug business is driven by huge payoffs. It involves complex logistical processes in the transportation of drugs from producing countries to markets. Thousands of miles have to be covered by air, sea and land; the merchandise has to go through country borders before arriving at the final destination. In this elaborate process there are many opportunities for interception; hence, it is a key objective of the trafficker to make the journey as smooth as possible. And what better way to insure a smooth journey than to pay for safe-conduct in advance? What is there to prevent the drug trafficker from making arrangements ahead of time with the authorities along the way to insure safe passage? Nothing! Therefore, that is what happens. It is true that many national authorities report significant drug interdictions, but it is also a fact that illicit drugs continue to flow into the hands of consumers, and drug traffickers receive billions of dollars in revenues. The Golden Rule comes into play: "He who has the gold sets the rules." In the process, the moral fiber of society is weakened and society as a whole becomes feebler, unable to cope effectively with this and other ills. The corruption driven by the illicit-drug trade inflicts severe damage on society.

The murder of honest law enforcement agents. It is a well-known practice of drug traffickers to bribe high-ranking law enforcement authorities in order to obtain safe passage for their drug shipments. The officials are only asked to look the other way on a specific day and time-frame, simple enough. Their subordinates do not even have to come into contact with the drug operation; they just have to be far away. This can be seen as a business proposition that cannot be refused, but it is not just that, it is actually a life proposition. Refusing it is like signing your own death sentence, once the official receives such a proposal, either he accepts it or he is dead. There are hundreds of cases in the annals of drug trafficking to support this assertion. More than one honest law enforcement agent in different countries has paid with his own life for refusing to accept the offer and look the other way. The loss of valuable, honest law enforcement officials is another casualty of the illicit-drug trade.

Except for the visible neighborhood drug peddler, the business structure — the DTOs — delivering the drug supplies to the drug peddler's doorsteps remains out of sight to the common person — it runs on silent mode. Nevertheless, it manages to deliver tons of drugs from the farm gate or the laboratory all the way into the hands of the consumers. In the process, fortunes — illicit fortunes — are made, drug traffickers are becoming very rich and very powerful, and this is a true nightmare taking place behind the scenes, out of sight, in silence. This is another piece of this silent and puzzling nightmare.

3

THE WAR ON DRUGS

Nobody dares predict an end to the war on drugs. All accounts by the anti-drug warriors themselves suggest that the war will go on forever given the current rules of engagement.

3.1 The Declaration of War

President Nixon declared the War on Drugs [1] at a press conference on June 17, 1971. Nixon named drug abuse as "public enemy number one in the United States" and two years later the Drug Enforcement Administration (DEA) was in place to handle all aspects of the drug problem facing the U.S. The DEA consolidated agents from various agencies including Customs, the CIA, and ODALE (Office of Drug Abuse and Law Enforcement). To this day, the DEA remains the legacy of Nixon's war on drugs.

Why declare a war on drugs? Wars are declared to fight and defeat an enemy perceived as a threat. In war, belligerent parties make use of the most advanced strategy and weaponry at hand and strive to achieve victory. Why did the U.S. need to declare a war on drugs back in 1971? Were we being attacked by a belligerent army or nation? It is true that the U.S. was faced with an increase in the use of illicit drugs and that trend required the urgent attention of the authorities. However, did the increase in the use of drugs require some sort of military strategy or was it more of an educational and health issue? The facts show that, after more than thirty years fighting the so-called war on drugs, there are more drugs being sold in the streets of U.S. cities than before the war got started. Still the premises leading the Nixon administration to start a war have been upheld by all subsequent administrations, and today the U.S. continues to fight a "war on drugs." How come all these administrations have perpetuated the war when the signs suggest there is no end in sight? There does not seem to be a real opportunity to win this war. As presented in the previous chapter, the illicit-drug trade has thrived during the past three decades. In the process, civilians continue to be the main casualties. Drug addiction is prevalent in all segments of our society, and the country has managed to condemn over half a million people to serve long jail sentences for drug-related crimes. Many of those sitting in jail are young people who are being deprived of a proper education; instead, they are exposed to the worst schooling possible, they are graduating from a sophisticated crime school in an overcrowded prison system. This is the type of labyrinth a nation can be trapped in by not exploring all the angles of a particular problem. The U.S. government defined, and continues to uphold, the drug problem as a supply problem and has a policy in place to attempt to destroy the supply chain. However, in economics, there are no stand-alone supply issues. The supply comes along with the demand, and in the absence of a proper demand for a given product, nobody in his or her right mind would venture into the business of supplying that product. The people who generate the demand for drugs are the same people meant to be protected by current drug policy. From the supply side perspective, society is faced with an economic issue and it must be handled as such. From a demand side perspective, the problem is much more complex, there are many societal issues — single parent families, working mothers, focus on the easy way out, lost of traditional values, and many others — which make children more vulnerable to the lure of drugs. Though these societal issues must be brought to bear in any effective drug policy, they are not at the core of this presentation; they deserve a presentation of their own. After thirty years of failing to eradicate illicit drugs, there is a need to review the current war on drugs strategy and the current drug policy.

The evolution of drug trafficking during the war. Whatever size the illicit-drug industry was back in the early 1970s when the war on drugs was declared, it has grown dramatically to the astonishing amount of $322 billion at retail and $94 billion at wholesale in 2003. As presented in the previous chapter, this is a very significant number rivaling many important industries and commodities trade. No small feat for an industry that grew under the siege of war. What drives the growth of any industry? Demand is definitely at the head of the list, but there are other drivers that are fundamental to the development of any industry; they are: the presence of suppliers in the marketplace and the price of the product which will make it attractive for potential suppliers to deliver the product to market. What role has the war on drugs played in the development of the illicit-drug industry? The war, the persecution of those daring to enter the business, introduces additional risks that in the eyes of the law enforcer are meant to deter suppliers from servicing the market. However, a higher risk commands a higher price, which operates as a surcharge, and a higher price becomes an incentive for suppliers to persevere or enter the marketplace. These higher prices also contribute to covering the increased operating costs of the trafficker who needs to acquire sophisticated technology, weaponry, telecommunications, and computers, to offset the actions of law enforcement. Therefore, it can be argued that the war on drugs is one of the driving forces behind the growth of the illicit-drug industry over the past thirty years. By driving prices up through the surcharge introduced by the additional risks facing the DTOs, the war on drugs makes the business more attractive.

Supporters of drug prohibition highlight that the decline in drug production over the last century did not occur by accident. According to Antonio Maria Costa, Executive Director of the United Nations Office on Drugs and Crime (UNODC), the decline "reflects serious, real-world efforts to eliminate drug cultivation and production. And it proves, beyond a doubt, that governments with the political will, strong legislation, and effective law enforcement and economic development policies can tackle this enormous problem, and solve it." [2] Costa's statement, though perhaps accurate when looking back into the late 19th and early 20th centuries, overlooks that the drug promotion paradigm a century ago was radically different from the drug prohibition paradigm in the latter part of the 20th and early part of the 21st centuries. The former was one of promotion and support by the colonial powers, while the latter is absent of such support. It is to be expected that under a drug-promotion environment, drug consumption would be significantly higher. The drug problem of the 21st century must be looked at within the context of the current socio-political-economic environment. The events of the late 19th and early 20th centuries — opium promotions by the colonial powers — are a poor reflection of today's drug market reality. There ought to be a logical way to face the multiple challenges confronting society on the subject of illicit drugs. Today's reality reveals that after more than thirty years of fighting the war on drugs, the streets of America continue to be flooded with drugs. Why insist on the survival of a failed policy when there are more promising options that have gone unexplored for so long?

3.2 The Battleground

Battlegrounds are the trademark of wars. World War II carved a presence all over Europe, in Northern Africa, and in many Asian countries. The fight against the illicit-drug industry is taking place all over the world; DTOs are global enterprises, not just in terms of the markets they serve, but also in terms of the sourcing and transportation of the drugs. This is the age of technology and globalization; actually, technology has made globalization possible for many industries, and the drug industry is no exception. Technology has also added flexibility to the DTOs. It is very easy to change smuggling routes on last-minute intelligence information; a simple telephone call over a mobile phone can do it. Therefore, the battleground is everywhere.

Where is the war being fought? From the U.S. perspective, the primary battleground of the war on drugs is on the home front, within the borders of the U.S. This is where the largest concentration of illegal activities takes place and where the largest monetary transactions are closed. As presented earlier, the U.S. accounts for almost 40% of the global drug business and contributes with 17% of the worldwide population of drug users. The large price differentials between the farm-gate, wholesale, and retail prices discussed earlier suggest that most of the money generated by the industry in the U.S. market is generated in U.S. territory at the retail level. This leads to a significant concentration of war related activities within U.S. territory. At the same time, there are a few foreign countries, source and transshipment countries, where there is significant involvement of the DEA and other U.S. authorities. These are the foreign battlegrounds of this war. The primary countries are Colombia, Mexico, and Afghanistan because of their relevance in the drug trade, but Peru and Bolivia are also important as well as a number of Latin American and Caribbean countries serving primarily as transshipment platforms. Besides Afghanistan, there are other countries in Asia involved, either as producers or transshipment locations.

The U.S. home front. The DEA has spearheaded the war on drugs since it was created in 1973. Extensive DEA reports attest to the many activities of DEA agents and to the overall anti-drug strategy conducted by all Federal Government administrations since President Nixon. One such report, the "Drug Intelligence Brief, The Evolution of the Drug Threat: The 1980s through 2002" [3] cited earlier, describes the evolution of the drug threat to the U.S. over more than twenty years. Throughout those years the DEA progressively increased its anti-drug activities on many fronts. At the same time, the DTOs discovered new opportunities, applied state of the art technologies, and expanded into new products and markets. Market conditions propelled the drug business to new highs during the 1980s and 1990s, and this in turn led to the intensification of DEA actions. The DTOs did not remain passive or idle; to every DEA action there was a forthcoming reaction from the DTOs. The increasing power of the DTOs became evident during two decades of war. The escalation of the war on drugs was under way, not only was it being fought on the home front, new fronts were being opened in the territories of supplying and transshipment countries in order to guarantee the stability of U.S. friendly countries and protect the security of the U.S. However, the DTOs operate in a dynamic and flexible environment; they do not face the same restraints faced by law enforcement agencies. DTOs need not abide by a code of ethics or a rulebook and the business generates abundant resources to facilitate access to state of the art technology and allow them to pave their way with generous contributions to those willing to cooperate with their endeavors.

When the Colombian drug lords feared extradition to the U.S., they did not hesitate to outsource the transportation of their drugs to the fledgling Mexican trafficking organizations. They actually introduced the convenient payment-in-product mode to compensate their Mexican counterparts; this new modality avoided large financial transactions and made life easier for the Colombians. This new process gave birth to the Mexican DTOs, making them just as powerful, or even more powerful, than their Colombian counterparts and opened additional fronts in the war on drugs. From this point on, the DEA found it necessary to include the Mexican drug cartels in the war on drugs and Mexico has since become the most important battleground outside the U.S. Regardless of the intensity of the anti-drug operations conducted by the DEA, the DTOs continue to adjust to the new habitat and the flow of drugs into the U.S. only suffers minor interruptions from time to time. Not only did the Colombians adjust their operations to the new conditions, in doing so they empowered their Mexican transshipment allies into becoming powerful DTOs and turned them into major competitors in the U.S. drug business. Three decades after the war started, the DTOs are stronger than ever, their business has grown beyond anybody's wildest imagination, and the DEA is facing a much more experienced and powerful enemy. Today, DTOs have the resources to acquire the latest technology to support their operations. The use of large jet aircrafts to transport multi-ton shipments of cocaine from Colombia to northern Mexico, the most up-to-date communications gear, and the Internet, have become some of the tools of the trade for the DTOs. Resources readily made available to them thanks to the deep pockets created by the drug business. In the end, the DEA efforts have succeeded in the interception of significant, but not sufficient, drug shipments. The 34.4 metric tons of cocaine reportedly intercepted by the DEA in 1998 barely accounted for 11.2% of the estimated cocaine consumed during that year in the US; even the reported 61.6 tons intercepted in 2002 accounted for only 20% of the cocaine consumed. These are optimistic percentages given that prices dropped 27% from 1998 to 2002 and this price drop suggests an increase in the supply of the drug on the streets. Only 371 kilos of heroin were reportedly intercepted in 1998, this is less than 1% of the heroin consumption estimate for that year; even the 705 kilos intercepted in 2002 does not exceed 1% of the heroin consumed. For 1998 the DEA reported the interception of 262 tons of cannabis, which is about 5% of the cannabis consumed.

The final outcome so far on the home front is not encouraging in terms of stemming the flow of illicit drugs. The DEA leadership claims progress has been made and that the agency is on the right track. However, to truly take drugs away from the streets of America, what would be the intensity required of the current war on drugs? Can the current drug policy embodied in the war on drugs deliver a drug free America or even reduce drug use to minimal levels? Thirty years of meager results should be enough to open the eyes of policymakers and deliver the message that new options ought to be explored. But if the outcome on the home front is not clear enough, a look at other fronts of this war should shed additional light on this controversial subject.

The war in Afghanistan — the war on drugs that is! As presented earlier, Afghanistan, after the toppling of the Taliban regime by the U.S. led NATO forces in 2001, became the world's leading supplier of heroin. It is estimated that almost 90% of the world supply of heroin in 2004 originated in Afghanistan under the new U.S. sponsored government of Afghan President Hamid Karsai. Afghanistan is a country at war; even though the Taliban regime was deposed in 2001 and 20,000 U.S. troops and 8,600 troops from NATO countries remain in the country, most of the country in 2006 was not under effective control of the central government of Karsai. Tribal chiefs seem to be in control of most of the countryside. In this environment opium poppy cultivation has again be-

85

come the major source of income for many Afghan farmers. Listen to Antonio Maria Costa, the chief anti-drug UN official:

"Afghanistan is both the largest cultivator of opium in the world, and the world's largest supplier, a double record. In spite of this distinction, only 3% of Afghanistan's growing fields are devoted to the cultivation of poppies, and only 10% of the population is involved in the drug industry. ... That may not sound like much but in Afghanistan; the revenue derived from opium is almost *twice* the amount of money the country has been taking in international aid. An acre of poppies returns twenty-seven times more than an acre of wheat." [4]

The incentives for the Afghan farmers are evident, so the country returned to the pre-Taliban dubious honor of being the world's leading cultivator of opium poppies, the raw material for the production of heroin. And this transition took place while U.S. and NATO forces were in charge of the country. Either the war on terror did not assist the war on drugs or the market forces are so great that even in the presence of a large military force in the country the drug business still flourished.

On May 22, 2005, The New York Times published a report accusing President Karsai of not doing enough to control poppy cultivation in Afghanistan [5]. This increase in opium poppy cultivation is crucial in light of the Taliban recovering strength in Afghanistan and the opium business helping them finance their operations. The New York Times reported that the production of opium had soared since the fall of the Taliban government in 2001 and warned that the former al-Qaeda haven was turning into a 'narco-state' despite the presence of more than 20,000 foreign troops. It highlighted that "cultivation reached a record 323,700 acres and yielded nearly 90% of the world's supply."

The New York Times report reflected an increasing interest on the part of U.S. authorities in engaging on a war on drugs in Afghanistan, "Washington has already set aside $780 million to train Afghan anti-drug forces and help farmers switch to legal crops this year." This is no different from similar commitments made by the U.S. to other drug producing countries — Colombia for instance — and the facts speak for themselves: drugs continue to flow in the streets of America. At the end of the road, the underlying issue has an economic ring to it. If an Afghan farmer can make twelve to twenty-seven times more money growing opium poppies instead of wheat, that farmer is very likely to assume the risks associated with opium. There is nothing wrong with the strategy to provide incentives to the cultivation of food crops; it is a healthy strategy in many ways. However, to think that doing so will be enough to stop the cultivation of opium poppy is naïve. It is naïve to presume that the drug lords making multimillion-dollar fortunes from the illicit trade of heroin will give up on their attempts to obtain the necessary raw materials; if not from Afghanistan, they will get them from some other country or countries capable of delivering. The law of supply and demand will not evaporate just because the U.S. is earmarking $780 million to prevent the growing of opium poppies in Afghanistan; the laws of economics will prevail, so the farm-gate price of opium may experience an increase over the coming years resulting from a more active war on drugs in the country. But the overall opium and heroin production will not be affected in any significant way in the medium and long term as long as the current drug prohibition policy is upheld.

The Afghan front of the war on drugs does not look very promising. The Karsai government does not really have control of the countryside, Afghan warlords do. The Taliban as of 2006 seem to be regaining influence in many Afghan provinces, and they are financing their activities with proceeds from the opium poppy crops. U.S. policy — the war on terror — created the conditions for the resurgence of the opium industry in Afghanistan therein counteracting another U.S. policy — the war on drugs. The booming opium industry is fueling the forces that the war on terror strategy is meant to destroy — al-Qaeda and their Taliban allies. This is a vicious cycle that is bound to gain strength as long as current the drug policy prevails.

The war in Colombia: crime, corruption, and the FARC. Colombia has for many years been the main sourcing country for cocaine, and the U.S. is its the primary market. It was illustrated earlier that Colombia, Peru, and Bolivia are the most propitious countries to grow the coca bush, the leaves of which are the raw material for the production of cocaine. However, for many years and as the result of actions taken in Peru and Bolivia to combat the cultivation of coca bush, most of the cultivation shifted to Colombia in the late 1990s. As of 2004 Colombia was responsible for 68% of cocaine production. The DEA with the collaboration of the Government of Colombia (GOC) has taken the war on drugs to the Colombian battlefield. Through the Plan Colombia, as this particular joint venture is called, the U.S. has funneled close to $5 billion to the GOC since 2000 to eradicate coca bush cultivation and the production of cocaine. This has proven to be a long and costly battle for the U.S. and its Colombian allies. The Drug Trade in Colombia: a threat assessment report published by the DEA in March 2002 provides relevant information on the war on drugs' Colombian front [6]. The report, apart from describing the many DEA supported GOC's anti-drug strategies, sheds light onto the ability of the DTOs to adapt to new conditions and provide continuity to their illicit activities. Some excerpts follow:

"In July 2000, the U.S. government (USG) enacted a comprehensive $1.3 billion assistance package in support of the GOC's Plan Colombia — an integrated strategy focusing on Colombia's peace process, economy, counter drug strategy, justice reform, human rights protection, democratization, and social development. Under the Plan Colombia assistance package, which supplements ongoing U.S. counter drug assistance, the USG is supporting Colombia's overall development strategy. On the counter drug front, the USG is providing equipment, training, and technical assistance to the Colombian National Police (CNP) and the Colombian military to increase their capability for eradication of coca leaf and opium poppy, and to conduct interdiction operations.

"If the Colombian Government significantly expands and sustains aerial coca eradication operations into southern Colombia as part of Plan Colombia, the DEA anticipates that the initial 'spillover' effect in coca cultivation will be limited to Colombia. The DEA would expect to see a shift in coca cultivation back into the traditional growing areas of central Colombia (the Guaviare), as well as expanded new cultivation in northern Colombia (Norte de Santander and San Lucas).

"If the Colombian Government is able to expand and sustain coca eradication operations in central and northern Colombia — while maintaining pressure on southern Colombia — the DEA expects to see some of Colombia's coca cultivation and cocaine base processing operations driven into Ecuador and Venezuela. Traffickers would also be expected to encourage expanded coca cultivation and cocaine base production in Peru and Bolivia — two countries that collectively produced about two-thirds of the world's cocaine base as recently as 1995.

"The DEA has already documented some spillover from Colombia into Ecuador. Limited reporting indicates that some Colombian traffickers are transporting cocaine base out of Colombia's Putumayo Department through northern Ecuador and into Colombia's Nariño Department in an effort to avoid insurgent interference and taxation. Some Colombian traffickers reportedly also use the reverse route — from Nariño to Putumayo via northern Ecuador — to smuggle the essential chemicals used to produce cocaine." [6]

When the activities of the DTOs come under severe attack in Colombia, they simply shift from one region of the country to another. Even the DEA predicted the spilling over of some of their activities to neighboring countries like Venezuela and Ecuador. The 2005 UN World Drug Report reflected a drop in Colombian cocaine production in 2003 and 2004 to 440 and 370 metric tons respectively. These figures were revised upward to 550 and 640 metric tons in the 2006 UN World Drug Report. This upward revision resulted from the discovery that the DTOs had shifted coca bush cultivation to regions of Colombia not previously inspected. This discovery brought to an end the hypothesis that cocaine remained abundant and relatively inexpensive because it was believed the DTOs were supplying the market from existing stockpiles — a self-delusion of the authorities. The fact seems to be that worldwide production of cocaine for 2004 increased to 937 metric tons in 2004, and not decreased to 687 metric tons as previously reported. The 2004 cocaine production turned out to be the second highest since 1990, only exceeded by the 950 metric tons produced in 1996. The DTOs are highly sophisticated, cash rich, global organizations capable of adjusting successfully to changing operating conditions.

The DEA report points to insurgent interference and taxation. The insurgency in Colombia is a phenomenon going back more than four decades, but in more recent years it has established close links with the DTOs. The DEA reports:

"The FARC employs a wide variety of tactics to meet its goals, and has greatly emphasized its military capability. Over the past two decades, the FARC has controlled large areas of Colombia's eastern lowlands and rainforest, which are the primary coca cultivation and cocaine base processing regions in the county. However, the FARC also engages in traditional terrorism and criminal activities such as kidnapping, extortion, assassination, and bombing oil pipelines." [6]

Press reports in the first half of 2005 showed the FARC involved in criminal activities outside Colombia. One such involvement was reported by Miami Herald reporter Gerardo Reyes in its Spanish edition, El Nuevo Herald, on March 27, 2005 [7]. According to this report the FARC had been involved in the kidnapping and murder in Asuncion, Paraguay, of the thirty-two-year-old daughter of the former president of Paraguay, Raul Cubas. Later on, reports surfaced linking the FARC in a trade of arms for drugs in Honduras, Central America. It is currently believed that because of the opportunities provided them by the resources derived from the drug trade, the FARC have extended their reach to a number of Latin

American countries. Therefore, the Colombian front of the war on drugs, instead of coming under control, is spilling over into other countries. The long-term consequences of this trend are hard to predict, but they could be catastrophic so long as the financial resources from the drug trade continue to engross the coffers of the DTOs and their allies.

Regarding the DTOs and the AUC self-defense groups, the DEA reported:

"…illegal self-defense groups do not appear to be directly involved in any significant coca, opium poppy, or cannabis cultivation. Paramilitary leader Carlos Castaño-Gil has admitted in press interviews, however, that his group receives payments from coca growers in southern Colombia to protect them from guerrillas." [6]

The DEA believes these groups are involved with the drug trade. Subsequent reports established a definite connection between the AUC and drug trafficking. The following is an excerpt from a press conference given by U.S. Attorney General John Ashcroft on September 24, 2002[8] just six months after the assessment by the DEA. Ashcroft stated:

"Today the Department of Justice is unsealing an indictment charging leaders of the United Self-Defense Forces of Colombia, or AUC, with trafficking over seventeen tons of cocaine into the United States and Europe since 1997. The AUC is a Colombian paramilitary group listed on the State Department's Foreign Terrorist Organization List.

"The indictment charges AUC leader Carlos Castaño-Gil and two other AUC members with five counts of drug trafficking. Also named in the indictment are AUC military commander Salvatore Mancuso and AUC member Juan Carlos Sierra-Ramirez. The United States has requested the extradition of all three of these defendants from the Republic of Colombia, one of our closest international law enforcement partners. They face sentences up to life imprisonment if convicted of all charges." [8]

91

Judging from the above reports by the DEA and U.S. Attorney General, the Colombian front of the war on drugs is a mess. The lure of big profits converted the self-defense groups, who presumably were fighting the FARC and other leftist guerrilla groups already cooperating with the DTOs, into willing partners of the DTOs. However, that is not everything going on in Colombia. The state of lawlessness prevalent in Colombia has driven the country into a nightmare of crime and violence. The DEA revealed in 2002:

"Colombia is one of the most dangerous countries in the world. According to the U.S. State Department and GOC statistics, Colombia had a 1999 per capita murder rate of 77.5 murders per 100,000 inhabitants, about thirteen times higher than that of the United States. Murders in Colombia increased from 24,358 in 1999 to 26,250 in 2000. Insurgent groups have routinely conducted bombings in and around major Colombian cities. Although drug-related and insurgent-related violence accounts for a significant portion of the murders in Colombia, common criminals are responsible for an estimated 75% of the reported murders.

"In addition, Colombia is the kidnapping capital of the world; with an estimated 2,000 to 3,000 people kidnapped each year. According to the U.S. State Department, from 1980 to 2000, nearly 120 U.S. citizens were kidnapped, primarily by leftist insurgent groups. Insurgent groups frequently establish roadblocks in order to rob and/or kidnap travelers. Colombian law mandates that individuals must coordinate their efforts to resolve kidnapping cases with the *Ministerio de Defensa/Programa Para la Defensa de la Libertad Personal* (Office of the Anti-Kidnapping Director)." [6]

This ally of the U.S., a major battlefield of the war on drugs, is in disarray. The power delivered to the DTOs by the huge financial resources generated through the drug trade does not allow for a level playing field, lawlessness prevails. The dice are loaded in favor of the DTOs and will continue that way unless a different drug strategy can be designed and implemented to dry up the huge stream of financial resources available to them under the current rules of engagement.

The war in Mexico: rampant crime and corruption on the U.S. doorstep. The closest Latin American neighbor, Mexico, shares a 2,000-mile border with the U.S. The illegal migration of Mexican workers seeking better opportunities for themselves and their families has been in the front pages of the U.S. press for many years. This border, extensive and porous, is an enticing magnet to those looking to improve their way of life. This privileged geographical situation did not pass unnoticed to the DTOs looking for better and safer smuggling routes into the U.S. Mexican grown cannabis has been entering the U.S. for almost half a century; more recently, Mexican heroin has also found its way through the Mexican border, though in much smaller quantities than the Afghan product. The most significant evolution to take place in the past quarter century was the increased use of Mexico as a transshipment country for the Colombian cocaine entering the U.S. Because of the pressures placed on the Colombian smuggling routes through the Caribbean, the Colombian DTOs turned to Mexican cannabis smugglers to move cocaine across the US-Mexican border. By the mid-1980s, this border became the major transportation route for cocaine into the U.S.

The evolution of Mexico as a major base of operations for DTOs is broadly documented in the DEA Drug Intelligence Report, Mexico: Country profile for 2003. [9] This report provides substantial information on the status of Mexico's involvement in the drug trade. The report is not a victory report; it is rather a state of affairs report that in many respects should raise serious questions about the effectiveness of the war on drugs strategy. In the executive summary of the report, Judith E. Bertini, Acting Assistant Administrator for Intelligence states:

"In its struggle against drugs, Mexico still faces daunting challenges. The drug trafficking organizations that control the production and shipment of drugs, related money laundering, and criminal activities remain powerful. These well-organized groups possess abundant financial resources and are adept at corrupting or intimidating public officials. Such organizations pose a serious threat to the United States because of their control of drug distribution networks throughout much of the United States." [9]

Not only are Mexican DTOs involved in cocaine transshipment activities, they are actually involved in the business of almost all major drugs of abuse in the U.S. and control distribution networks throughout the country. As a result, they are sharing not just in the wholesale margins of the business, but also in the more juicy retail margins. The drug business in Mexico is not monolithic. There are a number of illegal organizations competing for the markets and for the sources of supply. The competition amongst rival groups has produced a major increase in drug-related violence in the past decades. The DEA reports:

"The precise number of drug-related murders in Mexico is difficult to estimate, but drug-related violence accounts for hundreds of murders each year [10]. Typically, drug-related violence in Mexico is centered on retaliatory killings of individual traffickers. Murders of Mexican law enforcement officials, lawyers, politicians, and innocent citizens are also prevalent. In 2002, federal officials Juan Carlos Ventura-Moussong, Mario Roldan-Quirino, and Juan Palafox were brutally murdered. The U.S. Consulate in Nuevo Laredo, Tamaulipas, reported that eighteen active and former police officers were murdered, kidnapped, or wounded in shootings in 2002. Violence perpetuated by Mexican drug trafficking organizations persists with relative impunity because of law enforcement corruption, a scarcity of resources to properly investigate these crimes, and a lack of resolve due to the threat of retaliation.

"Many narco-assassinations in Mexico take place using assault weapons, such as AK-47s and AR-15s. These weapons are often used during high-profile drive-by shootings and other executions. Victims are sometimes kidnapped and then murdered, and their remains dumped along roadsides or in isolated desert areas. In addition, many drug-related murders are characterized by heinous acts of torture, including severe beatings, burnings, the severing of body parts, and other gruesome tortures. Drug-related violence is prevalent in the states of Baja California, Nuevo Leon, Tamaulipas, and Sinaloa due to ongoing struggles between groups rivaling for control of these strategic drug producing and transit regions. For example, the Mexican press reported that Tijuana, Baja California, saw 249 violent deaths among the general public in 2002, of which at least 70% of those deaths were drug-related. The Mexican press also reported that 25 executions occurred in the state of Nuevo Leon during 2002." [9]

The DEA depiction of drug crimes in Mexico befits the most macabre novel. The sad part is that it is a true account; it is not fiction. Mexican traffickers will stop at nothing needed to achieve their goals. Murder is used to eliminate enemies, or as a tool to intimidate those who might interfere with the business, it is common currency in the Mexican landscape. Impunity, together with deep pockets provided by the drug business itself, go hand-in-hand to keep the business rolling. The war on the Mexican front persists and is most likely to carry on without any sign of victory as long as the rivers of cash keep flowing into the hands of the DTOs. To stop this flow of money, the current drug prohibition policy must be overhauled. It is imperative that the fundamental issues are focused on and that a sound policy is developed. An effective policy must come together with enforceable legislation to have a good chance of success.

3.3 War Stories and Numbers

There are always statistics and war stories associated with any war, and the war on drugs is no exception. A visit to the DEA web site, www.dea.gov, leads into a vast information pool on the activities of the DEA and the war on drugs. There the reader can learn about drug and drug money interceptions. A large variety of intelligence reports and country specific assessments add to the pool of knowledge for the reader. The book *HEAVY TRAFFIC: 30 years of headlines and major ops from the case files of the DEA* [11] illustrates the tremendous effort made by DEA agents over the years in the continuation of this war. There is no questioning the valor and dedication of the thousands of DEA agents who, risking their lives, have struggled for years to try to bring to an end the scourge of illicit drugs on society. Unfortunately, this is a very complex war because it finds its roots in very complex issues and premises. This war is being fought because the federal government back in 1971 decided that a war must be fought to eliminate drugs from the streets of America, and the same message has been repeated year after year by the administration in charge. American society has grown accustomed to the war on drugs, some believe it is the wrong way to address the drug problem, but others are faithful supporters, somehow the war is perceived by the latter as "fighting the bad guys." The back cover of *HEAVY TRAFFIC* reads as follows:

"Since its inception in the 1970s, the Drug Enforcement Administration has fought an ever-growing battle against drugs — and against those who make, distribute, and abuse them. After billions of dollars spent and countless lives destroyed, the war is still being waged with no end in sight. Dedicated men and women continue to put their lives on the line every day to combat a social plague that knows no boundaries.

"In this compendium, the history of the United States' war on drugs is told through more than three decades of news stories and DEA case files that bring readers into the violent, shadowy world of drugs. From the cocaine cartels of Colombia and back-alley basement methamphetamine labs to the narco-terrorist connections that link drug lords to the war on terror; these are true stories of the crime, punishment, power, and politics that have defined America's campaign to eradicate a global scourge." [11]

Should society not review the premises that led to a war that judging by the warrior's own accounts cannot be won, "a war…with no end in sight"? A review of the numbers and some of the stories helps find a path to the answer.

United States war-on-drugs budget. How much money is America spending to fight this war? The fiscal year 2006 budget for the Office of National Drug Control Policy (ONDCP) alone was $12.4 billion, an increase 2.2% over the FY 2005 level of $12.2 billion. Most of this money, about 60%, is earmarked "disrupting the market." The rest is for education, community action and for treatment. Nonetheless this is not all that America spends on drug-related activities. An analysis made by Steven T. Jones of New Times (CA) in June 24, 1999 [12] revealed that the federal government was spending $17 billion per year fighting drugs through its Office of National Drug Control Policy. Jones pointed out that the figure was equivalent to what the government was spending on the Food Stamp program at the time, and on the country's entire General Sciences, Space, and Technology program. He pointed out that the actual financial cost of the drug war was much higher — as high as $50 billion — and equal to the combined budgets for all of our country's agriculture, energy, and veteran's programs. He stated that close examination could demonstrate that the total annual costs of the drug war would exceed $50 billion.

Jones was quick to highlight that state and local governments contributed $15.9 billion to the fight against drugs in 1991, and that this was the last year for which the federal government tallied that figure. At that time federal spending on drug eradication was only in the order of $8 billion. Of the $17 billion the federal government was directly spending in 1999 to control drug use, 61% went for criminal justice and interdiction, while only 30% went for treatment and prevention programs according to Jones.

Additionally, Jones pointed out that the California Department of Corrections had an annual budget of $3.9 billion to deal with 161,000 inmates, 46,655 of whom are being incarcerated for drug offenses at a cost of about $1.1 billion each year. In addition, nationwide, federal government figures revealed there were more than 1.7 million people in prisons and jails, 22% to 33% of those for drug offenses. At an average annual cost of about $20,000 per inmate, that added nearly $7.8 billion to the drug war price tag. Then there were the soft costs of the drug war, which may be impossible to calculate. Jones believes this data needs to be taken into account during any serious debate over whether the drug war is worth its costs.

Steven T. Jones' New Times publication brings economics into the discussion arena by illustrating how various elements associated with the war on drugs have a significant economic impact on the nation. These elements deserve careful consideration when working out the real numbers surrounding the war-on-drugs strategy, they add to the puzzle that America needs to put together if an effective drug policy is to materialize for future generations.

DEA success statistics: drug interceptions and drug-related arrests. The DEA has war trophies to show. From 1986 through 2002, the number of arrests made by DEA agents in the U.S. total 443,600. This number does not take into account the arrests made by local law enforcement agents. The yearly DEA figures range between 19,693 in 1986 to 27,635 in 2002, with a peak of 39,500 arrests in 1999. Figures are also available for drug seizures by DEA agents from 1986 through to 2002. They range from 28 metric tons (1997) to 75 metric tons (1999) of cocaine, 320 kilograms (1996) to 1,170 kilograms (1991) of heroin, and 98 metric tons (1991) to 630 metric tons (1987) of cannabis, among others; definitely not sufficient to seriously disrupt America's drug market.

These war trophies on the DEA mantel do little to stem the flow of drugs in America. As a matter of fact, the Bureau of Justice statistics [14] reported 1,745,700 arrests for drug abuse in 2004 of which 11%, or 194,200, were juveniles. The total number yields one person arrested in the U.S. every eighteen seconds. The U.S. prison population has grown by an average of 43,266 inmates per year since December 31, 1995; about 25% are sentenced for drug law violations. Regardless of these law enforcement "successes" the DTOs continue to pump huge quantities of illicit drugs into the market and continue to fill their coffers. The extradition to the US, from Colombia primarily, of some of the key DTO leaders in recent years has not made any significant dent in the operational capabilities of the DTOs. As mentioned earlier, the departed leader is quickly replaced by an associate, or a competing DTO takes over the operation. The fundamental profit incentive does not disappear and the economic laws continue to rule. This reality has not and will not disappear because of the war on drugs.

Casualties at the front lines: murdered in the line of duty — the Enrique Camarena story. Many DEA agents have fallen in the line of duty fighting the war on drugs. However, none has received more coverage than the story of Enrique Camarena's abduction, torture and murder. Camarena was an undercover DEA agent first assigned to the agency's Guadalajara, Mexico office in 1981. He had served for two years in the United States Marine Corps before joining the DEA in 1974. Before his death his work became famous all over the U.S. and Latin America. He successfully infiltrated drug trafficking bands and helped disrupt the activities of many of them. His name became well known, though he managed to keep his face out of the newspapers. Eventually he was identified by one of the drug trafficking groups he was trying to infiltrate. He was kidnapped, tortured and murdered in 1985 by members of the Caro-Quintero drug trafficking organization, a leading DTO operating in Mexico. Hours after Camarena's abduction, Alfredo Zavala-Avelar, a Mexican agriculture department pilot working with anti-drug authorities, was also abducted. Camarena's body was found on March 5, although forensic studies suggested February 9 as the date of death. The story of Camarena's demise is well told in the DEA museum publication on the Department of Justice website [14]. Rafael Caro-Quintero, a leading suspect in the Camarena abduction and murder, left Mexico on a flight to Costa Rica, where he stayed until he was finally apprehended by Costa Rican authorities on a lead from local DEA agents and extradited back to Mexico. He was judged in Mexico and sentenced to serve forty years in a

Mexican prison. The Caro-Quintero organization under his command continues to operate under the leadership of his brother. The death of agent Camarena led to widespread investigation by U.S. authorities.

The Camarena story is one of heroism and dedication. However, it also reveals the powers behind the scenes in Mexico; it is not a story about doing justice. Justice failed in many ways, the story of a Mexican physician linked with the torture episode is but one example of this failure. Dr. Humberto Alvarez-Machain was allegedly involved in the kidnapping, torture and murder of Enrique Camarena by prolonging his life so that others could further torture and interrogate him. Alvarez-Machain was kidnapped himself in Mexico by DEA agents or bounty hunters because of the difficulties encountered by U.S. authorities to obtain his extradition to the U.S. His case lasted two years in court and was later dismissed by the judge on the basis of insufficient evidence. Another person implicated in the murder of Camarena, Ruben Zuno-Arce, also a Mexican citizen, was detained in the US, brought to trial and convicted in 1992 of complicity in the death of Agent Camarena. Zuno-Arce happens to be the brother-in-law of former Mexican president Luis Echeverria-Alvarez (1970-1976).

Throughout the struggle of U.S. authorities to bring to justice all those thought to be implicated in the death of Agent Camarena, there was little cooperation from Mexican authorities, who had a long list of reasons not to cooperate, some of them technical, some political, and maybe some motivated by the long tentacles of the Mexican DTOs extended throughout the structures of power in Mexico. Another instance of apparent justice was the trial in Mexico of Rafael Caro-Quintero, though he denied any implications with Camarena's death, he was tried and convicted of kidnapping, murder and other drug law violations and was sentenced to serve forty years in a Mexican high-security prison on December 12, 1989. Regardless of various appeal processes being used by Caro-Quintero's lawyers, he continues to serve his sentence. However, the prison system in Mexico is not immune to the plague of corruption covering the country. Early in 2005 a controversy arose regarding the conditions of privilege of a number of prisoners in the high-security prison of La Palma, state of Mexico. This is the prison where Caro-Quintero has been serving his sentence. On January 11, 2005 the prison authorities, alleging security measures, transferred fifty prisoners from La Palma installations to a new prison in Puente Grande, state of Jalisco; Caro-Quintero was among those transferred. On January 28, he was again transferred to a high-security prison in Matamoros, state of Tamaulipas. His brother Miguel Angel Caro-Quintero is also serving a sentence in this prison. These shuffling of prisoners during the month of January was the result of attempts by the Mexican government to bring to an end the lax security conditions enjoyed by Caro-Quintero and a number of high-risk detainees, many for drug law violations. It turned out that these drug lords found a way to corrupt prison officials and were able to operate their illicit-drug businesses from inside the prison. Evidently justice is not being done to Enrique Camarena if the objectives he fought and gave his life for are being trampled under foot. However, can justice prevail when the money in the hands of the DTOs overshadows any reasonable attempt to curtail their activities? It is very unlikely, that is one lesson of the Camarena story. Big money is the master key of the DTOs; it opens the way for them to continue their thriving business.

3.4 The Corrupting Power of Drugs

Everybody has a price! Some people are driven by need, so all it takes is a bit of money to have them do whatever is required. Others are moved by greed, it takes a bit more money to get them to comply with somebody else's wishes. There are some individuals in the human landscape who claim they do not have a price, that there is no money in this world that will make them do something they believe to be wrong. It is certainly possible to find this kind of individual, they have no monetary price; there is no amount of money capable of making them break their principles. However, the rule may not apply when non-monetary retribution or even outright threats are at play. Are these righteous individuals immune to those also? The DTOs' most powerful asset is money, and they have plenty of it. Their industry commands at least $322 billion every year. It is possible to buy a great many loyalties with that kind of money. For those who do not have a dollar sign in their forehead, that same money is available to pay off the henchmen needed to make good on a threat; whether the threat has to be executed on the uncooperative party or on an unsuspecting relative. Therefore, the thesis that everybody has a price is fairly accurate when we move beyond the realm of monetary rewards and enter the world of non-monetary retribution.

LAPD policemen turned drug dealers. The temptation of easy money can lure police officers into the drug business. This definitely has to do with greed, but it is a fact that many police officers day in and day out risk their lives in the fight against drug organizations. While doing their job, they come into contact with the people they are fighting only to discover that these individuals live very wealthy lives and very often come out of detention a few hours after being taken in. The power of drug money becomes evident, and with it the temptation to change sides, to move into the business themselves. The story of Ruben Palomares, a Los Angeles Police Department (LAPD) officer involved in many illicit activities, including drug trafficking, made the pages of the Los Angeles Times in October 20, 2004 [15]. Palomares and his associates stole hundreds of thousands of dollars worth of drugs, cash, guns and other items over a four-year period beginning in 1998. The Times reported that Palomares' criminal rampage ended in June 2001, when he was arrested in San Diego, together with four other men, in a DEA cocaine sting operation. The collaboration of one of the detainees led to the uncovering of Palomares' gang modus operandi. He pleaded guilty to the San Diego drug charges in 2003 and was sentenced to fifteen years in federal prison. After his arrest, a team of FBI agents and LAPD detectives pieced together the extent of his criminal activity. It extended into a 1999 police shooting by former LAPD Officer William Ferguson. Authorities believed Ferguson was a member of Palomares' crew.

The Palomares story is not unique; it is one of many stories uncovering how greed or need may lead to the corruption of police officers.

102

The temptation is big, though there is no apparent objective justification for a police officer to betray his oath of duty. But it happens, and when the subject of illicit drugs is involved, with its path to easy and big money, it is bound to happen often. Those who stand behind the perimeter of risk within their zone of comfortable safety do not experience the many risks to which police officers expose themselves when fighting drug traffickers. The combination of these risks together with the opportunity to make big money to address their needs or greed make for an explosive cocktail capable of leading the most honest cop astray; it is difficult to keep their hands off an open coffer. This is not meant to be a justification for crooked cops; it is more of a warning to society that law enforcement will be in a better position to serve the community if it did not have to face the powerful criminal organizations that flourish with the nourishment provided by the same laws that are supposed to prevent such crimes.

Edward K. O'Brien — DEA supervisory special agent gone sour. On August 14, 1989 Edward K. O'Brien, a seventeen-year DEA veteran, was arrested by fellow DEA agents at Boston Logan airport and charged with transporting more than 62 pounds of cocaine in exchange for thousands of dollars in cash. O'Brien had had a successful DEA career which won him commendation after commendation for his work as an agent, but all of the sudden he became the highest DEA agent to be charged with smuggling drugs. Many hypotheses were brought forward to try to explain what had happened to this hard-driving law enforcer. Some speculated that O'Brien might have been conducting a sting operation of his own in an effort to reach higher ups in a drug distribution network. Others suspected that he was overwhelmed by family and debt problems and searched for a way out by collaborating with the same kind of people he had been so successful in bringing to court. In the end the records show he was prey to a DEA sting operation. Even though the DEA was aware of his personal and financial problems, rather than providing support to a successful warrior of the war on drugs, they chose to set him up and entrap him. Maybe this was the DEA way of telling its agents that Big Brother will show no leniency to those who stray from the path of

103

faithful adherence to duty. Whatever the ultimate cause was, the results show that even a DEA agent, a warrior of the elite corps fighting the war on drugs can go sour, can change sides under the lure of the wealthy lifestyle of the drug traders. Finally, in January 1991 O'Brien entered a guilty plea, almost two weeks before he was to go on trial for four counts of conspiracy and bringing 116 pounds of cocaine to Boston from Florida. As part of the plea bargain agreement, he pleaded guilty to one of the four counts and admitted he was paid $39,000 to transport cocaine from Florida to Boston in the summer of 1989. O'Brien was sentenced in March 1991 to six years in prison.

O'Brien's story speaks of the temptations of the drug trade even for those at the front lines of the war on drugs. Back in August 19, 1989, at the outset of the O'Brien case, Boston Globe reporter Michael Kranish wrote: [16]

"FBI Director William Sessions, whose agency was recently rocked by news that a Chicago agent had been charged with selling cocaine, said in a breakfast with reporters last week that the temptations are enormous. 'The opportunity to make $25,000 by just turning your head is readily and routinely available. . . . I think any time you have such tremendous quantities of money that are available, both for action and inaction on the part of police authorities, it is logical to have it.' Sessions said of corruption. 'I don't know that anybody in any element of law enforcement can escape that. People will try to bribe judges, prosecutors, law enforcement people. But the affirmative side of it is we have so little of it.'

"But Hubert Williams, president of the Washington-based Police Foundation, said the pervasiveness and acceptance of drugs, and the huge amount of money tied to the drug trade, will inevitably lead to more police corruption. Among other potential responses, he suggested drug testing of police officers and a crackdown on drug users as a means of warning officers that illicit-drug activity will not be tolerated. 'I don't think corruption is pervasive at all right now, but the seeds are there for it to become a major problem,' he said. 'I don't think it has any way to go but up, and I think it will go up unless there is a radical change.'

"Convicted drug smuggler Max Mermelstein told the Senate Judiciary Committee last week that drug dealers sometimes give an ultimatum to those they are trying to bribe. 'Either they take the money or they die,' Mermelstein said."

Back in 1989 former FBI Director William Sessions had it very clear; there were plenty of opportunities for law enforcement agents to be corrupted, the sheer power of money knocks at the doors of those enforcing the law. Those challenges have not been reduced in the past fifteen years; on the contrary, they have increased. The DTOs are more powerful today than they were back in the late 1980s. Hubert Williams was right when he said back then that corruption had nowhere to go but up. For the law enforcement agent it is like being between a rock and a hard place. On one hand the agent risks his life day in and day out in the war against drug criminals, and on the other he is constantly presented with the possibilities of a more financially rewarding life if he chooses to cooperate with them. O'Brien's case brought under the spotlight the vulnerability of law enforcement to the corrupting power of drugs. How extended corruption is today within law enforcement is hard to tell, but the threat is pervasive. The war on drugs is an uphill struggle for those fighting on the side of the law, and to make matters worse, there is no victory in sight.

General Jesus Gutierrez-Rebollo — the Mexican anti-drug czar surprise. The Los Angeles Times correspondent, Mark Fineman, writing from Mexico City, reported on December 6, 1996 [17] on the background and impeccable credentials of the newly appointed Mexican anti-drug czar, General Jesus Gutierrez-Rebollo.

Fineman described some of the successful actions undertaken by Gen. Jose Gutierrez-Rebollo, a member of Mexico's presidential guard and military commander in Guadalajara, when he confronted Hector Luis "El Guero" Palma, the high-profile leader of one of Mexico's main drug cartels, who enjoyed the protection of federal police officers on his payroll. This confrontation led Gutierrez-Rebollo to mobilize 200 soldiers to surround the house where "El Guero" Palma was hiding and arrest him and thirty-three police officers under Palma's orders without firing a single shot.

The operation was heralded as a model of the Mexican military's new high profile in the Mexican government's war on drugs and police corruption. Gutierrez-Rebollo, described as a low-profile and press-shy general, was appointed in early December 1996 Mexican anti-drug czar as head of Mexico's elite National Institute for Combating Drugs. He was sixty-two at the time and the first military officer to serve in the post traditionally reserved for well-connected politicians. In this capacity Gutierrez-Rebollo became the key point man working with U.S. law-enforcement in the war on drugs.

The appointment of Gen. Gutierrez-Rebollo to his new position was openly welcomed by U.S. anti-drug czar retired Gen. Barry R. McCaffrey. In McCaffrey's own words as reported by the Los Angeles Times, his Mexican counterpart "has a public reputation of absolute integrity." The Times went on to say: "It was precisely to improve performance and to attack enduring police corruption that officials said (Mexican president) Zedillo [18] turned to a senior officer of the Mexican army — a disciplined force that remains largely untouched by corruption."

The Los Angeles Times report was certainly loaded with optimism following what seemed continuous failure by the Mexican authorities to strike sufficient points in their own war on drugs. There was hope in the general's "public reputation of absolute integrity" in the eyes of Mexican and U.S. authorities, including then U.S. anti-drug czar Gen. Barry R. McCaffrey. The Mexican general had built a strong reputation by his unquestionable actions against some of the most powerful Mexican drug cartels. However, there were many surprises in store for everyone. Only a couple of months after his appointment as Mexican anti-drug czar, Gen. Gutierrez-Rebollo was taken into custody accused of collaborating with a rival drug cartel. It was true that the general had been fast on the tracks of the Tijuana Cartel, one of the most important drug cartels operating in Mexico, but in doing so he had come very close to the drug leaders and had got to know their ways. As it turned out, the general had established a very close working relationship with Amado Carrillo-Fuentes, head of the Juarez Cartel; maybe that was the reason why his predecessor as Mexican anti-drug czar, Francisco Molina, was having extraordinary difficulties delivering results during his anti-drug tenure. The general's act of betrayal turned out for the worst, it actually sent a cloud of mistrust amongst U.S. and Mexican anti-drug warriors. This was reflected in a Washington Post article published on November 5, 1997, which stated: "Top U.S. officials are acutely aware of the dilemma, having been scorched themselves. Today, the enduring symbol of the U.S.-Mexican partnership against drugs is a photograph of White House anti-drug policy chief Barry R. McCaffrey and the former Mexican anti-drug chief, army Gen. Jesus Gutierrez Rebollo, taken in January during their first meeting in Washington. During the session, McCaffrey lavished praise on his counterpart. Three weeks later, Gutierrez was jailed on allegations that he was on the payroll of Mexico's most notorious drug kingpin, the late Amado Carrillo Fuentes, head of the Juarez Cartel." [19]

General Gutierrez-Rebollo is now serving a seventy-one-year prison sentence for a number of drug-related crimes. This long sentence may be viewed as a sign of victory over the Mexican drug cartels, and the corrupt officials who betrayed the trust of their society. Unfortunately, it may only be the façade of a farce going on at the core of the spheres of power in Mexico. The combination of drug trafficking, ingrained corrupt practices within the echelons of government in Mexico, and the outright disregard for the law, might be of no concern to the typical American citizen if Mexico were located on a different planet. But the naked truth is that Mexico shares a 2,000-mile border with the U.S., it is America's third largest trading partner, and has become the source of a very large share of the imported illicit drugs consumed by Americans. Mexico and Mexican security are crucial to American security; there is no way the U.S. can pretend to develop a secure drug environment without taking Mexico into account. The fundamental issue is how to design an effective drug policy, taking Mexico into consideration, which would allow the U.S. to minimize the risks from illicit drugs.

The current course of the war on drugs has proven ineffective. The three stories of corruption presented above are a sample of what is very likely happening on a much wider scale within the spheres of law enforcement. Even though back in 1989 former FBI Director William Sessions believed that incidents of corruption were actually the exception, the fact is that the law enforcement agents involved in the previous stories had an impeccable reputation until the evidence surfaced to demonstrate the contrary.

3.5 The War on Drugs as a Business Driver

More than thirty years at war and there is no end in sight. Drug trafficking continues to thrive all over the globe. A $322-billion-a-year business is the most reasonable estimate at the present time, and it seems to have been at that level for the last ten years (1996-2005). If it is assumed it was $225 billion per year for the previous ten years (1986-1995) and $125 billion for the ten years before (1976-1985), the last thirty years yields cumulative revenues of $7,720 billion. Though this may turn out to be a very conservative estimate, the sheer size of the numbers is terrifying. This is plenty of money to buy many loyalties; a fraction will certainly suffice to buy the necessary ones. Those whose loyalties cannot be bought can be removed from the playing fields, exterminated, through the services of faithful henchmen, at a lower cost. Why has the war on drugs not been able to squelch the drug business and reduce the flow of fortunes into the coffers of the DTOs? Is it a matter of insufficient resources allocated to fight the war? Certainly, after thirty years, the true believers — the anti-drug warriors — are more entrenched in their ways; every new drug or drug money interception is a reason for joyful celebration. Hope is boosted by the apparent progress being made in their crusade. They have come to believe that more resources will do the job; hence, they turn into an interested party in the squabble for government funds, they will fight hard for additional taxpayer's money to fund their crusade.

The economics of the drug business. The drug business is no different from any other business, and as such it is ruled by economics. The law of supply and demand explains the workings of the drug market. What does this mean for the drug trade and for the war on drugs? It has many implications. In terms of the drug trade, the demand curve reflects how much of a particular drug will be bought by the consumers at different price levels — the lower the price, the higher the demand for the drug. Likewise, the supply curve reflects how much of the drug will be supplied by the vendors, the drug traffickers; as the price increases, the drug traffickers will deliver more drugs to the market. The point where these two curves intersect will determine the market price and the quantity transacted (see Chart 3.1). Simple enough, there will be no supply of the drug if there is no demand, i.e., if there are no consumers wanting to buy the drug. Furthermore, as the war on drugs intensifies, the suppliers — the DTOs — face greater risks; they may be intercepted, brought to court for drug law violations, and be convicted and sentenced to serve many years in prison; they also may be killed during a face off with law enforcement or with a rival trafficker. As the risk to the DTOs increases, the supply curve shifts from Supply 1 to Supply 2 (see Chart 3.2), representing the increased risk to the DTO supplying the market — the supplier will, under the new market conditions, request a higher price to deliver the same amount of drugs as before. The additional business risks created by the war on drugs generate a new supply curve — Supply 2 — reflecting a surcharge to the original drug price introduced by the additional risks. The point of intersection of the Supply 2 curve and the Demand 1 curve is the new market equilibrium. The result of the increased market risk is that less drugs are transacted, but at a higher price. Business is still good for the supplier — perhaps even better — less product volume but at a higher price. The higher price is bound to attract new and possibly more innovative vendors into the market. Independent of the increase in market risk that may occur, the business motivation of the suppliers is bound to lead

109

to better and more effective marketing and promotional schemes: Distributing drugs in elementary schools to expand the market base or the creation of new varieties of the drugs to increase appeal and maybe create more addicts; for instance, crack cocaine is smokable and is supposed to be more addictive than powder cocaine, and powder heroin can be snorted without the stigma of injection; both are innovative products. These new products and marketing actions on the part of DTOs will impact the demand curve, creating a new consumer paradigm. The demand curve will shift to the right, representing the new market demand conditions; at a given price more drugs will be demanded by the consumers (see Chart 3.3). The new demand curve — Demand 2 — will have a new intersection point with the supply curve —Supply 1. This new intersection point represents a higher price being charged for the drug and a larger volume of the drug being transacted in this market. Finally, if both events happen simultaneously — higher market risks and a bigger demand driven by innovation — the new intersection point (see Chart 3.4) will yield a higher price and a higher volume. The new equilibrium point has shifted from the low price and low volume position (P1, Q1) to a higher price and higher volume position (P4, Q4).

CHART 3.1 DRUG SUPPLY MEETS DEMAND

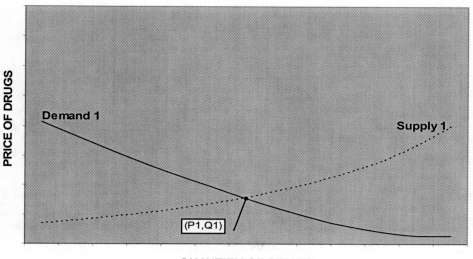

CHART 3.2 SUPPLY SHIFT DUE TO ADDED RISK

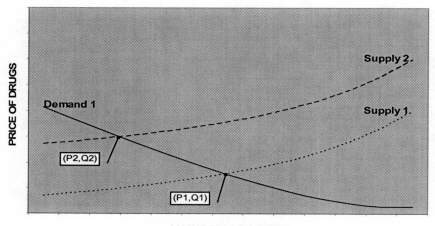

CHART 3.3 DEMAND SHIFT DUE TO PRODUCT OR MARKETING IMPROVEMENT

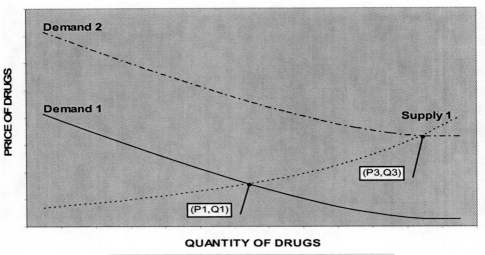

CHART 3.4 DRUG SUPPLY AND DEMAND SHIFT

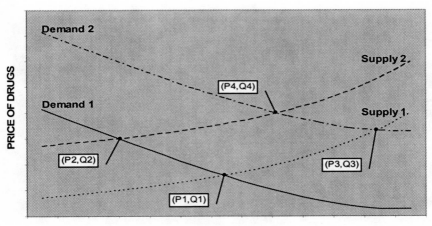

The net result of the war on drugs in the face of the inviolable laws of economics is to make the drug business more lucrative for the DTOs. The advocates of the war on drugs seem to believe in the possibility of neutralizing the effects of the law of supply and demand. However, in reality the laws of economics continue to operate, the only difference is that the business becomes riskier for the traffickers, but the rewards are plenty to compensate for those additional risks. Chart 3.4 can also be used to illustrate what may have happened from 1990 to 2000 with the cocaine and heroin market in the U.S. (see Tables 2.2 and 2.3). Over this time period the prices of both drugs dropped as the consumption increased. If we assume the demand curve remained constant during this time period (say Demand 1), the drop in price with an increase in the quantity consumed has to be explained by a shift in the supply curve (say from Supply 2 to Supply 1), moving the point of equilibrium from (P2, Q2) to (P1, Q1). It was during this decade that the big Colombian drug cartels came under severe attack from drug enforcement, giving way to the emergence of a myriad of drug trafficking organizations that replaced the handful of monolithic cartels. This event — a more competitive marketplace — may have led to the new supply curve paradigm, a direct result of the war on drugs.

The management of the drug business. DTOs are very resilient organizations; they are used to managing very complex global businesses with the most advanced technology and are proficient in the use of the tools of the trade. They have no respect for the lives and/or suffering of their adversaries and no qualms about using whatever means are necessary to further their goals. The most grotesque acts of torture have been documented. Their organizations follow a cell structure — typical of any clandestine group — to increase their chances of survival when under attack. DTO's management has survived over thirty years of war; as a matter of fact they have thrived and become more powerful. Their business has been made more attractive by the war itself. They have improved their organizational methods and figured out ways to replenish their ranks. When a top leader finds his way into a long prison sentence, the DTO ei-

113

ther replaces him with somebody from their ranks, or they fight it out amongst the aspiring lieutenants; whoever wins takes over. Their own operating rules do not preclude any of these options. Sometimes the replacement is only so in appearance, somebody takes the visible leadership of the organization, but the jailed leader continues to run the DTO from his prison cell. On occasions a competing DTO may take over the business of a DTO in disarray. In summary, DTOs do not seem to lack resources to replace a missing leader if the need arises. Therefore, as the facts of the war on drugs show, the business of illicit drugs continues to flourish even after thirty years of continuous warfare. The DEA Drug Intelligence Report-Mexico: Country Profile for 2003 [9] illustrates the resiliency of the Mexican DTOs. The report reads:

"The most prominent Mexican drug trafficking organizations that impact the United States include the Arellano-Felix organization, the Vicente Carrillo-Fuentes organization, the Armando Valencia organization, the Miguel Caro-Quintero organization, and the Osiel Cardenas-Guillen organization. These five organizations are responsible for the majority of the cocaine, heroin, methamphetamine, marijuana, and precursor chemicals that enter the United States.

"In early 2002, **the Arellano-Felix organization (AFO)**, historically one of the most powerful drug trafficking organizations in Mexico, was dealt two huge blows: the death of its notoriously brutal enforcer, Ramon Arellano-Felix, on February 10, 2002, and the arrest of its overall chief of operations, Benjamin Arellano-Felix, on March 9, 2002. For more than a decade, the AFO had been one of the strongest and most violent drug trafficking organizations operating in Mexico, primarily in Tijuana, and in the United States, mainly between San Diego and Los Angeles. While these two events impacted the overall operations of the AFO, the organization continues to operate.

"**Since the death of Amado Carrillo-Fuentes in July 1997**, the structure of the Carrillo-Fuentes organization, for the most part, remained intact with key lieutenants retaining control of specific geographic areas.

These key lieutenants — who include Amado's brother Vicente Carrillo-Fuentes, Juan Jose Esparragosa-Moreno, and Ismael Zambada-Garcia — work cooperatively to move cocaine north to major U.S. cities.

"Mexican national **Armando Valencia-Cornelio** is one of the most significant drug traffickers operating in the Republic of Mexico and a key figure in the interrelationship between major Mexican and Colombian drug trafficking organizations. During Operation MILLENNIUM [20], the Armando Valencia organization, whose primary bases of operation are in Guadalajara, Jalisco, and the State of Michoacan, was receiving approximately 20 tons of cocaine on a monthly basis. These shipments were transported primarily to the west coast of Mexico from the north coast of Colombia via maritime vessel, and subsequently moved north for ultimate smuggling into the United States. Despite the successes of Operation MILLENNIUM, Armando Valencia continued to traffic in cocaine, heroin, and marijuana. On August 15, 2003, Armando Valencia-Cornelio and seven of his associates were arrested in Mexico at a restaurant near Guadalajara. Armando Valencia is facing drug trafficking charges in both Mexico and in the United States, where he is wanted in a Miami investigation.

"Based in Sonora, Mexico, the **Caro-Quintero organization** is involved in the trafficking of large quantities of cocaine and marijuana. The organization was initially headed by Rafael Caro-Quintero until his arrest in 1985 for his involvement in the murder of DEA Special Agent Enrique Camarena. Following the incarceration of Rafael, Miguel Angel Caro-Quintero ascended to the leadership of the organization until his arrest in December of 2001. Subsequent to Miguel's arrest, the brothers, Jorge and Genaro Caro-Quintero, and sister, Maria Del Carmen Caro-Quintero, assumed control of the organization.

"Until his March 14, 2003, arrest, **Osiel Cardenas-Guillen** was a major marijuana and cocaine trafficker and leader of the Gulf Cartel, formerly led by the now-incarcerated Juan Garcia-Abrego. Additionally, Cardenas-Guillen is responsible for the November 9, 1999, attempted assault and abduction of a DEA agent and a FBI agent in Matamoros,

Tamaulipas. On May 18, 2000, a Mexican judge issued arrest warrants for Cardenas-Guillen and twelve co-conspirators following their indictments in Mexico on charges of attempted murder, drug trafficking, and illegal possession of firearms based on the November 9, 1999, assault. On December 14, 2000, a U.S. federal indictment was unsealed against Cardenas-Guillen charging him on two counts of possession with intent to distribute more than 100 kilograms of marijuana and three counts of assault on a federal officer (18 United States Code (USC) 111). Three criminal associates of Cardenas-Guillen are named in the same indictment. Cardenas-Guillen is currently imprisoned in Mexico awaiting trial and possible extradition to the United States. Despite his incarceration, his organization remains active in drug trafficking."

There is no better evidence of the resiliency of Mexican DTOs than the above excerpts from the DEA report. These five DTOs continued to operate successfully even after their leaders had been imprisoned with very long sentences. So business is good for the DTOs in spite of the war on drugs, or perhaps because of it.

3.6 Can the War on Drugs be Won?

The Geneva Convention establishes the rules of warfare between belligerent countries; it is supposed to bring civility onto the battlefield. Former President Nixon may have been searching for emphasis when he declared the war on drugs back in 1971. However, fighting crime, or even fighting the ills of a society, does not necessarily call for a declaration of war. War defines clear enemies and in the quest for victory the belligerent parties aim at defeating the adversary, this may translate into killing as many enemy soldiers as possible. The goal is the destruction of the enemy. Who is the enemy in the war on drugs? Is it the hopeless junky, or maybe the regular drug user? What about the occasional drug user, is he the enemy too? Certainly the people running the DTOs look unquestionably like enemies, they are the largest beneficiaries of the drug trade. The definition of who the enemy is, is not an easy one. This dilemma results from calling law enforcement a war. From the perspective of law enforcement, of any law, the players may be classified in a different way. There are the criminals, those who are breaking the law and by doing so inflicting damage on other members of society. Then there are the victims, those members of society upon who damage is being done by criminals. In addition, there are the law enforcement agents and the judicial authorities in charge of enforcing the law and dispensing justice. In the so-called war on drugs there seems to be some confusion regarding who the victims are. Certainly there are innocent victims sometimes caught in the crossfire between law enforcement and criminals, or the citizen held up by a drug addict looking for money to pay for his addiction. Therefore, the addict becomes a criminal in this particular story. However, is this addict a criminal because he is an addict, or because he robbed an unsuspecting citizen, or both? The targets selected by the war on drugs have generated discomfort and confusion in many quarters of American society and this environment imperils its success. Detractors of the war on drugs argue that a drug user, any drug user, cannot be marked as a criminal. Some will even go as far as to say that any adult citizen has the right to introduce into his body whatever substance he chooses to, and that as long as he does not place any other citizen in danger when doing so, he is not committing a crime. But the law, as it is interpreted under current drug prohibition policy, classifies the drug user as a criminal and that introduces a whole new set of rules. So in a world which classifies victims as criminals, and makes law enforcement initiatives a synonym of war, the fundamental issues associated with today's illicit drugs remain in the dark; and the so-called war goes on without an end in sight.

The lessons of thirty years at war. David Robbins [11] has managed to put together a compendium of thirty years of escalating war stories reflecting the struggle against the violent and shadowy world of drugs. The number of DEA arrests and drug seizures mentioned earlier reflect, in most cases, a rising trend, an illusion of successful actions led by DEA agents. The history of the war on drugs has been one of ever-growing battles against those who make and distribute them, but also against those who use and abuse them. The drug user is treated in the same league as the manufacturer and the distributor. In spite of this growing battle, drugs continue to be available in the streets of America. Could it be that battles are being won, but the war is being lost? Alternatively, is America determined to continue fighting a war that has no end in sight? Year after year the federal budget to fight the war on drugs has been increased, with more funds going towards law enforcement and not enough toward prevention and treatment. There is a definite focus on the belligerent component of the struggle. As discussed earlier, billions of dollars are directly and indirectly associated with the war on drugs at the federal, state, and local levels. There are many families whose livelihood depends on these specific budgets and this may be an inducement to continue with the war. Very seldom an institution will propose an initiative that will threaten its own survival. So, if the DEA's reason to exist is the war on drugs, is it reasonable to expect the DEA to propose alternative drug policies that might include more emphasis on prevention and treatment rather than on interdiction? Common sense suggests they will not; doing so will imply that many current DEA employees will find themselves out of a job. So the war turns out to be self-perpetuating, with no end in sight. Hence, what are the lessons of this thirty-year long experience? They follow:

- Nobody dares predict an end to the war on drugs. All accounts by the anti-drug warriors themselves suggest that the war will go on forever given the current rules of engagement.

- The DTOs have prospered during the war; as a matter of fact, elementary economic analysis suggests that the war itself has been a major driver of the ever-expanding drug business.

- By equalizing the victims of illicit drugs (the addict and occasional user) with the beneficiaries (the producers and distributors) the prison population of the U.S. has grown to a level that places the U.S. in the first place amongst developed countries in terms of prisoners per 100,000 inhabitants. Drug-related sentences account for 25% of current prison population. About 500,000 inmates are serving sentences for drug-related crimes.

- Billions of dollars generated by the drug business are finding their way into the legitimate economy every year. This should be a reason for concern, as economic power always leads to political power, and the security of the U.S. may be at risk if political power falls into the wrong hands.

Unfortunately, these are not lessons for rejoicing; they forecast rough times ahead. Under the current drug policies, drugs will continue to flood the cities of America, including elementary schools; the DTOs will become wealthier and their wealth is bound to buy their way into the echelons of power; the brave men who, out of conviction, are fighting this war on the side of the law will continue to risk their lives in an unwinnable struggle; and the prisons of America will continue to provide residence for hundred of thousands of Americans while they move from relatively minor drug offenses into the more sophisticated world of high crime.

3.7 Collateral Damage

War comes along with a lot of collateral damage. Civilians killed by military miscalculations, soldiers killed by friendly fire, all innocent victims of the conflict. The war on drugs carries its own victims, they are the result of collateral damage inflicted on people not necessarily involved with the war or, if somehow involved in the drug puzzle, they find themselves caught into an asphyxiating web dispensing punishment out of proportion.

Young people in prison instead of college. The current legal and judicial system in the U.S. is designed to harshly punish the players in the illicit drugs supply chain. As a result, a multitude of young Americans are serving long jail sentences instead of attending college or getting some sort of education to help them craft their way through life as productive members of society. The lure of high profits from dealing drugs leads

119

these young people into the easy-money fast track. The system, rather than providing them with a viable alternative to redirect their lives, has chosen punishment as the expedient way out. Not that the overall problem of illicit-drug dealing is better addressed by this approach, it is not. However, it serves well to engross the statistics supporting the war on drugs. Some may think that one more drug dealer in jail is one more battle won; but it is more likely that we are winning skirmishes and losing the war. Judging by the availability of drugs in the streets of America, it certainly does not look like the war on drugs is being won. The war on drugs conceived as an isolated effort rather than as a component of a more encompassing integral initiative does not deliver a long-term viable solution to the drug problem in America. It inflicts undue punishment on the youth of America and cancels out their hopes and aspirations for a better and productive life. It becomes part of a bigger problem weighing heavily on the shoulders of a segment of America's youth and their parents, rather than providing an effective solution. This flavor of collateral damage resulting from the war on drugs places a heavy burden on the society the war was meant to protect.

Mandatory jail sentences. Current drug legislation requires the imposing of mandatory prison sentences for specific drug crimes. This has resulted in a disproportionate increase in the jail population in the US, and gives the U.S. the dubious honor of being the country with more citizens incarcerated per 100,000 of population amongst the industrialized democracies. Human Rights Watch [21] reported that more than two million men and women were behind bars in the U.S. in April 2003. In their report they stated:

"Contrary to popular perception, violent crime is not responsible for the quadrupling of the incarcerated population in the United States since 1980. In fact, violent crime rates have been relatively constant or declining over the past two decades. The exploding prison population has been propelled by public policy changes that have increased the use of prison sentences as well as the length of time served, e.g. through manda-

120

tory minimum sentencing, "three strikes" laws, and reductions in the availability of parole or early release.

"Perhaps the single greatest force behind the growth of the prison population has been the national "war on drugs." The number of incarcerated drug offenders has increased twelve fold since 1980. In 2000, 22% of those in federal and state prisons were convicted on drug charges."

Human Rights Watch source of data is the Bureau of Justice Statistics of the U.S. Department of Justice. These numbers speak of the crude fact that the war on drugs itself has become a source of significant damage to American society. This has to do with the slanted approach taken in the execution of the war; the anti-drug warriors place the emphasis on fighting the enemy rather than protecting the citizens.

The Bill of Rights under fire. The execution of the war on drugs leads law enforcement to apply tactics and procedures which infringe on the civil rights of Americans, more collateral damage of the war. Whether it is the forfeiture of assets resulting from some accidental connection with illicit drugs or low flying helicopters inspecting private fields in search of cannabis cultivation, or some other infringement of the bill of rights, law enforcement finds itself trampling over the constitutionally guarded rights of Americans. Judge James P. Gray in his 2001 book *Why Our Drug Laws Have Failed and What We Can Do about It* [22] makes an extensive analysis of the erosion of protections of the Bill of Rights. His analysis leads him to conclude:

"Our Drug Prohibition laws have not worked, but we have lost, perhaps irretrievably, valuable civil liberties in our futile and expensive attempts to stem the flow of illicit drugs. Long ago, Abraham Lincoln told us what would happen with laws of this kind: 'Prohibition goes beyond the bounds of reason in that it attempts to control a man's appetite by legislation and makes crimes out of things that are not crimes. A prohibition law strikes a blow at the very principles upon which our government was founded.' We should have heeded Lincoln's warning."

121

Judge Gray and President Lincoln make a good point, but Americans are not listening hard enough yet to rise to the occasion and drive the necessary changes in our current drug policies and legislation. The time has come for those who most fear the devastating potential of drugs, the parents of America's children — after looking at the bare facts associated with drug use and abuse, the illicit-drug trade, the war on drugs, and drug money laundering — to drive the search for a lesser evil to replace the impossible dream that has mangled up the hopes for a solution to the drug problem for over thirty years.

The above three pieces of collateral damage should reinforce the warning that something is not right with the war on drugs and the rules of engagement that come with it. As mentioned before, the illicit-drug problem is not a trivial one, it has many facets and they must all be looked at and taken into consideration if society is to come up with a better drug policy.

A war meant to protect society by eliminating mind-altering substances from the streets of America has in turn become a major business driver of the illicit-drug trade — a true nightmare. Because key drug-related issues are not openly debated in national forums — they are kept silent — a consensus has not developed among Americans to demand a revamping of the current prohibitionist drug policy. The absence of debate on a policy that chases an impossible dream — the elimination of narcotics — but ignores the realities of the laws of economics and keeps society engaged in the un-winnable war on drugs, is the silent accomplice of this American nightmare.

4

DRUG MONEY LAUNDERING

Because of the structure of the U.S. illicit-drug retailing net-work worth $125 billion, at least 65% of the proceeds get laundered within the U.S., up to 25% in Mexico, and the balance in Colombia and other countries.

4.1 Laundering Drug Money — How is it Done?

Much has been said about money laundering in recent years. The annual figure ranges between $600 billion and trillions of dollars. Of these, approximately $322 billion are associated with the illicit-drug trade; the rest comes from other illicit activities as the ones highlighted in *ILLICIT* [1], by Moises Naim. These activities run by organized crime include illegal gambling, prostitution, extortion, human traffic, and the illegal sale of arms. In addition, a portion of the laundered money results from graft and corruption involving government officials and private sector executives. Our presentation focuses on the laundering of the $322 billion generated by illicit drugs; nevertheless, the mechanisms and vehicles used to launder the rest are similar or the same as those used by the DTOs. This chapter takes a look at money laundering as one of the fundamental issues to be addressed, together with the use and abuse of drugs, the illicit-drug trade, and the war on drugs, to conduct a comprehensive analysis of the overall illicit-drug problem engulfing American society and the world at large.

123

Laundering through the financial system. What is the meaning of money laundering and why does it become necessary to launder money? Money derived from illicit activities cannot be used openly without drawing attention from interested parties, such as tax collectors or law enforcement agencies; it needs to go through a cleansing process to look legitimate. This legitimization process is what is known as money laundering. Laundered money can be used in business or private transactions without attracting anybody's attention. It flows freely within the worldwide financial system traveling in the form of checking accounts, savings accounts, CDs, treasury bonds, or even stock certificates of publicly traded or privately held companies. The only requisite is that the money be under the name of an individual or a corporation and that its source be no longer subject to questioning by the authorities.

There are many stories from the early days of the war on drugs, in the 1970s and 1980s, telling of drug traffickers walking into a branch of a U.S. bank within U.S. territory with a suitcase full of cash; through the goodwill and cooperation of the friendly banker, and in exchange for a commission, that money made its way into the drug dealer's bank account with no questions asked and no regulatory reports filed. From then on the money would move from bank to bank, even country to country, always within the legitimate financial system. By the time the owner, the drug trafficker, made use of the money, it had been sitting or traveling within the legitimate financial world for a while with no real tracks to trace it back to its origin — the cash deposit. This simple and straightforward method came under the scrutiny of the authorities, and banks were required to comply with a number of additional regulations and reporting requirements. Over the years, such money-laundering techniques came under intense scrutiny by U.S. banking regulators like the Office of the Comptroller of the Currency (OCC) and the Federal Reserve Board (FRB). Specialized units were created and strengthened over the years to prevent such blatant money-laundering practices. Nevertheless, the financial system in a global economy is a global system. The money-laundering activity, previously taking place within U.S. borders, moved to offshore banks where regulations did not call for the reporting requirements imposed by U.S. regulatory agencies upon U.S. banks. This new laundering mode also came to the attention of American authorities. Over the years, through bilateral and multilateral treaties, the anti-money laundering regulations extended worldwide. Therefore, the opportunities for money laundering directly within the financial system have shrunk as banking and government authorities all over the world have agreed to cooperate in the prevention of money laundering. The Financial Crimes Enforcement Network (FinCEN) of the U.S. Department of the Treasury plays a critical role in combating money laundering. Its network links the law enforcement, financial, and regulatory communities, in the U.S. and abroad for the purpose of preventing, detecting, and prosecuting financial crime. This network together with the regulations imposed by agencies like the OCC and the FRB provide the backdrop for the operation of U.S. banks, subsidiaries of U.S. banks, and foreign branches of U.S. banks; also foreign banks doing business with U.S. banks have to comply with current U.S. banking regulations. FinCEN also gets involved with other financial institutions beyond the banking system. Many foreign governments, following the U.S. model and complying with international treaties, have enacted legislation regulating banking transactions designed to thwart money laundering within their own countries. These regulations impose a heavy operating burden on the banking industry, but they have been incorporated in their cost of doing business.

FinCEN was established in 1990 by the U.S. Department of the Treasury to provide a government-wide, multi-source intelligence and analytical network. FinCEN operation was broadened in 1994 to include regulatory responsibilities, and in 2001, the USA PATRIOT Act elevated FinCEN to bureau status and emphasized its role fighting terrorist financing. Today, FinCEN is one of three entities — besides the Office of Foreign Assets Control-OFAC and the Internal Revenue Service Criminal Investigation Division — within the U.S. Department of the Treasury responsible for combating money laundering and terrorist financing. In their own words:

"FinCEN works to accomplish its mission in two ways. First, FinCEN administers the Bank Secrecy Act (BSA), America's comprehensive anti-money laundering statute, and is responsible for expanding the regulatory framework to industries vulnerable to money laundering, terrorist financing, and other crime. Second, FinCEN analyzes and shares the BSA information with U.S. law enforcement at the federal, state, and local levels, and its international counterparts, to help them identify and track the financial aspects of criminal investigations. Because it both collects and analyzes the BSA data, FinCEN is able to assess and demonstrate the value of the data and suggest ways to increase its value. FinCEN seeks to strike a balance between meeting law enforcement's information needs, minimizing the burden on regulated industry, and protecting individual privacy."[2]

In pursuing its goals, FinCEN reported in its Strategic Plan 2003-2008 the intention to expand the industries covered by anti-money laundering regulations as shown in Table 4.1. All industries included in the table are of a financial nature and fertile ground for money laundering. To enhance their supervision FinCEN launched several modernization efforts to accelerate the flow of valuable information from regulated industries, and provide that information in a timely, efficient, and secure manner to law enforcement. Furthermore, FinCEN is determined to continually enhance its analytic capability — both for investigative case research and strategic analysis. It also seeks to enhance the quality and value of its strategic analytical services by providing a broad range of short and long-term analytical products to law enforcement, regulators, and the regulated industries.

Table 4.1 Industries Covered by Anti-Money Laundering Regulations [2]

FY 2001	FY 2003 Estimated	FY 2005 Projected
Depository institutions	Depository institutions	Depository institutions
Casinos	Casinos	Casinos
Card clubs	Card clubs	Card clubs
	Money services	Money services
	Broker-dealers	Broker-dealers
	Credit-card operators	Credit-card operators
	Mutual funds	Mutual funds
	Futures commission merchants	Futures commission merchants
		Insurance companies
		Precious metals, stones & jewels
		Commodity trading advisors
		Unregistered investment
		Companies
		Investment advisors

Thus, anti-money laundering progress is viable and progress has been made to stem money laundering within these industries in recent years. It is a task calling for permanent monitoring of transactions within those industries; the focus is usually on unusual transaction activities within them. Regardless of FinCEN's focus, which has made great contributions to anti-money laundering worldwide, the universe of money-laundering opportunities open to DTOs goes beyond these financial institutions.

The gray economy and laundering. Not all monetary transactions are subject to scrutiny by government authorities. Anybody getting paid in cash for goods or services and who does not issue a receipt or invoice is in a position to hide this income. Through this act, the money does not immediately enter the formal economy. It is not until the holder of the cash uses it to pay for products or services within the legitimate or formal economy that the money makes a definite entry. How is the money introduced in the formal economy? In many ways, for instance, by paying for groceries at the supermarket, buying lunch in a cafeteria, or purchasing some new tools at a hardware store. The minute the cash is used to acquire goods or services in a legitimate tax-complying business, the money enters the formal economy. Even if the original cash transaction did not involved any illicit business, the individual receiving the cash chose to handle the money in "black" to avoid paying taxes for this portion of his income. This is known as the gray economy. This particular economic environment is also available to the drug trafficker and is most likely widely used by the lower echelons of the drug distribution networks. A drug dealer who makes $2,000 a week will not go to the bank to deposit his money. Instead, he will keep the cash and use it to pay for his necessities: food, clothing, shelter, entertainment, and even a car if he can get the car dealer to accept cash for his purchase. The instant he uses the cash to acquire goods and services in any legitimate business, his money becomes legitimate and starts circulating within the legitimate financial system.

The owner of a legitimate **construction business** may be willing to accept cash payments — without issuing an invoice — for a portion of the construction work being done on behalf of a client. This, as explained earlier, is a gray market transaction. The money exchanging hands could easily be drug money, but to the construction businessman it is all the same. He can use this cash to pay some of his workers off the books. Once the cash is in the hands of his workers, they can use it to pay for their necessities, thereby transferring the cash from the gray economy to the legitimate financial system. This is one example of how proceeds from the illicit-drug trade may find their way into the formal economy through the gray economy. Similar transactions take place everyday even though this is not a straightforward way of laundering drug money, but it certainly serves the interest of the less sophisticated links in the drug distribution networks. Still, there are more intricate and effective ways to launder drug money which bypass the supervision of FinCEN and do not go through the cumbersome labyrinths and limitations of the gray economy.

Laundering in the formal economy. Money laundering commands a fee which is accepted as a cost of doing business by DTOs. Laundering drug proceeds through the financial system today faces very high risks associated with bypassing the monitoring and controls implemented by FinCEN and similar government organizations in other countries where money laundering is a persecuted crime. Gray market operations are rather cumbersome and it is not easy to cleanse large volumes of money through them. How do DTOs launder the bulk of their ill-obtained fortunes? There is a straightforward answer: they use the formal economy. Any business or industry where cash is accepted as legal tender is an excellent vehicle for money laundering. To the unsuspecting observer it may come as a surprise that such a possibility is open to the DTOs for cleaning their drug proceeds, but it is. In the early days of big money-laundering operations within the financial system, back in the 1970s and 1980s, a 5% commission paid to the friendly banker was not unusual. Today the risks involved in money laundering are far bigger and hence command a bigger fee. How big? It is hard to tell without being in the midst of the operation itself. But standing in the shoes of a drug trafficker, what would be preferable, to have one billion dollars of drug proceeds stashed under the mattress or $500 million of cleansed money in a bank account? DTOs are willing to pay a hefty fee to safely receive clean money in exchange for their drug money. How is it done?

The **retail industry** is a good example: supermarkets, auto parts stores, department stores, pharmacies, and similar businesses. All these businesses accept cash as legal tender. They also have a common trait, large volumes of articles are stocked and sold to customers, and it is not feasible to track every single item in the accounting books. Many of these stores sell thousands, tens of thousands, or even hundreds of thousands of different products. There is no way in which accounting can keep track of the activity of each individual item. Hence, it is a generally accepted ac-

129

counting practice to use what is known as the **retail method** of accounting to keep the books of retail merchandising businesses. The retail method allows for the inventory accounts to be carried in currency terms — dollars in the US, euros in Europe — and there is no record kept of the number of physical units of the product associated with the total dollar figure registered in the inventory accounts. A typical store is divided into departments comprising of similar type items — canned groceries in a supermarket, or men's shoes in a department store — and each department may carry hundreds or thousands of different products. When a specific purchase is made for a particular department, for instance, 1,000 cans of string beans with a unit cost of 80 cents to be sold for 90 cents to the public, the inventory account for the canned groceries department receives an entry of $800 at cost and $900 at sale increasing the value of the inventory on hand; the gross profit margin provided by the purchase and sale prices of this particular purchase of the product is $100, or 11.1% of the sale price — the gross margin of this product is 11.1%. Because the individual items do not get tracked in the accounting books, and every canned grocery purchase and sale gets registered to the canned groceries department, the store management, by looking at the accounting books, knows the performance of the department, the combined effect of all the articles included in that department, but not the individual performance of each item — not from the accounting books anyway.

How can drug money be inserted into a retail business like the one described above? The procedure is simple, just ring as many sales of specific articles as required to add up to the amount of drug money to be introduced into the business at any particular moment. To continue with the string beans example, if the sales tax is 10% and the requirement is to introduce $990 of drug money into the business, it may be done by ringing the sale of 1,000 cans of string beans at 90 cents each: $900 for the product value and $90 for the sales tax. The store may have only bought a hundred cans, but because there is no record of the actual number of cans available to sell, the sale can be registered without the cans being delivered. As a matter of fact, in money-laundering operations, no product or service is delivered in exchange for the money being laundered. The money goes fully into the business, except that the store pays the sales tax associated to the tax authorities. In the above example, the DTO introduced $990 into the business of which $90 will go to the tax collector. This procedure shows how the drug money goes into a legitimate retail business. The payback to the DTO can be similar in any industry and can be implemented in many different ways; the payback step of the laundering process is discussed later.

The **hospitality industry** is another industry where cash is legal tender and it brings additional opportunities for money laundering. Take for example a hotel with a hundred rooms. It is unusual for a hotel to achieve full occupancy all the time, actually most hotels have a break-even point at between 50% to 70% occupancy. Introducing drug money for laundering purposes only requires reporting a larger occupancy than the actual one and bringing the drug cash to the hotel. Assuming the hotel example has on average a real occupancy rate of 70% and each room rents for $100 a night plus a 10% tax; the legitimate revenue of the hotel is on average $7,000 per night, and $700 are collected in taxes. This hotel presents an opportunity to receive $3,300 of drug money per night; $3,000 going into the business and $300 for the tax collector, it will show occupancy of 100% for that particular night. There is no difficulty introducing the money into any legitimate unit of the hospitality industry. Here again, the initial cost of laundering is 10%, equal to the taxes to be transferred to the tax collector. The payback to the DTO is covered later.

The **repair/maintenance services industry** also accepts cash as legal tender. Take for example a home appliances or computer repair business selling service policies to the consumer. Maybe a $100-dollar-per-year service policy will cover the repair and parts of the particular appliance or PC covered by the policy. Some legitimate customers may be interested in buying such a policy, but is there any impediment to registering sales of a service policy to everyone listed in the phone book? None whatsoever! It is perfectly feasible to register such a policy to everybody in the phone book. If they have a phone, they are certainly going to have electricity and hence are candidates to own an appliance or a PC covered by the service policy. To complete the example, if the tax rate is again 10% and there is $110,000 of drug money to be introduced into the legitimate service industry, the operation requires the registration of 1,000 service contracts; this will generate $100,000 in revenue to the business and $10,000 in taxes to be transferred later on to the tax collector. There are no obstacles to the introduction of the drug money into the business. By the way, those individuals whose names show up in the service policies will never request service; they do not even know their name is on a service policy. Hence the cost of servicing these customers is zero.

The **restaurant industry** is another vehicle to receive drug money without any hassle — it accepts cash as legal tender. A restaurant can easily register, within reason, as many sales as it wishes. For a typical restaurant the direct cost of food is in the range of 15% to 40%. By registering fictitious sales the accounting books will show a reduced cost of food. Hence, if a restaurant is selling $10,000 per day with a cost of food of 40% or $4,000 and a tax of $1,000 (assuming a 10% rate), it can easily register additional sales of $10,000 per day with the corresponding $1,000 taxes. This operation will yield a cost of food of still $4,000, now at the rate of 20% of sales, just an apparently more efficient restaurant operation.

The four industries illustrated above, as well as other candidate industries where cash is accepted as legal tender, are excellent vehicles for laundering drug money. These drug money laundering surroundings may be easier to find in some countries, but it is available, one way or another, everywhere DTOs may wish to launder drug proceeds. The laundering procedure requires the participation of a core of reliable associates to register the sales and provide proper custody of the drug proceeds entering the legitimate business. Such laundering processes cannot be carried out without the compliance of the owners of the business. There has to be a close relationship between the DTOs' drug lords and the legitimate business owners. It is required for the introduction of the money into the business, but fundamentally to complete the cycle by which the drug lords receive their share of the laundered money.

The **payback to the DTOs** for the money entering the legitimate business may take different forms; all of which require that drug lords be properly camouflaged to avoid identification by authorities. The camouflage may come in the form of corporations with a pyramidal ownership structure and/or where relatives or friends of the drug lords serve as front owners distancing the drug lords from the operation. With the appropriate camouflage, the drug lord and the legitimate businessman are well set up to carry out the payback phase of the laundering process. How much this service is worth to the DTO is anybody's guess. The question is how much a particular drug lord is willing to accept in perfectly clean money in exchange for drug money filtered through his legitimate business partner. The answer is suggested in the different payback mechanisms discussed further down. Definitely, there is never any money going directly to the drug trafficker, it must go to corporations, domestic or foreign, which are directly or indirectly controlled by him; the payback can also go to individuals, family or friends, who will benefit personally or to make payments for goods and services for the benefit of the drug trafficker. In today's global economy, such corporations can be incorporated in the country where the money is being laundered or in another country; as a matter of fact, there are countries where tax benefits attract the incorporation of companies and where even the identification of the bona fide proprietor is not required by law. These corporations are free to do business worldwide, as there are many legitimate corporations making legal use of these arrangements. Bermuda is a case in point where the offshore incorporation of companies takes place, but it is not the only country. In the following discussion, the entity benefiting from the receipt of the cleansed money is referred to as **the beneficiary** and the legitimate business doing the laundering is called **the business.**

The fees-paid model. In this payback mechanism the business pays the beneficiary for fictitious services provided by the beneficiary to the business. For instance the beneficiary may be a media corporation owning radio and TV stations as well as printed media. Through a formal contract the business agrees to pay the beneficiary for advertising services that will not be delivered or will only be partially delivered. Table 4.2 illustrates this operation where the DTO delivers $1,100,000 of drug money to the business as fictitious sales; $1,000,000 goes into the business and $100,000 is used to pay the sales tax — a 10% tax rate is assumed. The remaining million is available to distribute between the business and the beneficiary. Suppose 70%, or $700,000, is paid by the business to the beneficiary as the agreed upon service fee for fictitious media services; $300,000 remains in the business to engross its profit margin. As there is no cost associated with the original sale, the $300,000 goes directly into profits before taxes of the business because there are no goods delivered. If the corporate income tax rate is 30% of the profit before taxes, the business will show an increase in net earnings of $210,000 after deducting $90,000 for income taxes on the gross profit generated by the drug money being laundered. There are no real costs associated with the original one million dollar transaction. At the same time, the books of the beneficiary will show total fictitious revenue of $700,000 — the example assumes no sales taxes between corporations. If the beneficiary chooses to leave the money in the company, it will pay income tax on this gross profit (assuming there are profits and the corporate tax rate is 30%) of $210,000. On the other hand, the money can be used to pay the expenses of the company, which may include salaries and other expenses which would benefit the owners of the beneficiary, its employees' friends and family. In summary, the drug trafficker through the beneficiary will receive net benefits of at least $490,000 of unblemished money; this figure is 44.5% of the $1,100,000 originally introduced into the legitimate business. Not a bad deal while escaping the eyes of the authorities. The associated legitimate business receives net after tax benefits of $210,000 for operating the laundry. There is no cheaper money in the market to finance the expansion of legitimate businesses! Of course, these numbers will shift if the split of the clean money between the business and the beneficiary varies, but the total of laundered money ($490,000 + $210,000 = $700,000) will not change. In summary, 63.6 % of the original amount introduced into the legitimate business by the DTO is back under the control of the drug trafficker and/or his legitimate business associate — and it is clean money. Most intriguing is what happens to the remaining 36.4% and why DTOs may be willing to part with it. The money went towards paying sales and income taxes in the total amount of $400,000 (Table 4.2). The obliged question is then: do the tax authorities, and the governments they are part of, want to stop this cleansing process? Very unlikely, they are not in any way privy to the laundering process, all they see is a law-abiding corporate citizen paying all due taxes. For the DTO it is one more cost of doing business.

Table 4.2 Money Laundering Through a "FEES-PAID" Model (Thousand $) *

	DTO	BUS	BENEFIC	GOVT
Money Entering the Laundering	(1100)			
Fictitious Sales		1000	700	
Sales Tax Collected (10%)		100		
Total Cash Flow In		1100	700	
Fees Paid to Beneficiary (70% per contract)		(700)		
Sales Tax Paid (10%)		(100)		100
Total Cash Flow Out		(800)		
Gross Profit		300	700	
Income Tax (30%)		(90)	(210)	300
Net Profits		210	490	
Government Tax Revenue				400

* A figure in parentheses ( ) reflects money leaving the particular entity.

135

The above fees-paid model describes the laundering process within any service industry acting as the beneficiary. Take for instance a **beneficiary** public relations firm in Argentina under contract by the **business** operating in Mexico. This contract is justified by the expansion plans of the Mexican business to open the way for future or additional investments in Argentina. This is a legitimate and not uncommon setup; it is a normal day-to-day business practice. Therefore, it will not stand out as an unusual activity of the business or the beneficiary. Complexity in the web of interrelated companies participating in a money-laundering scheme will add protection to the laundering process. The more corporations that are involved with the money, the more difficult it will be for a curious anti-money laundering agent to track or even suspect any wrong doing. This type of operation does not seem to be the focus of anti-money laundering agencies in any country. They are actually very difficult to identify unless some prominent drug trafficker shows up in the roll of owners or management of the beneficiary. The amount of investigative resources required to go after this kind of laundering operation will go off the chart if compared with the resources currently assigned to anti-money laundering. To thwart this laundering model the cash based businesses described above will have to be subjected to a police state type of supervision. Such a scheme will place an unbearable burden on these industries and turn them into unproductive enterprises and eventually force them out of business.

The stock-transaction model. Another compelling payback mechanism involves a private and public stock transaction combination of the stock of the company laundering money. The model is illustrated in Appendix A, which uses the same definition of beneficiary and business as used in the fees-paid model example above. The operation is designed as a medium to long-term payback vehicle. This particular example illustrates how $275 million of drug money introduced into a laundering process can yield $220.55 million of clean money to the beneficiary company controlled by the drug lord, a conversion factor of 80% — not a bad feat. Through this process the legitimate business associate increases the value of his company, thanks to the drug money being laundered, by $236.7 million — a nice reward for the stealth operation. The conversion factor is 86% in the case of the legitimate business associate. And finally, the government tax collector gets $100 million just for fulfilling its responsibilities, a conversion factor of 36%; not bad for standing on the sidelines.

One important observation regarding the stock transaction model is the fact that $275 million of drug money introduced into the business delivered $220.55 million to the beneficiary/DTO, $236.7 million to the business, and $100 million to the government tax collector; a total of $557.25 million! Where did this money come from? The government tax revenue came directly from the money being laundered in the form of sales and income taxes, the beneficiary's capital gain came from the new stockholders who bought the beneficiary shares in the company, and the increase in value to the original stockholders came from half of the retained earnings and the premium paid in capital for the new issue of stock sold to the public stockholders at the time of the IPO. These new stockholders — most likely a large number of different stockholders — are not aware of the laundering operation, they have bought into the IPO with the information available through the published financial statements, which are certainly backed up by a proper audit performed by a reputable CPA firm. The future value of the stock will depend on a number of different factors, but it will be subject to fluctuations, as with any stock traded on the stock market. Some may be tempted to argue that such a scheme does not stand a chance under the watchful eyes of the SEC and other financial authorities. Wrong! Many corporate frauds have been uncovered in the U.S. in recent years involving multibillion-dollar operations, such as Enron and WorldCom, and they went on for many years. Besides, this laundering model does not have to be implemented in the U.S.; it can be implemented in countries, such as Mexico, Brazil, Argentina, and Colombia among others. In these countries the securities markets are not under the strict supervision imposed by the SEC on U.S. publicly traded companies.

The real estate - transaction model. There is a variation of the stock-transaction model — involving the business and the beneficiary.

This variation brings into the picture the construction business gray economy mechanism discussed earlier. The model creates a joint venture between the business and the beneficiary for the purpose of investing in real-estate construction projects. Drug money goes into the construction of the real estate using the gray economy mechanism; once completed, the project will be worth at least as much as was invested in it, except that the drug money pumped into the project will not show in the accounting books. The sale of the real estate will yield huge capital gains which will be shared between the business and the beneficiary. In this model there are no stock transactions, real estate is built and real estate is sold at a significant capital gain; all leveraged by drug money.

Whether it is through the **fees-paid**, the **stock-transaction**, or the **real estate-transaction** model the DTOs have an effective way of laundering drug money with minimal or no risk. The legitimate businessman, in close concert with the drug trafficker, is able to set up a money-laundering operation which is practically impossible to uncover. Besides, the tax authorities have a lot to gain from standing on the sidelines. But even if they wished to interfere with this money-laundering arrangement, it is not humanly possible to do it, short of placing an incorruptible policeman next to every cash register in the country or countries where the laundering takes place.

4.2 How Much Drug Money is Laundered and Where?

As mentioned earlier $322 billion is the estimated global revenue generated by the illicit-drug trade. Our estimates, as reflected in Chapter II, indicate the U.S. accounts for $125 billion or almost 39% of the worldwide business. Where are the U.S. drug proceeds laundered? A look at the mix of the illicit U.S. drug business and the structure of retail, wholesale and producer prices leads to a close approximation. Because of the relative importance of the drug retailing network, it is likely that anywhere between 67% and 70% of the proceeds get laundered within the U.S., 18% to 22% in Mexico, about 6% in Colombia and other Latin

American countries, and about 5% in other countries. Table 4.3 contains the UN 2003 reported retail and wholesale prices in the U.S. for all drugs included in the analysis, it also contains the Mexican wholesale prices for Latin American heroin and for cocaine, these two products either have production in Mexico or travel through Mexico on their way to the U.S. In addition, the producer prices are obtained from the UN report. There is no Mexican wholesale price for Asian heroin, as it is assumed that no Asian heroin travels through Mexico. Ecstasy is produced in Europe, the U.S., and Mexico, but there is no wholesale market price reported for Mexico, and the ATS/methamphetamine wholesale price in Mexico is not reported by the UN even though Mexico is considered a significant supplier to the U.S. market. The wholesale price reported for cannabis in Mexico is $80 per kilo, which does not make much sense compared with the reported producer price of $936 for North America. The $80 price is most likely a price particular only to Mexico, while the $936 must reflect the U.S. and Canadian producer price. Cannabis retails in Mexico at 20 cents [3] a gram, or the equivalent of $200 a kilo, which is reasonable in light of a wholesale price of $80.

Table 4.3 UN Estimated Drug Prices for 2003 ($/Kg)

Drug Type/Source	Retail U.S.	Wholesale U.S.	Mexico Wholesale	Producer
Heroin				
Latin America	115,800	71,000	32,850	4,136
Asia	115,800	60,000	N/A	3,495
Cocaine	74,600	21,500	7,880	808
Cannabis	11,400	2,035	80	936
Methamphetamine	153,000	31,000	N/A	3,028
Ecstasy	260,000	103,000	N/A	24,483

N/A: Not applicable or not available.

The value added to each one of the drugs by the wholesale and the retail networks is calculated in Table 4.4 using the figures in Table 4.3 together with the UN estimated consumption levels for each drug shown in Table 2.8 (Chapter II). The initial producer value of $6 billion for all

139

drugs sold in the U.S. is incremented by $25 billion in the wholesale network and by $93 billion in the retail network. It is the retail network that is taking the biggest chunk of the business. This does not necessarily mean that $93 billion stays in the U.S. and requires laundering domestically.

Table 4.4 Estimate of Drug Proceeds from U.S. Illicit-Drug Business (Million $)

Drug Type	Metric Tons	Retail Value	Value Added at Retail	Value Added at Wholesale	Producer Value
Heroin	67	7,800	3,581	3,973	246
Cocaine	363(a)	38,890	27,689	10,780	421
Cannabis	4,798	54,700	44,936	5,273	4,491
ATS/Meth	103	15,700	12,519	2,870	311
Ecstasy	33	7,700	4,650	2,325	725
TOTAL		124,800	93,374	25,232	6,194

(a) This number represents the tonnage of pure cocaine, which is equivalent to 521 metric tons of 70% purity cocaine.

Additional elements need to be introduced before determining with reasonable accuracy the final destination of the money. Based on a variety of U.S. government and UN reports, a set of assumptions can be made to explore the possible destination of drug proceeds. There is a general group of assumptions as follows:

- All the Colombian and Mexican heroin comes into the U.S. market. That would account for 16 metric tons — 8.4 MT from Mexico and 7.6 MT from Colombia. This is out of a total consumption of 67 metric tons in the U.S. The remaining 51 tons come from Asia.

- Two-thirds of the cannabis is produced in the U.S. and two-thirds of the imported cannabis comes from Mexico; the rest comes from Canada.
- All the ATS/Methamphetamine is produced in North America, but it is not clear from the data where in North America. In the following calculations two-thirds is assumed to be produced in the U.S. and one-third in Mexico.
- Two-thirds of the ecstasy is produced in Central and Western Europe and one-third in North America. In the following calculations two-thirds of the North American production is assumed to take place in the U.S. and one-third in Mexico.
- The wholesale price of heroin in Mexico is $32,850 per kilo and for cocaine it is $7,880.
- Colombian DTOs are involved only in the wholesale business and do not get involved with the operation of the drug distribution retail networks. Hence they only repatriate the wholesale drug proceeds from the drugs they introduce to the U.S.
- The wholesale value of all drugs goes to the country of origin. Except for the cocaine paid by Colombian DTOs to Mexican DTOs as payment-in-product for transshipment services through Mexico, this wholesale value goes to Mexico.
- Colombian DTOs pay-in-product 50% of the cocaine shipped through Mexico to Mexican DTOs.
- Mexican DTOs control their own retail distribution networks in the U.S.

On top of these fundamental assumptions, two scenarios are presented with two complementary but different sets of assumptions.

Scenario A assumes:
- Seventy percent of the cocaine entering the U.S. comes through Mexico and is introduced by well-established Mexican DTOs.

141

- Mexican controlled retail networks repatriate back to Mexico 65% of the value added to the drugs by the retail network.

Scenario B assumes:

- Eighty percent of the cocaine entering the U.S. comes through Mexico and is introduced by well-established Mexican DTOs.
- Mexican controlled retail networks repatriate back to Mexico 75% of the value added to the drugs by the retail network.

Tables 4.5a and 4.5b below, illustrate Scenarios A and B.

Table 4.5a SCENARIO "A" DISTRIBUTION OF U.S. DRUG PROCEEDS

(MILLION DOLLARS)

DESTINATION OF PROCEEDS

DRUG TYPE/Origin	US	MEXICO	COLOMBIA+LA	OTHER	TOTAL
Heroin					
Latin America	475	846	543	0	1864
Asia	2860	0	0	3076	5936
Total Heroin	3335	846	543	3076	7800
Cocaine					
Through Mexico	14456	8850	3924	0	27230
Other Route	8307	0	3363	0	11670
Total Cocaine	22763	8850	7287	0	38900
Cannabis					
US Domestic	36467	0	0	0	36467
Imported	8488	8661	0	1085	18233
Total Cannabis	44954	8661	0	1085	54700
ATS/Meth					
US Domestic	10467	0	0	0	10467
Mexican Source	1461	3773	0	0	5233
Total ATS/Meth	11927	3773	0	0	15700
Ecstasy					
US Domestic	1711	0	0	0	1711
Mexican Source	181	675	0	0	856
Europe Source	3100	0	0	2034	5133
Total Ecstasy	4992	675	0	2034	7700
TOTAL DRUGS	87972	22804	7830	6194	124800

143

Table 4.5b SCENARIO "B" DISTRIBUTION OF U.S. DRUG PROCEEDS
(MILLION DOLLARS)

DRUG TYPE/Origin	US	DESTINATION OF PROCEEDS MEXICO	COLOMBIA+LA	OTHER	TOTAL
Heroin					
Latin America	437	884	543	0	1864
Asia	2860	0	0	3076	5936
Total Heroin	3297	884	543	3076	7800
Cocaine					
Through Mexico	14966	11670	4484	0	31120
Other Route	5538	0	2242	0	7780
Total Cocaine	20503	11670	6727	0	38900
Cannabis					
US Domestic	36467	0	0	0	36467
Imported	7489	9659	0	1085	18233
Total Cannabis	43956	9659	0	1085	54700
ATS/Meth					
US Domestic	10467	0	0	0	10467
Mexican Source	1043	4190	0	0	5233
Total ATS/Meth	11510	4190	0	0	15700
Ecstasy					
US Domestic	1711	0	0	0	1711
Mexican Source	129	726	0	0	856
Europe Source	3100	0	0	2034	5133
Total Ecstasy	4940	726	0	2034	7700
TOTAL DRUGS	84207	27130	7270	6194	124800

With the above assumptions in mind and as illustrated in Tables 4.5a and 4.5b, it is estimated that the U.S. retail drug revenue staying in the U.S. ranges between $84 and $88 billion, or 67% to 70% of the total

U.S. drug proceeds, that Mexico receives between $23 and $27 billion from the U.S. drug business or anywhere between 18% and 22%, and Colombia and other Latin American countries get around $7 billion or about 6%. Other countries receive in the order of $6 billion or about 5%.

Mexican DTOs repatriate to Mexico between $22.8 and $27.1 billion in drug revenues requiring laundering; Colombian DTOs repatriate and need to launder between $7.3 and $7.8 billion. Altogether, these two countries repatriate between $30.6 and $34.4 billion according to the estimates from Tables 4.5a and 4.5b. The cash requiring repatriation to Mexico, Colombia, or other countries has to go through an additional cross-border operation. Because the financial system has become more and more inhospitable for this kind of money, the DTOs need to physically transport the drug proceeds back to those countries. The logistics of delivering the cash abroad adds to the complexities of the DTOs' business processes. Once transported, the cash will need to make use of the three basic laundering models described earlier, or similar ones, to insert the money into the legitimate financial system. Some of the cash enters the gray economy as payment for goods and services received by the DTOs in their illicit business world. Due to the proximity of Mexico to the U.S. and the bulky nature of the cash shipments required to repatriate their share of the U.S. drug proceeds, it would not be a surprise if a significant portion of the Colombian share travels through Mexico before arriving at its final destination. Other countries in Asia and Europe, and Canada face a laundering task of about $6 billion altogether. Money laundering is another area where the authorities, and particularly the DEA, have placed significant emphasis in recent years; trying to hurt the DTOs where it hurts most — in their pockets. Hence, drug money interdictions are among their activities of choice, as they rightly believe that the most effective way to hit the DTOs is in their pockets, though they seem to be taking a never-ending route to get there.

The interception of drug money. Intercepting drug money is one strategy the anti-money laundering authorities use in their struggle to thwart DTOs' operations. The DEA reports less than one billion dollars of

145

drug money intercepted [4] annually in recent years, and there are stories published on specific operations dealing with the breaking up of money-laundering rings, including the confiscation of drug money. One billion intercepted out of $125 billion does not seem to be a good indication of thwarting the DTOs; nevertheless, every drug money interception does get ample publicity. Some interception stories have been widely publicized. Operation Casablanca, which took place in May 1998, is a good example of the type of drug money interception conducted by U.S. authorities. Operation Casablanca was conducted by the United States Customs Service and billed at the time as the most comprehensive and significant drug money laundering case in the history of U.S. law enforcement. Following are some excerpts reproduced from the Money Laundering and Financial Crimes Report on March 1, 2000 published by the U.S. Department of State: [5]

"This undercover money-laundering investigation resulted in the seizure of over $98 million in U.S. currency ($67 million from bank accounts and $31 million in cash from drug traffickers), over four tons of marijuana and two tons of cocaine. The indictment, which was issued in U.S. District Court in Los Angeles, charged twenty-six Mexican bank officials and three Mexican banks, CONFIA, SERFIN, and BANCOMER with laundering drug money. The indictment alleged that officials from twelve of Mexico's largest nineteen banking institutions were involved in money-laundering activities. Additionally, bankers from two Venezuelan banks, BANCO INDUSTRIAL DE VENEZUELA and BANCO DEL CARIBE were charged in the money-laundering scheme.

"Operation Casablanca was significant for a number of reasons: (1) because of the sheer volume of the amounts of money involved, and (2) because it represents the first time Mexican banks and bank officials have been directly linked to laundering the Cali and Juarez cartels' U.S. drug profits, and (3) because it uncovered a systematic scheme to launder money via a large number of Mexican institutions.

"The money-laundering scheme worked in the following manner:

146

- Undercover agents were introduced to financial managers from both the Cali Cartel and the Juarez Cartel and obtained contracts to "pick up" drug proceeds on the streets of major U.S. cities.
- The agents were also introduced to Mexican bankers who then opened bank accounts for them.
- The funds that were "picked up" were then transported back to Los Angeles, California where they were deposited in U.S. Customs Service-controlled undercover bank accounts.
- The funds were then wire transferred to accounts opened by the Mexican banking officials. After taking out their commission, these officials then issued Mexican bank drafts drawn on the U.S. accounts of the Mexican banks. These bank drafts were delivered back to the undercover agents in the U.S. either in person or via courier.
- The funds were then disbursed at the direction of the money launderers. A large percentage of the money seized during Operation Casablanca was as the result of the use of "substitute assets" laws. Substitute assets are assets owned by a business or individual and seized by the government in lieu of the actual property (in this case money) that was used to further a criminal enterprise.

"Court orders were obtained allowing for the seizure of the total amount of drug money laundered through the accounts and the amount of commission money paid to the bankers. Because the Mexican bank drafts were drawn on the U.S. accounts of the Mexican banks, court orders were obtained allowing for the seizure of the aforementioned funds from those U.S. accounts. As a result:

- BANCOMER and SERFIN each pleaded guilty to criminal money laundering violations and together forfeited a total of $16 million to the government. Each bank was also fined $500,000.
- CONFIA settled the indictment with a civil plea and forfeited $12 million.

147

- Twenty-eight individuals, including twelve Mexican bankers and their associates, have pleaded guilty to money laundering and/or drug smuggling charges.
- Three Mexican bankers were convicted, and three Mexican bankers were acquitted of money-laundering charges in trials in Los Angeles.
- Three Venezuelan bankers were convicted in December 1999 on money-laundering charges.
- $64 million of the $98 million seized during this investigation has been forfeited to the government of the United States."

Operation Casablanca was hailed as a great success for the U.S. Custom Service anti-money laundering activities. According to the above report it obtained guilty pleas to money-laundering and/or drug-smuggling charges from twenty-eight individuals, including twelve Mexican bankers and their associates. However, the operation also raised many objections from Mexican government officials, including Ernesto Zedillo, at the time the President of Mexico. Many arguments were waged by the Mexican government to object to this operation and the way it was conducted. In the final analysis the operation was a sting operation, and this type of operation is illegal under Mexican law. It is not legal in Mexico to induce somebody to commit a crime; hence, sting operations are not valid in a Mexican court of law and this was at the root of the strong controversy emanating from Mexican government circles following Operation Casablanca. Not that Mexico can stand as a paladin of law and justice, but the use of sting operations very often only demonstrate that somebody can be induced to commit a crime; it does not necessarily demonstrate that the "criminal" was so before the sting. Besides, Casablanca was said to deliver an important sum of drug money to the U.S. authorities, $98 million to be exact; but, how important is this sum in light of the almost $30 billion sent to Mexico for laundering from proceeds of the illicit U.S. drug business? The answer: about three-tenths of one percent, precisely 0.3267%; not even a drop in the ocean! The real drug money keeps going

148

back to Mexico by the truckload or is laundered in the U.S. in plain view of the authorities, and uses the more sophisticated mechanisms described in this chapter.

From money bags to the money laundry. How is it feasible for $30 billion plus to make its way into Mexico undetected? Thirty billion dollars in small denomination bills require many truckloads. The repatriation of U.S. drug proceeds is one of the links in the overall illicit-drug operation chain; it is an intrinsic part of the DTOs' business. According to the DEA:

"Mexico continues to be one of the primary money-laundering centers in Latin America. Sophisticated polydrug trafficking organizations capitalize on the voluminous trade and traffic between the two countries to facilitate the movement of bulk-cash shipments between the United States and Mexico. Bulk currency shipments continue to be the most prevalent method used by Mexican drug traffickers to move trafficking proceeds. U.S. currency is concealed and transported by courier or cargo, either overland or by air. The money often travels in the same vehicle or airplane that originally transported the drugs into the United States. Concealment methods used by drug traffickers are often difficult to detect and are constantly changing. DEA reporting, however, indicates that the concealment of narco-dollars in luggage, and the smuggling of those funds to Mexico via commercial airlines and personal vehicles is the most common method of moving drug proceeds. DEA reporting has also indicated that transportation companies are recruiting drivers to transport drug proceeds from the United States to Mexico." [6]

Back in the 1990s some of the drug proceeds traveling to Mexico may have used US-based money service businesses. This may have accounted for a significant portion of the proceeds during those years. However, since August 18, 1999, the U.S. Department of Treasury's FinCEN published regulations requiring money-service businesses to comply with currency transaction reporting as required by the Bank Secrecy Act, and on August 20, 1999, FinCEN published regulations requiring money-service businesses to register with FinCEN by December 31, 2001. Registration requirements include providing information on ownership, geographic locations, and operational details. These regulations have strengthened law enforcement's ability to fight money laundering through this type of businesses ever since. These measures contributed to curtailing the transfer of drug proceeds though financial mechanisms.

The DEA agrees that drug money finds its way into Mexico with little impediment, just a scuffle here and there. Some of the $30 billion plus going through Mexico may move on for laundering in other countries of the region, but it is highly probable that a significant portion stays in Mexico using the very secure laundering models described earlier. Mexico actually provides a fertile economic environment that allows for these laundering mechanisms to work effectively. These models can be applied in other countries of the region as well. For every billion dollars that gets laundered in Mexico, by applying the percentages arrived at in the fees-paid model example, the Mexican government would receive around $364 million in sales and income taxes and the DTOs and their stealth business associates would get about $636 million of perfectly clean money. The DTOs and business associates would get more under the stock-transaction model mechanism. Is it possible to prevent this laundering activity? Very unlikely, as to do so the authorities, even if willing to try, would have to establish very strict controls on many truly legitimate businesses and doing so would negatively impact the Mexican economy. Therefore, it is easy to imagine the building of a huge economic empire financed with the fortunes of perfectly clean money derived from the proceeds of the illicit-drug trade.

4.3 Building Economic Empires—a Realistic Scenario

Drug money is in dire need to find a legitimate venue, and legitimate businessmen can use inexpensive cash to further their legitimate business objectives; by putting aside ethical considerations, the two have an opportunity to come together in a mutually beneficial partnership, a partnership capable of building economic empires. DTOs have the option of using the financial system (currently under constant surveillance by the authorities), the gray economy, or the formal economy to channel their money. Some drug proceeds will be used to finance the day-to-day operations of the DTOs, including payments to the drug producers. Of the estimated $30 billion plus going to Mexico and South America, less than $1.5 billion will go to pay the producers of Colombian and Mexican heroin, South American cocaine, and Mexican cannabis, ATS and ecstasy. Some of the money will be used to cover operating expenses, transportation, weaponry, computing and telecommunications equipment, precursor chemicals, the DTOs' payroll, bribes, and protection, among other things. Some of these expenditure will require clean money, but some will take place in the gray economy and will not require laundering by the DTO — some other entity will take care of the laundering. Taking all of the above into consideration, it is very likely that an amount in the order of $20-$25 billion will require laundering in Mexico; the higher figure presumes the South American DTOs choose to launder their proceeds in Mexico. Whatever the final amount laundered, while these funds make their way into the formal economy, they have the power to finance the building of truly mammoth economic enterprises.

Building an effective money-laundering operation. Putting together an effective money-laundering operation is not trivial; it can be very complex and requires the concurrence of the best creative and innovative minds. Implementing a laundering process using the many instruments available in the financial industries is a very risky proposition for the DTOs; as mentioned earlier, these vehicles are closely watched by law enforcement authorities in most parts of the world. In addition, the creation of superficial front companies is easily detected. A truly effective laundering organization requires the participation of a myriad of companies, the bigger the number, the more difficult they are to track. Essentially laundering drug money in the formal economy seems to be the most effective way of obtaining a certificate of legitimacy for the drug money. The following is required:

- A closely knit team integrated by the **DTO,** which delivers the drug money and the legitimate businessman with a **legal business** structure to receive the money and transform it into sparkling clean financial instruments.

- The legal business must be one that accepts cash as legal tender in the normal conduct of business, no questions asked and no reporting requirements to the authorities.

- The payback mechanism must satisfy the conditions described in the illustration of the fees-paid, stock-transaction, and/or real estate-transaction models, or something similar.

- The DTO must set up a structure of **beneficiary** companies through which it will receive the payback from the legitimate business. This may be seen as a difficult task, as it needs the camouflaging of the DTO to prevent suspicion by law enforcement authorities. In today's global economy this is not difficult at all; setting up new companies may take more or less time depending on the country of incorporation, but it is a straightforward activity. Certainly the experienced legitimate businessman can assist the DTO in this process.

- The **pyramidation** of beneficiary companies will contribute to confusing any investigator looking for illegal tracks.

- The **diversification** of the legal business providing the terrain for money laundering will add obstacles to anybody trying to follow the money track. This would suggest the creation of a conglomerate of companies including banks, insurance companies, securities brokerage houses, manufacturing, retailing, services, and many other legitimate businesses. The conglomerate will include — but not be limited to — those accepting cash as legal tender. It will contain companies that serve as receptors of the drug money and companies that provide temporary transit for the money, as well as legitimate companies that are the final destination of the laundered money.

- The **globalization** of the legal business will further enhance the cover of the laundering operation. It will be more difficult to track and trace the laundering operations as the money moves across borders in a labyrinth of multinational companies.

Appendix B includes a detailed illustration of how an economic empire can be built through the laundering of drug money over a period of twenty years. It illustrates how $40 billion of drug money is converted into $32 billion of legitimate money for the stealth business associate, $38.7 billion for the beneficiary of the DTO, and $14.5 billion is collected by the tax authorities. The model illustrates the transfer of wealth amongst the different players, some as active participants made out like "bandits", others as passive players register substantial benefits — the government tax collector. The other set of players — the unsuspecting stock market investors — end up footing the bill. It may be argued that the model is somewhat simplistic, and it is so in as much as there may be some additional costs associated with keeping the legal business structure of the beneficiary, which are not included in the model. Also, not all the profits shown may materialize, as the beneficiary may choose to use some of the money to pay salaries and/or bonuses to its employees and/or associates of the DTO or the beneficiary organization instead of reinvesting it. On the other hand, the model could very well reflect a complementary drug laundering operation on top of an existing legitimate business structure. In reality such a laundering machine could be built and it would be practically impossible to discover by law enforcement, as it operates within the rules of the legitimate business world in the formal economy.

Back in the 1980s the Guadalajara (Mexico) drug cartel, under the leadership of Rafael Caro-Quintero, currently serving a forty-year sentence in Mexico for his participation in the murder of DEA agent Enrique Camarena, used a less sophisticated money-laundering process. By working within the gray economy, Caro-Quintero invested heavily in real estate construction. Construction costs were understated by paying suppliers off the books. Laundering the money then became the responsibility of his suppliers. The real estate properties were leased to legitimate businesses who did not know Caro-Quintero was behind the landlord's organization. From these leases Caro-Quintero was able to obtain perfectly clean money in the formal economy. But his legal business structure was rather superficial and not properly camouflaged; when the prosecutors started looking into his sources of income, as a result of the Camarena murder investigation, Caro-Quintero's laundering setup was brought out into the open and confiscated. Using drug money in an isolated fashion like Caro-Quintero and many others have done is easy to identify. The operation is not so easy to uncover if the mechanism is used to enhance the real-estate holdings of a large and intricate conglomerate making use of drug money to finance the expansion of otherwise legitimate businesses. This mechanism, as a complement to the one shown in Appendix B, cannot be ruled out in a sophisticated money-laundering operation. The quantity of these laundering operations in place today is hard to tell, but there may be more than a handful. Mexico, being a key provider of illicit drugs to the U.S. and the receptor of around $30 billion of drug proceeds, seems like an ideal environment for the setting up of such operations. As mentioned earlier, the DEA considers Mexico to be one of the most important locations for money laundering and so far very little money laundering has been uncovered in Mexico. The above laundering operation model may very well explain why.

The sharing of the spoils of drug money. The distribution of the drug money spoils illustrated in the laundering operation in Appendix B shows the DTO beneficiary, the legitimate businessman, and the tax collector getting substantial benefits. Not a bad deal for the three of them and particularly for the DTO. The DTO just has to have patience and trust in their legitimate business-world partners. The business partners must be truly legitimate businessmen; otherwise, their activities could attract the attention of the scrutinizing eyes of law enforcement. For their collaboration and services, the legitimate businessman gets compensated handsomely. Through inexpensive cash resources, the business partner finances legitimate business operations with a clear advantage over competitors who do not have the benefit of easy and inexpensive cash. In the process, there is enough money to buy many loyalties and friends all over the global landscape. Those loyalties within the business and government communities become very handy to enhance their image. Moreover, last but not least, the government tax authorities need do nothing extra to increase tax revenues — just their everyday tax collection work. These are tax revenues derived from well-established businesses. Why would the tax authorities interfere with the legal operation of a tax paying corporate citizen? There is no argument in the world to compel them to question the legitimacy of the business operation. Frankly, to the naked eye, no law has been broken and hence there is no reason to rock the boat. Therefore, except for the unsuspecting stock market investor caught in the middle, this is a win-win-win situation, and nobody gets any medals for disrupting this peaceful and highly profitable arrangement.

Who is in command, the DTO or the business partner? In the business world, partnerships require the care and goodwill of the partners. It is not always easy for the participating partners to agree on every issue that comes to their attention, even if their values and ethics coincide. The partnership involving DTOs and legitimate businessmen is no different on the fundamentals; nevertheless, it contains elements not present in the run of the mill partnerships. To begin with, the DTOs have unique ways of doing business. They happen to be in the illicit-drug trade and used to confrontations with law enforcement and rival organizations all through their business processes. More often than not they rely on the use of force, sometimes very violent force, to overcome the obstacles that come across their path. Murder, preceded by torture if necessary, is one of the tools of the trade. The DTOs have no scruples, and they have plenty of resources, financial and technological resources. They can get the best technology money can buy to further their business interests. Are these traits sufficient to grant the DTO the command of the laundering partnership? There is no simple answer. The business partner is the DTO's gateway into the legitimate business world and the legitimization of their drug fortunes; without the full cooperation of these partners the DTO would have to rely on less robust corporate setups like the one used by Caro-Quintero back in the 1980s and risk being discovered by the authorities. In addition, going back to Appendix B, under the stock-transaction model the business delivers the payout in a five-year cycle. In the model presented there is money in the pipeline most of the time. Hence, this is one more good reason for the DTO to be on good terms with its partner. In a way, the laundering operation would suggest the need for a system of checks and balances in the partnership that calls for a tight and close relationship between the partners. If the laundering companies within the overall legitimate business conglomerate are not managed with a strong hand, they may become a black hole for the money being introduced by the DTO and the stock-transaction, or even the fees-paid model, may be jeopardized and no payback to the beneficiary will be possible. To answer the question as to who is in command, the best answer is that this partnership is more like a marriage; it ought to work until "death do them part." It is definitely not a one-night stand!

4.4 Is Drug Money Transferring Power?

Money is not everything in life, but it certainly has a soothing effect on the human nervous system. Money delivers financial security, which is an important ingredient in today's complex world. To a corporation, having money or liquid assets allows it to embark on new ventures, to expand into new markets, to successfully face unforeseen events, and to finance growth. In difficult economic times the availability of money in the company coffers can make the difference between life or death, between staying in business and going under. A bad economy is often in the background of many companies' bankruptcies, but it is also the scenario for those who have cash available to find opportunities. During bad times some companies go under and others survive or even thrive; liquidity, the availability of cash, becomes the crucial ingredient for survival. There are many opportunities available to companies with access to easy and inexpensive sources of cash, in particular during hard economic times when other companies, compelled by the lack of liquidity or on the verge of bankruptcy, are forced to sell out at very low prices. Imagine the DTO-legitimate business partnership coming into this scenario.

The opportunities of easy cash. As mentioned earlier, a money-laundering operation requires the existence of specific laundering companies within the legitimate business corporate structure. The cheaper it is to obtain control of these companies the more efficient the laundering operation can be. Besides, in a complex conglomerate of companies, it is easier to hide the movement of large amounts of drug money in the process of being laundered. Easy cash, such as the one provided by drug money, is a basic ingredient underlying the growth of substantial money-laundering enterprises. When bank interest rates are very high, those who have access to large quantities of cash have the upper hand, they can go on a shopping spree and add significant companies to their enterprise, either as legitimate business or as a legitimate business doing the laundering work within the conglomerate; both are equally in demand.

Our earlier analysis suggests that the U.S. based illicit-drug business is generating $125 billion in revenues (Table 4.4). A significant portion, around $86 billion, is likely to be laundered in the U.S., some entering through the gray economy given the retail nature of this income, but all of it eventually entering the legitimate world. About $30 billion is expatriated to Mexico for laundering or on its way to the final destination. As previously mentioned, anywhere in the range of $20-$25 billion is likely to be laundered in Mexico every year. This figure hovers around 2.0%-2.5% of Mexico's GDP, and between 10%-12.5% of the Mexican Federal Government Budget for 2007. This huge sum poses significant challenges and opportunities to the DTOs and their legitimate business associates. As illustrated in Appendix B, over a period of twenty years, a laundering operation can build a legitimate business empire — DTO and stealth business associate owned — worth $70 billion from a yearly contribution of $2 billion of drug money. The resulting empire can serve as

157

solid testimony to the power of easy cash in the hands of highly sophisticated legitimate businessmen. These conclusions may entice dedicated law enforcement agents to pursue an investigation, but there is little, if anything, they can do to prevent sophisticated laundering operations, short of turning the world into a police state where huge resources are focused on watching the everyday activities of its citizens. In the final analysis, the DTO-legitimate business partnership has a foolproof method of turning drug proceeds into sound and legitimate investments — risk free.

The power of easy cash in a lax-control environment. The above analysis and DEA reports point towards Mexico as a highly hospitable money-laundering turf for DTOs doing business in the U.S. With a population over 100 million and the eleventh largest economy in the world, Mexico provides fertile soil upon which to grow a thriving money-laundering venture. Even though Mexico has made, and continues to make, significant progress in the development of its modern institutions, today Mexico does not have the same quality of institutional controls in place as the U.S. The Mexican Stock Exchange (Bolsa Mexicana de Valores-BMV) and the Mexican equivalent of the SEC, the Comisión Nacional Bancaria y de Valores (CNBV), are not on a par with their counterparts in the U.S. Therefore, there is ample room for any legitimate business to operate within the stock exchange without the strict supervisory controls imposed by the SEC in the U.S. This lax habitat makes it easier to implement a money-laundering operation like the one described in this chapter. The fact that Mexico has a laxer investment control environment does not mean that money is not laundered within the U.S. As mentioned earlier, in the order of $86 billion of drug proceeds is estimated to enter the formal economy in America. Given the retail level origin of most of these drug revenues, as mentioned earlier, a significant portion of the money is probably going through the gray economy on its way to the formal economy through retail transactions, though other vehicles described in this chapter — mostly the fees-paid and the real estate-transaction models — are very likely used to launder drug proceeds within the U.S.

Whatever the vehicle used, the combination of easy cash and a lax-control environment provide fabulous terrain for the transfer of power. Economic power leads to political power in any society. Even the American democratic political system is under the influence of the economic interests of various flavors; this happens in the midst of an open society with widespread political participation. Most Latin American countries do not enjoy the democratic maturity prevailing in the U.S.; thus, they are more vulnerable to the influence of economic groups with substantial resources at their disposal. For example, in the last three decades of the 20th century, Mexico went through a number of economic crises during which individuals and corporations having cash in hand were positioned to acquire economic assets in the auction block and build economic empires — the cheaper the cash the greater the opportunity. Those were also the days in which Mexico began to play a bigger role in the traffic of illicit drugs into the U.S. Hence; drug money began to flow in large quantities into the Mexican economy, opening the way for many investment opportunities in the legitimate business world. Truly genuine economic enterprises developed in Mexico during the later half of the 20th century, but, in parallel, the opportunity flourished for the laundering of large sums of drug money; this environment contributed to strengthening the power of DTOs and their stealth business partners. How much economic power has been transferred to these partnerships is hard to tell, these transactions are clandestine in nature and there are no reliable statistics. Combining the laundering operation model with the amount of drug money estimated to have entered Mexico during the last thirty years suggests that the opportunity to create huge economic empires with the support of drug money was pervasive. It is very likely that legitimate businesses, under the stress of the multiple economic crises which lashed Mexico for three decades, became prey to the voracious appetite of cash-rich enterprises financed with drug money. Hence, a process of economic power transfer and/or accumulation into the hands of those with access to

159

easy cash could have taken place during the last 30 years. This has many implications, economic power transfer activates political power transfer and also the possibility of extending, both economic and political power, beyond the original borders of the enterprise given today's global economy.

Border crossing of power made easy. The world today is like a village of the early 20th century. It is as easy to do business in any part of the world and practically at any hour of the day as it was to transact business within a small village a century ago. The Internet, for one, has shrunk the world. Money can be transferred from practically anywhere in the world to the most remote location provided there is access to the World Wide Web. Goods can be purchased also through the Web and they can arrive in a matter of hours to the selected location. Virtual meetings, if preferred to physical ones, can take place with just a few minutes notice. Physical ones would take no more than a day to arrange no matter how far away the parties are. In summary the world has shrunk!

In this global economic environment, it is natural for businesses of any nationality to look for opportunities beyond their borders; this has given birth to the multinational corporations. A few decades ago multinational corporations used to be the exclusive domain of U.S., European, and Japanese companies; usually also of large corporations from these countries. This is no longer true; the global village has opened the way for companies of any nationality or size to enter the international arena. This opening is available for any legitimate business operating under the rules of the game. It is certainly not open to the DTOs; they must continue to operate outside the law. However, it is not a problem for their stealth business partners to benefit from this opportunity; they are legitimate and therefore protected by the rules of the game of international business.

What is there to prevent a Mexican DTO-legitimate business partnership from setting up a laundering operation within U.S. borders? As mentioned earlier, it is estimated that $30 billion from the illicit-drug trade travels back to Mexico. This operation involves the bulk shipment of cash, which in itself is a rather complicated operation with many hurdles and risks involved. Would it not be easier to deliver the drug cash to a laundry within U.S. borders? Absolutely! All it takes is for the legitimate business partner to set up a laundry within the U.S. with the characteristics already described to receive the drug money; the payback can use the same ingenious fees-paid, stock-transaction, or real estate-transaction models with the additional advantage that the payback can be made in a country other than the U.S. if so desired. The economic and political powers of the partnership can easily move across borderlines without being identified as part of a drug trafficking operation.

4.5 The Multi-functional Money-Laundering Operation

As mentioned earlier, annual worldwide money laundering is estimated in the $600 billion to trillions range, depending on the source of the data. Money laundering is not limited to drug money, there are many illicit activities requiring the services of money laundering. Organized crime activities, together with government and private sector graft, all have a need to launder their ill obtained proceeds.

Sharing the money-laundering machine. The money-laundering vehicles available to DTOs are also within the reach of others. Besides, since the attack on the World Trade Center in New York on September 11, 2001, the issue of money laundering by terrorist organizations has taken center stage. These organization need to channel resources to finance their terrorist activities and, besides engaging in illicit activities to obtain resources, they may transfer otherwise legitimate money from presumed charitable organizations, or even businesses, to the coffers of terrorist entities like al-Qaeda. The analysis of terrorist money laundering is not at the center of this research; hence, it is not covered. Nevertheless, there are organizations currently labeled as terrorist which happen to be linked to the drug trade, such as the FARC and the AUC in Colombia, and al-Qaeda and the Taliban in Afghanistan. These organizations are of

161

interest to this presentation as they are today, or may in time, evolve into a major threat to the security of many countries, including the U.S.

Graft money sharing the money-laundering machine. Graft money is always eager to find its way into the formal economy as the only real safe way to become useful to its owners. It is not uncommon for politically connected individuals to receive kickbacks for arranging business deals with government entities. Those proceeds are not legal even on their home turf and need laundering. As more recent strategies implemented by FinCEN show, the financial system is not as safe today as it used to be only a few years ago for the laundering of illicit proceeds, whether from drugs or graft. The participation of various types of illicit proceeds in a laundering operation makes it more difficult for law enforcement to investigate any particular illicit money-laundering activity.

4.6 Is Drug Money Threatening America?

Drug money is an effective tool for exercising violence by the DTOs, it can buy the latest weapons and technology to support their illicit activities; it can also buy loyalties by appealing to human greed or the survival instinct. Drug money can reward partners in crime or cancel law enforcement initiatives. It empowers the drug trafficker to pose the fundamental live and let live proposition to law enforcement agents: "Help me and live, do not help me, and die."[7] Not a difficult choice to make for law enforcement in countries like Colombia and Mexico, where the salary of a municipal police agent may not exceed $350 a month. However, laundered drug money has a different kind of power; it has the power of a stealth hand capable of penetrating unnoticed — in silence — into the most intricate places. This power can go beyond anybody's wildest imagination into the highest circles of influence in any country, including the United States. Where might it lead? This is a question that should be in the mind of every citizen and political leader.

The penetration of strategic industries. The money-laundering operation presented earlier suggests the possibility of generating huge fortunes for the DTOs and their stealth business associates. The U.S. is amongst the most attractive places and fertile grounds to invest. What would be the implications for any country of receiving investments from the DTOs' stealth associates in strategic industries? Industries like tele-communications, broadcasting, and media communications, besides high-tech of many flavors, are strategic to the security of any nation, and the U.S. is no exception. Laundered drug money is no different from genuine legitimate money; it has the same look and feel. Therefore, the danger of penetration of strategic industries will be present for as long as the pipe-line of drug money remains full. Developing and implementing an effec-tive policy aimed at drying up the drug money pipeline is a great chal-lenge facing modern society at the dawn of the 21st century.

4.7 Collateral Damage

There is significant collateral damage to society associated with the laundering of drug money. Easy money as a temptation is one thing, but easy money in the hands of certain individuals grants them an unfair advantage. In the end, it will be hard to develop a sound and solid busi-ness culture if it is always easier to make a fat profit by laundering money.

The charm of easy money. In a society assigning great value to financial success, the lure of making big money can lead young valuable talent to willingly participate in illicit activities, including money launder-ing. Effective money laundering is not for the mentally challenged, it is an activity requiring bright individuals if it is to be successful and comply with all the requirements for proper concealment. Hence, it is an activity likely to attract young capable talent with the lure of big profits; young people who would choose to abandon other more valuable occupations from society's perspective. Talent is also a scarce resource, diverting it to money-laundering activities is collateral damage inflicted on society.

Unfair business competition. In difficult economic times, like the ones Mexico and other Latin American countries have gone through over the past thirty or forty years, it is a scary business weakness to run out of liquidity. The availability of cash to face difficult economic conditions is a lifesaver for many businesses. Especially during those difficult times, with inflation running at an annual rate of over 100%, bank credit becomes prohibitive and usually runs into a two-digit monthly rate. However, liquidity is not a problem for those with access to the wonders of laundered drug money. It is under this environment that many companies go under or fall into the hands of the DTOs' covert business associates. This is unfair business competition. Legitimate businessmen, unable to obtain the cash needed to survive, end up going under or selling cheap to those with access to cash. Not all, but certainly some, of these buyers are the partners of the DTOs in laundering operations. This is another case of collateral damage from drug money laundering.

Cannot build a sound business culture and competitive enterprises with easy drug money. The long-term strength of the economy of any country is highly dependent on the strength of the individual enterprises which operate within it. And the strength of any individual business depends to a great extend on the corporate culture prevailing within the organization. An organization highly focused on servicing customer needs and lowering operating costs is very likely to be more successful than one that ignores the wishes and desires of the customer and does not strive to be more efficient. Focusing on customers' needs and corporate efficiency requires certain leadership traits in the organization; such traits will encourage or even empower company employees to take customer satisfaction and corporate productivity into their own hands. This approach will usually come hand in hand with compensation schemes that reward good performance and punish bad ones. When money laundering becomes the main focus of any legitimate company, customers' needs quickly become relegated in the priorities of the organization. Security and the securing of a safe environment for the money to be laundered becomes the most important priority. Why security? Security becomes important to make sure that the money being laundered is not stolen by customers or employees in the form of petty theft or internal fraud. Security is also important to running a tight operation where the drug money can be safely introduced into the business without causing any suspicion. Even if the cynical approach were taken, suggesting that laundered drug money can be a vehicle to further the sound development of certain countries, the above observation will prove that presumption wrong. The true health of a company cannot be measured by good-looking financial statements reflecting the magic of laundered money. The ultimate test of a company's health, besides the financial statements, is the concurrence of satisfied customers who choose to buy from that company and not from its competitors. The lack of sound business cultures resulting from easy laundered money adds to the collateral damage inflicted on society by money laundering. The minute the drug money pipeline dries up, real opportunities for the development of sound business cultures and a level playing field for all business enterprises will come to be. Money-laundering enterprises, and the business conglomerates they are part of, will not be able to survive intact in a business world without a pipeline of drug money.

In spite of all the fireworks that go off every time law enforcement strikes a blow at some drug money laundering operation, the laundering of drug money is a silent, covert activity. It is truly a stealth operation, away from any law enforcement radar. Less than 1% of the proceeds from the illicit U.S. drug business are intercepted according to the DEA's own account, the other 99% flows smoothly into an effective money-laundering operation which in silence is helping transfer power into the hands of DTOs and their stealth business associates. Some of them may even be buying into strategic U.S. industries. A true nightmare for U.S. national security, but also for the national security of U.S. allies; they are not immune to these events taking place on their own turf. One more piece of this puzzling silent nightmare.

5

THE BOTTOM LINE — MYTHS AND

REALITIES

Three very specific myths stand out, they are: Drug use leads to drug addiction, drug use leads to a life of crime, and the war on drugs is being won.

5.1 Sorting Out the Mythical from the Real World

Illicit drugs are at the center of a crucial controversy in American society and all over the world. Current drug policy finds strong backing in large segments of the population primarily concerned with the negative effects drugs — narcotics and other mind altering substances (OMAS) — have on humans, particularly the young and unwary. At the same time, there are groups of citizens who champion radical changes in current policy. These groups may seek change for a variety of reasons; some stake a claim on the medicinal qualities of cannabis and/or its low addiction level, others just want to exercise their individual right to introduce into their body whatever they choose to without causing any harm to their fellow humans. However, there are some who, regardless of the medicinal properties of cannabis or their individual rights as citizens, are concerned with the lawlessness and power transfer that results from the current drug prohibition policy. The lawlessness goes beyond street crime and the blatant disregard for the restrictions imposed by current policy; it is delivering huge wealth and power into the hands of those who have chosen to break the law by trafficking with drugs and their stealth business associates who help them turn drug money into legitimate financial instruments and wealth. In today's global village, huge power in the hands of unscrupulous and power thirsty individuals may pose serious risks to the security of many nations, including the United States. Supporters and detractors of the current drug policy believe their position furthers the greater good of society, but somehow they find themselves walking on opposite sides of the aisle; many emotions come into play as the parties engage in a sort of dialogue of the deaf. As presented in earlier chapters, there are plenty of facts surrounding the crucial drug issues addressed in this presentation; they are solid elements to better understand drug use and abuse, the illicit-drug trade, the war on drugs, and drug money laundering. Unfortunately the drug problem is surrounded by many myths — these myths must be dealt with. Sorting out what is truly real from the mythical is vital if society is ever going to effectively address the drug problem. This is the quest for the bottom line.

Bringing in the facts. The drug problem is overshadowed by many myths — broadly held beliefs perceived and treated as facts by the people. A comprehensive analysis and diagnostic of the drug-related issues covered in this presentation requires sifting the facts and discarding the myths. Scientific research is one tool to assist in this process; such research ought to be conducted in an environment of scientific freedom without coercion and with adequate data derived from an unmarred research environment. Statistical data and analytical methods can also support the process. Statistical analysis helps to measure progress of programs and adherence to policy. The interception of less than one percent of the drug money generated in the U.S. is not a credible indicator of the war on drugs' success. It is urgent for America — and the world — to do away with the myths and face reality, this is the only path capable of leading toward a coherent and successful drug policy.

The drug problem is officially defined along the following line: Illicit drugs — narcotics and OMAS — are detrimental to human health; therefore, the state assumes the responsibility of prohibiting the consumption of such substances to all citizens — adults and juveniles.

168

With this basic conception of the problem a **drug prohibition policy** has been in place since the beginning of the 20th century:

- Legislation was enacted to address the violation of the prohibition to consume or commercialize narcotics.

- In the face of prohibition, the illicit commercialization of drugs makes it possible for adults and juveniles to acquire and consume these substances. Therefore, it becomes the responsibility of the state to take whatever measures are deemed necessary to prevent the use and trade of illicit drugs.

- Law enforcement is entrusted with the responsibility to persecute and bring to justice those engaged in illicit commercialization and use of drugs.

- The judicial system is entrusted with the application of the prohibition legislation to those in violation, following precise guidelines provided by the legislation itself.

The above succinctly summarizes the rationale and modus operandi behind the current drug policy and its enforcing arm, the war on drugs. In more recent times, the policy that was designed to prevent the use of drugs by adults and juveniles is currently faced with vigorous drug use and abuse. The same policy, which was meant to prevent the commercialization of narcotics, presides over a huge worldwide business of $322 billion and a domestic business in America of $125 billion. Besides, the policy which was expected to deliver results with a reasonable "war on drugs" budget thirty years ago has not been able to make a significant dent on the drug business with an ever-increasing budget. And finally, despite the huge investments to thwart the activities of illicit-drug merchandisers, the DTOs and their business associates have been able to amass huge fortunes thanks to the high price of drugs. Meanwhile there are 200 million consumers around the world — 34.8 million in the U.S. — eagerly waiting to pay the market price for their drug of choice. The fundamental objective behind current drug policy was to keep drugs away from human consumption; a look at the above facts, suggests that the government was trying to achieve an impossible dream.

What would have happened over the past thirty years if the drug problem had been defined differently? Perhaps it could have been defined as a health problem and treated as such, not as a criminal one. There is much to learn from looking at the current state of affairs, making an evaluation of the facts and from there designing and launching a new drug policy. In the end, the greater possible good to society should guide a new policy. There is no room or time to pursue impossible dreams, society must focus on achieving the greatest feasible good for its members, and that may very well mean accepting the littlest of all evils — the lesser evil.

5.2 Searching for the Bottom Line of Illicit Drugs

The bottom line of illicit drugs should distinguish what is truly relevant from what is not. It is crucial to sift through the maze of drug-related events to identify whether they have a significant — positive or negative — **impact on the democratic values of American society.** As a primary objective of society, the preservation of life, liberty and the pursuit of happiness must be achievable by society as a whole and not only by some of its members in detriment of others. The rights of any particular individual extend until they interfere with the rights of others. Some, in their desperation to find a quick solution to the drug problem, might be attracted to the methods applied by the government of Communist China in the late 1940s and early 1950s to eradicate their 15 million opium addicts. The Chinese, with the compulsory rehabilitation of opium addicts and the execution by firing squad of drug dealers, succeeded in their quest for eradication, but they did not have the U.S. Bill of Rights or democratic principles with which to contend. The Chinese approach would not meet the democratic standards of American society. "Mao Tse-tung was no Thomas Jefferson", as a high-school senior was quick to point out when discussing the subject with me.

Focusing on the primary objective of society — the preservation of democratic values — and being able to focus on root causes and not be sidetracked by symptoms, ought to be high in the priorities of policymak-

ILL:

Thank you for loaning us the following item:

Title: A silent nightmare : the bottom line and the challenge of illicit drugs /
Author: Ferragut, Sergio.

OCLC#: 144642621
ILL#:
ILLiad Transaction Number: 41248
Pieces: 1.0
Notes/Special Instructions:
Lending Library's Due Date:
12/30/2009 12:00:00 AM

This item is being returned to:

L.W. Nixon Library
901 S. Haverhill Rd.
El Dorado, KS 67042

If there are any questions about this item, please give us a call at (815) 753-9842 or e-mail us at illdept@niu.edu.

ers. Besides, it is crucial to assess the feasibility of achieving the objectives of a particular policy in the process of getting to the bottom line of drug-related issues. Sometimes, the **greater (feasible) good of society** may be better achieved through **the lesser evil**; a particular choice or decision may cause less damage to society than any of the alternatives at hand — less damage is inflicted upon society by choosing that particular option. Focusing on feasible alternatives and on the lesser evil to society in lieu of an impossible dream completes the criteria to proceed with the search for the bottom line of the illicit-drug controversy. Hence, the criteria stand as follows:

- Does the event under analysis further or obstruct the democratic values of society?
- Is the event under scrutiny a root cause — a root event — or a symptom or secondary event in the chain of events under analysis?
- Is the event under consideration — e.g., a policy, program, legislation — attempting to reach an impossible dream or is it delivering the lesser evil to society from all the available feasible alternatives?

Empowered with these criteria and with the documented facts covered in Chapters I through IV we proceed with the search for the bottom line — the relevant events — immersed in the four intertwined issues of the drug problem: drug use and abuse, the illicit-drug trade, the war on drugs, and drug money laundering.

5.3 The Bottom Line of Drug Use and Abuse

Mind altering substances — illicit drugs — have a direct effect on the human nervous system. Heroin, cocaine, cannabis, ATS, and ecstasy all have an effect on the brain; therein the attractions to those who experiment with, casually use, or abuse them. This effect is also true of licit drugs like alcohol and tobacco. As explained in Chapter I, the 2004 National Survey on Drug Use and Health — NSDUH [1] presents the population of illicit and licit drug users in three groups: those who have used drugs at least once during their lifetime, those who have used them during the past year, and the ones who have used them during the past month; the first group includes the other two, and the second group includes the last one. The survey also reports the number of drug dependents and abusers as reflected in Table 1.2, which suggests the highly addictive nature of heroin, followed by cocaine, and to a much lesser degree by cannabis, and ecstasy and ATS. This table also shows alcohol dependents and abusers at a rate close to the ATS and ecstasy use and a bit lower than cannabis. The data point to the fact that not all drug users become drug addicts and that some drugs are more addictive than others. Though this is a solid conclusion coming out of the cold numbers, it does not mean that drugs are necessarily good for human health; certain drugs can be more damaging than others, as illustrated in Chapter I. In summary, the percentage of dependents plus abusers for each of the drugs among the population using the drug during the twelve months prior to the survey was as follows: 65.5% for heroin, 27.8% for cocaine, 17.6% for cannabis, a combined 11.6% for ecstasy plus ATS, and 11.9% for alcohol. The percentage of dependents plus abusers among the population who have used the drug sometime during their lifetime was as follows: 31.1% for heroin, 4.6% for cocaine, 4.6% for cannabis, a combined 1.3% for ecstasy plus ATS.

Additionally, of the 83.1 million users of tobacco during the past year, 70.3 million have used it during the past month (including first-time users), which suggests an addiction rate below 84%, but higher than for heroin. The fact that alcohol and tobacco are addictive does not make these two legal drugs illegal. There are also well-known health and social issues associated with alcohol and tobacco use as illustrated in Chapter I, but that does not drive the drugs into illegality either. Keeping these two drugs legal makes it easier to obtain reliable data regarding their use and the related health and social effects. Besides, scientific research can be conducted in an environment of scientific freedom without coercion from prohibition rules.

The addiction statistics summarized above, together with the collateral damage resulting from the use and abuse of drugs presented in Chapter I, deliver **the bottom line of drug use and abuse** as follows:

1.   Illicit drug use does not necessarily lead to drug addiction, though some drugs are more likely to generate addiction than others. It is a **myth** that drug use — any illicit drug used by any person — will automatically lead to drug addiction.

2.   Prolonged use of any illicit drug is more likely to generate addiction. Some users are more likely to become addicts than others perhaps because of a genetic propensity. This happens to also be true of alcohol and tobacco.

3.   Illicit drugs may have a negative impact on the health of users — more on some users than others. But so do licit drugs like alcohol and tobacco.

4.   The illegality of drugs mars the scientific medical research required to get an effective handle on the health issues surrounding narcotic drugs. For one, it is difficult to obtain non-contaminated and quality-controlled samples of the drugs, and second, proper scientific research is frowned upon under the prohibition policy in effect.

5.   Current drug prohibition policy is a significant contributor to the widespread HIV/AIDS and hepatitis C infections because of the use of unsanitary injections to administer heroin and cocaine in an illicit environment.

6.   There is a high nationwide economic cost associated with illicit drugs — $97.9 billion per year.

7.   Current drug prohibition policy creates economic incentives for DTOs and drug peddlers to be in the drug business and promote the use of drugs. There are 34.8 million drug users in the U.S.; this is 17.4% of the worldwide population of drug users of 200 million and 14.5% of the U.S. population aged twelve and over.

5.4 The Bottom Line of the Illicit-Drug Trade

As illustrated in Chapter II, the UN estimated global illicit-drug revenue is in the order of $322 billion for 2003 at retail, $94 billion at wholesale, and $12.8 billion at the producer level. This is probably the best estimate available of the industry's worth and demonstrates that **the illicit-drug business is big business.** This data also reveals the composition of the production-distribution-retailing network. The drug producers, including the farmers cultivating the basic crops — opium poppy, coca bush, and cannabis plant — barely get 4% of the retail revenues, the portion received by the wholesale network is equivalent to 25% of retail revenues, and the retail network receives 71% of the revenue. This distribution of the proceeds speaks of the commanding role retail networks play in the business. Though the retail value of the illicit-drug industry is less than 1% of global GDP, it is still very significant in terms of other indicators; its value is higher than the GDP of 88% of the countries for which the World Bank has GDP data — 163 out of 184 countries. Thus, in relative terms, it is also a very important component of the global economy.

At $125 billion, the U.S. illicit-drug business accounts for almost 39% of the global business, though official U.S. government (USG) reports do not recognize this reality coming out of UN reports. Perhaps this unwillingness to publicly recognize reality results from the fact that 39% of the U.S. illicit-drug business is accounted for by U.S. domestically sourced cannabis, ATS and ecstasy, as illustrated in Tables 4.5a and 4.5b. By underestimating the domestic production of cannabis, ATS, and ecstasy, U.S. law enforcement focuses on foreign sources of supplies and diminishes the pressure on domestic producers. This is a point made by some foreign analysts who have looked at this particular contradiction.[2] The discrepancy surrounding the official USG figures and UN data on the size of the U.S. drug business, clouds the vision of any observer attempting to understand the motivations sustaining the current drug policy.

The above commentaries and the presentation in Chapter II lead to **the bottom line of the illicit-drug trade** as follows:

1. The global narcotic trade — $322 billion annually — is big business and a very important component of the global economy. Huge financial resources come into the hands of DTOs.

2. The illicit-drug business in the U.S. is estimated at $125 billion, though U.S. authorities publicly claim a much lower figure at $65 billion. This discrepancy adds confusion to the understanding of the illicit U.S. drug business and raises questions about the motivations of USG authorities for underestimating the size of the market.

3. Over the past three decades DTOs have successfully adapted their operations to changing markets and operating conditions and continued to supply an ever-present demand for illicit drugs in the U.S.

4. Mexican DTOs rose to occupy a prominent place in the international drug trade over the past twenty years or so by taking advantage of their privileged geographical location and the socio-economic-political environment in Mexico.

5. The drug trade is funneling resources to known terrorist organization which pose a threat to the U.S. and/or its allies.

6. A vigorous drug trade is also hampering the development of democratic institutions in countries close to the U.S., like Mexico, which shares a 2,000-mile border with the U.S.

7. Peasants in drug-crop producing countries abandon the cultivation of much-needed food crops in favor of drug crops.

8. Corruption is spreading and thriving in many countries as it is fed by ample resources from the drug trade.

5.5 The Bottom Line of the War on Drugs

Since the formal declaration of war by President Nixon in 1971, U.S. authorities have placed an ever-increasing emphasis on disrupting the supply chain of illicit drugs versus preventing and treating drug use and addiction. The federal government spends $17 billion per year on fighting drugs — some analysts estimate total nationwide spending to be as high a $50 billion. Most of this $17 billion expenditure goes on disrupting the activities of the DTOs, and a small portion is channeled toward prevention and treatment of drug use and addiction. More than thirty years have passed since Nixon's declaration of war, and the intensity of the war has been increasing since the beginning. In the midst of this aggressive law enforcement environment the DTOs have demonstrated great resiliency. Innovation and flexibility have been at the top of the DTOs' agenda and, as the evidence shows, during the past thirty years they have been able to change tactics and restructure to effectively respond to new threats. The net result is that drugs continue to be abundant in the streets of America and the price of drugs has dropped as a result of increased supplies and/or increased competition among DTOs.

In the midst of the war, many things have happened. In a way, the war on drugs may have become a driver of the drug business rather than a deterrent. **The bottom line of the war on drugs** can be summarized as follows:

1. The war places greater emphasis on disrupting the supply chain of illicit drugs than on educating the public — parents and children, adults and juveniles — to prevent the use of drugs, or on health programs to treat drug abusers.

2. In the midst of an aggressive law enforcement environment the DTOs have demonstrated great resiliency. They exhibit great capacity to adapt to new operating conditions and continue to deliver abundant drug supplies to the U.S. and other markets.

3. The war on drugs is global; it has battlefronts in many countries — producing, transshipment, and consumer countries alike. Except for minor accomplishments — more like skirmishes — the war has not delivered any significant reduction on the availability of drugs to the millions of American consumers.

4. Contrary to DEA's claims, the war on drugs is not being won. It has become a business driver and not an impediment. The war

puts upward pressure on drug prices, which in turn provide greater incentives to stay in or enter the business. As a result, drugs are easily obtained in any U.S. city and at lower prices than fifteen years ago because of the concurrence of competing DTOs to the marketplace lured by the big profit potential.

5. The destruction of the big Colombian drug cartels that dominated in the 1980s and early 1990s, gave rise to a myriad of loosely tied trafficking organizations and a more competitive and effective drug industry.

6. American society is bleeding with half a million inmates serving drug-related sentences; many of them youngsters wasting their lives in prison — specializing in high crime instead of attending college — became victims of mandatory jail sentences.

7. Certain law enforcement tactics and procedures violate the Bill of Rights, one of the pillars of the American democratic system.

8. Over thirty years of an endless struggle — evidenced by DEA and UN reports — ought to be enough indication that **the war on drugs can not be won. Those who assert the contrary support a myth** — some do so in good faith while trying to reach an impossible dream, others most likely have something to gain from keeping the myth alive.

9. Incorruptible law enforcement agents are murdered for refusing to cooperate with the DTOs, while others fall prey to the seduction provided by the lure of drug money.

5.6 The Bottom Line of Drug Money Laundering

Chapter IV revealed the straightforward and highly effective mechanisms available to DTOs for laundering their drug proceeds away from the otherwise watchful eye and highly ineffective actions of law enforcement. These mechanisms, together with the analysis of the destination of these proceeds leads to **the bottom line of drug money laundering,** as follows:

1. US drug proceeds in the order of $125 billion get laundered annually; 67% to 70% in the U.S., 25% to 28% in Latin America —— Mexico and Colombia primarily, and 5% in other countries.

2. DEA drug money interceptions amount to less than one billion dollar — less than 1% of the U.S. drug business and less than 4% of the drug money estimated to travel to and through Mexico for laundering.

3. The financial industry is no longer a good entry point to clean drug money; it is highly regulated and constantly monitored by the FinCEN and similar institutions in other countries.

4. The gray economy is probably a widely used channel in the U.S. where most of the money to be laundered comes from the retail network or from the domestic production of cannabis, ATS and ecstasy. Through cash transactions this money eventually enters the formal economy and adds to the U.S. GDP.

5. Economic empires are being built with the support of drug money. The advantage provided by easy cash drives the transfer of power from truly legitimate businessmen into the hands of drug lords and their stealth business partners.

6. In today's global village, the power acquired by DTOs and their business partners can easily cross borders and become a threat to U.S. national security and the security of its allies. This is even more so when there is an alliance between DTOs and known terrorist groups — a reality today.

7. The legitimate business community is hurt by the charm of easy money, which attracts valuable talent into drug laundering activities. In addition, easy cash grants the DTOs' business partners an unfair competitive advantage in detriment of truly legitimate business enterprises. And, customer service and business productivity take second place to money-laundering activities in businesses engaged in money laundering.

5.7 The Bottom Line

Current drug policy is predicated on the basis of protecting the public from the ravages of illicit drugs. For over thirty years a war on drugs has been waged in an attempt to implement the policy and enforce the drug laws enacted to support it. The bottom line of the four inter-twined drug-related issues — the use and abuse of drugs, the illicit-drug trade, the war on drugs, and drug money laundering — points towards a very complex maze of events which when placed in the proper context reveal the root causes of the drug problem in America. To unravel this maze it is crucial to begin by exposing the myths that have clouded the drug problem for so many decades. Three very specific myths stand out, they are:

- Drug use leads to drug addiction.
- Drug use leads to a life of crime.
- The war on drugs is being won.

As documented in this presentation, **not all drug use leads to addiction**. Research indicates that some drugs are more addictive than others, and some individuals are more prone to becoming addicts than the person next to them. To support the discarding of this myth, the 34.8 million American drug users are not all addicts, as a matter of fact, there are over 75.2 million Americans who have used drugs at some point in their lives and do not use them any more; this is the best proof that not all drug users become addicts.

Crime may be associated with drug use, but not in a cause-effect type of relationship. Certainly, drug use is in the menu of many criminals, but **drug use is not necessarily a driver of crime**. It is more likely that a drug user — perhaps an addict — would commit a crime to support his expensive habit. Many addicts would prefer to go to a social service clinic for their shot, if the option were available, rather than commit the crime. If drug use leads to crime, there would be 110 million criminals in the U.S. today — the individuals who used drugs sometime in their lifetime.

The interception of less than 1% of the U.S. drug proceeds and less than 10% of the drugs being sold — domestic and imported — in the U.S. is not a solid indication that the war on drugs is being won. Drugs have become cheaper in U.S. streets over the past two decades, in basic economic terms it means there are more drugs available; it could also mean that the increased competition resulting from more DTOs accessing the market lured by the huge profit potential leads to lower prices, as would happen in any other type of business. Hence, **there is no solid evidence that the war on drugs is being won**. This war has all the traits of an un-winnable war; prohibition policy is a drug business driver rather than an impediment. Those who herald success may do so in good faith, dazzled by an impossible dream.

Our analysis also leads to three root causes of the drug problem in America and in the world at large. They are at the bottom of the chains of events feeding the fundamental intertwined issues behind the drug problem. Earlier in the presentation we pointed out that our research did not focus on the demand component of the problem and recognized that it deserved a study of its own. However, two of the three root causes are demand related, and they are:

- Genetics, which may make one individual more prone to drug addiction than the next one under similar circumstances.
- The post-modernist social fabric, with changed social values, weak family structures, including deficient parenting when juveniles are involved, does not provide the necessary support to keep someone from using drugs or assist the user in his/her attempts to abandon drug use.

A third root cause is the current prohibition policy, making a crime of things that are not a crime goes beyond the bounds of reason by attempting to control a man's appetites by legislation. These words paraphrase Abraham Lincoln's words when he said: "A prohibition law strikes a blow at the very principles upon which our government was founded". [3] And prohibition together with its enforcing arm — the war on drugs — have become a driver of the illicit-drug business and both are way off the mark of becoming an effective deterrent.

The myths and root causes highlighted above are the pillars of the bottom line of the drug problem. The bottom line is complemented by those events — covered throughout this chapter — that ought to be considered in the design of a new policy and/or which can help as indicators of the policy's performance. The latter is indicated by a KPI (Key Performance Indicator) reference. Hence, the bottom line is complemented as follows:

- Drug use has an impact on the human body and may yield negative health results; the specific effect will vary from drug to drug. Solid scientific medical and psychological research, free from the coercive shadow of prohibition, is called for to get to the bottom of the human health realities of today's illicit drugs.

- Drug use induced HIV/AIDS and hepatitis C infections are more likely to come under control under a prohibition-free drug environment. The incidence of HIV/AIDS and hepatitis C infections can be used as a KPI.

- Proactive parenting — the development of strong family structures — should be at the core of any drug education campaign. Church groups and other non-governmental organizations (NGOs) have a significant role to play in this respect.

- The narcotics trade — the illicit-drug business — has become a major global industry with a strong foothold in the U.S. The industry is driven by current prohibition policy that, by raising the stakes involved, makes entering the business more profitable. The evolution of the illicit-drug trade can be a valuable KPI.

- Fighting the drug trade has also become a major industry; the billions of dollars that go into fighting drug traffickers provide sustenance to many interested parties who have a stake in keeping the war alive. The drug war budget can be a very valuable KPI.

181

- Neither the current drug policy nor the war on drugs has done enough to deter the DTOs. Their resiliency and flexibility have successfully overshadowed the actions of law enforcement.
- DTOs in certain countries are channeling resources to terrorist groups which are a threat to U.S. allies and can become a direct threat to U.S. national security. The transfer of drug money to terrorist groups is a valuable KPI.
- The shifting patterns of the drug trade over the past twenty years allowed Mexican DTOs to become a force to reckon with south of the U.S. border, a border spreading for 2,000 miles. This event has major implications for U.S. national security. The power exerted by Mexican DTOs in their own country is a valuable KPI.
- The vigor of the Mexican DTOs is a direct threat to the development of democratic institutions in Mexico. A stable and democratic Mexico is in the best interest of the U.S. The strengthening of Mexican democratic institutions is a valuable KPI.
- Corruption spreads with the expansion of the drug trade; money can induce many to cooperate with DTOs. Those who refuse sign their own death sentence. Drug driven corruption within law enforcement and among government officials is a valuable KPI.
- The world today is a village, the drug trade is a global business, the war on drugs takes place all over the world, and any solution to the current drug dilemma must be addressed globally.
- U.S. prisons are crowded with over half a million people serving drug-related sentences. The young are being trained in high crime while refused the opportunity to attend college. The number of prisoners serving drug-related jail sentences is a good KPI.
- The Bill of Rights and American democratic values are often at risk because of certain law enforcement tactics and procedures. The number of violations to civil liberties is a good KPI.
- Illicit-drug proceeds are filling the coffers of DTOs and their stealth business partners collaborating in very sophisticated but effective drug money laundering schemes far away from the reach

of law enforcement. The volume of drug money laundered is a good KPI.

- Laundered drug money is transferring power — economic and political — into the hands of drug lords and their stealth business partners.
- Economic empires can be built with the support of laundered drug money — inexpensive cash can go a long way.
- In the global village, power can cross borders easily. Down the road, it should come as no surprise to discover DTOs' stealth business partners sharing a meal with legitimate U.S. businessmen and politicians, or sitting on the board of directors of strategic U.S. corporations.
- Truly genuine businessmen are at a competitive disadvantage when facing those with access to inexpensive drug money.
- Corporate cultures are deteriorated when money laundering becomes the primary focus of the enterprise, and customer service, productivity, and competitiveness take second place.

This summary of drug-related events, the highlighted myths surrounding the drug problem, and the pinpointed root causes are the bottom line of the current drug problem in America and around the world. They come out of the comprehensive analysis in this presentation and are a solid foundation for the design and evaluation of the options facing society to overhaul the current drug policy and give birth to a more rational, humane and effective one.

The bottom line operates as a wake up call; it breaks the silence engulfing the four drug-related issues that have kept the drug problem alive in America for too long. The nightmare of drug use and abuse, the highly profitable illicit-drug trade, the un-winnable war on drugs, and the stealth drug money laundering can come to an end, and they ought to. It is possible for a new effective drug policy — rational, root-cause driven, and humane — to dawn on American society in this beginning of the 21st century.

6

LESSONS FROM

ALCOHOL PROHIBITION

This lesson of history brings hope to wake up from this silent American nightmare and opens new possibilities for a refreshing, rational, and effective drug policy.

6.1 Alcohol Prohibition Background

The bottom line of the illicit-drug problem unfolds the urgency for a new drug policy in America and the world. Illicit drugs are no trivial matter; current policy has been in place — in force — for over thirty years and a few persistent myths have clouded the landscape for too long. With the myths put aside and the fundamental root causes in open view, there is an enhanced understanding of the drug problem and a framework to explore the options open for a viable and effective new drug policy. This is the point where a journey through the Alcohol Prohibition Era of the early 20th century in the United States adds value to the search for a solution to the drug prohibition dilemma at the dawn of the 21st century.

The prohibition to consume alcohol was in effect in the U.S. from 1920 through to 1933. This episode of American history is almost a century old and just about every adult in America has heard of it. Unfortunately, most people have only heard of it from the movies, and very few have an in-depth knowledge of how it came about and how it ended. History's claim to being a great teacher can pass unnoticed when people do not learn from the mistakes it unveils, and those mistakes are repeated over and over. Perhaps this is happening with illicit drugs today. Is there any similarity between alcohol in the early 20th century and illicit drugs in the late 20th and early 21st centuries? Levine and Reinarman [1] definitely think so, and they thoroughly analyze the issue in their 2004 essay, *Alcohol Prohibition and Drug Prohibition, Lessons from Alcohol Policy for Drug Policy* [2]. Table 6.1 shows the timetable of events associated with alcohol prohibition in the U.S. from 1917 through to 1933. As it turned out, the prohibition to consume alcohol brought about an era of high disrespect for the law; large segments of the population were not in agreement with the criminalization of alcohol and chose to continue to consume it, albeit illegally. Organized crime, seeing the opportunity, got into the alcohol business, but also many small independent entrepreneurs delved into it.

"The many literary, photographic, and cinematic images of the prohibition era capture some of the essential features of the period. Prohibition was massively and openly violated, and alcohol was readily available in most of the United States. New institutions and cultural practices appeared: bootleggers and speakeasies, hip flasks and bathtub gin, rum runners smuggling in liquor and prohibition agents like Elliott Ness smashing down doors. Adulterated and even poisonous alcohol was sold and many people were locked up for violating prohibition laws." [2]

The advocates of repealing alcohol prohibition worked hard during the late 1920s and early 1930s to prepare the ground for effective post-repeal actions.

"In late 1933 and in 1934, bills creating state alcohol control agencies sped through state legislatures. The model for most of the legislation had been written by a group of policy-oriented researchers and attorneys associated with John D. Rockefeller, Jr., and with policy institutes he had created or financially supported. Within two years of repeal nearly every state had an agency to supervise the sale and distribution of alcoholic beverages, and alcohol had ceased to be a controversial and politically charged issue. The production, sale, and distribution of alcoholic beverages today is still largely governed by the alcohol control structures designed and implemented at that time." [2]

Thus came to an end an era whose roots went back to the anti-alcohol or temperance movement of the early 19th century. It was originally a movement of physicians, ministers, and large employers worried about the drunkenness of workers and servants, but it did not remain so. The Anti-Saloon League became the dominant force of the prohibitionist movement in the early 20th century.

"The League patterned itself on the modern corporation, hiring lawyers to write model laws and organizers to raise funds and collect political debts. The League put its considerable resources behind candidates of any party who would vote as it directed on the single issue of liquor. ... In 1913 the League finally declared itself in favor of constitutional prohibition. Increasing numbers of large corporations joined the many Protestant churches that had long supported the League. Prohibitionists mobilized the final support for prohibition during the hyper patriotic fervor of the First World War." [2]

187

Table 6.1 Alcohol Prohibition and Repeal Timetable

DATE	EVENT
12/1917	Both houses of Congress voted to require two-thirds majority to send to the states for ratification a constitutional amendment prohibiting the manufacture, sale, transportation, import, or export of intoxicating liquor.
11/1918	Congress passed the "War-Time Prohibition Act" banning the manufacture and sale of all beverages with more than 2.75% alcohol.
01/16/1919	Nebraska became the 36th state to ratify the 18th Amendment, to go into effect in one year.
10/1919	Congress overrode President Wilson's veto to the Volstead Act, which defined as intoxicating liquor any beverage with more then 0.5% alcohol content.
01/16/1920	The 18th Amendment took effect, and alcohol prohibition started in America.
1926	The Association Against the Prohibition Amendment (AAPA) took over the campaign for repeal of the 18th Amendment. Up until then the opposition had been fragmented. AAPA had the support of many of the rich and powerful, like Pierre DuPont and John D. Rockefeller Jr., who were concerned by the lawlessness brought about by alcohol prohibition.
11/16/1932	The Senate voted to submit the 21st Amendment (repeal of the 18th Amendment) to the states for ratification and return to the states the power to regulate alcohol.
03/13/1933	Shortly after being sworn in as president, Franklin D. Roosevelt asked Congress to modify the Volstead Act and legalize 3.2% alcohol (beer) to increase tax revenues.
04/07/1933	Beer was legal in most of the country.
12/05/1933	Utah became the 36th state to ratify the 21st Amendment and national alcohol prohibition was repealed immediately.

From a grassroots movement to a well-orchestrated lobbying campaign the prohibitionists succeeded in making alcohol illegal in America for fourteen years. However, reason and the understanding that legislation and law enforcement were not enough to stop human appetite for alcohol prevailed and alcohol returned to a legalized and controlled environment. The advocates of temperance, like John D. Rockefeller, Jr., who had turned in favor of prohibition in a spurt of idealism, hoping for a better society, came to the conviction that prohibition led to even worse evils and became strong proponents of repeal and favored a controlled environment for the consumption of alcohol. The alcohol experience of the 1920s and early 1930s suggests alternatives to the current drug prohibition policy, not just in the U.S., but all over the world. Drug prohibition is a global event supported by international drug treaties; hence, it requires a global solution strategy.

6.2 The Economic Results of Prohibition

In September 1932 Columbia University Press published the work of Clark Warburton, *The Economic Results of Prohibition,* [(3)] which addressed the impact the 18th Amendment was having on the U.S. economy and society in general. Warburton's work was initially financed by AAPA, but the work was concluded without their financial support. This work started in 1929, at the peak of prohibition, relying on meager statistical facts resulting from the illegality of the industry under analysis, the alcoholic beverages industry. Nevertheless, the book delivered valuable conclusions regarding the impact of prohibition. Warburton's conclusions:

(1) Regarding the effects of prohibition upon the consumption of alcoholic beverages.

- Prohibition reduced the per capita consumption of alcoholic beverages in terms of pure alcohol nearly one-third, when the years 1927-1930 were compared with the pre-war years 1911-1914; that is, from 1.69 to 1.14 gallons per year.

- The per capita consumption of beer was reduced about 70%, from 20.53 gallons per year in 1911-1914 to 6.27 gallons in 1927-1930; the per capita consumption of wine increased about 65%, from 0.59 gallons per year in 1911-1914 to 0.98 gallons in 1927-1930; and the per capita consumption of spirits increased about 10%, from 1.47 gallons per year in 1911-1914 to 1.62 gallons in 1927-1930.

- During the first three years of prohibition, the consumption of alcoholic beverages was curtailed to a much greater extent than since that early period.
- The per capita consumption of wine and spirits had been fairly constant since 1923, subject to annual variations as a result of business fluctuations and other disturbing factors; and the per capita consumption of beer increased steadily up to 1929, but dropped in 1930.
- Except for the first three years, the per capita consumption of alcohol was greater under prohibition than during the war period, with high taxation and restricted production and sale.

(2) Regarding the effect of prohibition upon national expenditure.

- The total expenditure on alcoholic beverages in the prosperous year of 1929 was nearly five billion dollars, and in the depression year of 1930 nearly four billion; that this was about what the liquor bill would have been if alcoholic beverages had been sold under the conditions of 1911-1914 and taxed at the rates imposed in 1917 (during the First World War); and that the expenditure on beer were less, but those on spirits more, than it would have been without prohibition.
- During the first three years of prohibition the liquor bill was reduced about two billion dollars per year.
- Prohibition was not a significant factor in the increased purchase of automobiles, radios, electrical appliances, household equipment or other consumers' goods during the period of business prosperity from 1923 to 1929; and prohibition, aside from the first year or two, had no appreciable effect upon savings deposits, life insurance carried, deposits in building and loan associations, or other forms of saving and investment.
- The consumption of milk, coffee and carbonated beverages increased considerably since the adoption of prohibition, and each of these, as well as distilled spirits, may have been a partial substitute for beer; but that it was not possible to determine the relative degree of substitution.

190

(3) Regarding the effect of prohibition upon industrial efficiency.

- Prohibition was not a factor of measurable significance in the increased industrial productivity of recent years; and that statistical evidence was lacking as to the effect of prohibition upon industrial absenteeism.

- Reduced consumption of alcohol under wartime restrictions and under prohibition may have been partially responsible for the decrease in the frequency of industrial accidents; but the data available did not show a measurable relation between prohibition and the frequency of fatal industrial accidents.

- There was a great economic waste in the decentralization of the alcoholic beverage industry, both in the use of productive resources and of labor.

(4) Regarding the effect of prohibition upon economic groups.

- Some farmers lost markets on account of prohibition, but the farming class as a whole gained more than it had lost.

- Under prohibition the working class consumed not more than half as much alcohol per capita as formerly; and the expenditure of this class upon alcoholic beverages was probably a billion dollars less than it would have been without national prohibition.

- The per capita, consumption of alcohol by the business, professional and salaried class was affected little by prohibition; and that was due to higher prices, this class was spending at least a billion dollars a year more for alcoholic beverages than it would have been spending without national prohibition.

- The wealthy class, with annual incomes per income-receiver of more than $25,000, made up in higher income taxes most of the loss of Federal revenue due to prohibition, amounting approximately to three-quarters of a billion dollars a year.

(5) The effect of prohibition upon public health and safety and upon public finance.

- Prohibition reduced to some extent the death rate from diseases directly associated with the excessive use of alcoholic beverages,

191

especially among the working class; but prohibition had no measurable effect upon the general health of the nation.

- As indicated by fragmentary statistics, there was some association between criminal activity and the use of alcohol, and that the frequency of some types of crime was reduced slightly by prohibition.

- The great increase in the use of automobiles during the past decade masked the effect of prohibition upon automobile accidents, so the relationship was not determinable by elementary statistical analysis.

- The federal government might collect a maximum of about a billion and a quarter dollars from the taxation of all alcoholic beverages, or a maximum of three-quarters of a billion from beer alone; and this would make possible lower income taxes than would otherwise be necessary.

In summary, alcohol prohibition did little to thwart the consumption of alcohol, though it changed consumption patterns toward higher alcohol content beverages. Savings, investments, and consumer spending on things other than alcohol did not register any significant impact from alcohol prohibition. Neither did prohibition have a significant impact on industrial efficiency. The working class ended up consuming less alcohol and spending one billion dollars less on alcohol, while the middle class consumed about the same and spent one billion dollars more on alcohol. The wealthy ended up paying more income taxes to make up for the loss of alcohol tax revenues. Finally, Warburton concluded that if legalized, all alcohol taxes could add $1.25 billion in revenues for the government; if beer only were legalized, the increase in government tax revenues would be $750 million. The above speaks to the failure of alcohol prohibition to reach the objectives it set out to achieve.

Table 6.2 reflects the alcohol consumption pattern before and during prohibition. It illustrates the conclusions of Warburton regarding the fall of consumption of all three kinds of alcoholic beverages in the early days following the enactment of prohibition. Nevertheless, it did not take long before the consumption of spirits and wine, the higher proof beverages, was up to the pre-prohibition levels. In 1923, the fourth year of prohibition, spirits consumption per capita was 1.96 gallons, 21% higher that the pre-prohibition peak of 1.62 gallons in 1917. A similar situation took place with wine in 1923 when a per capita consumption of 0.95 gallons exceeded by almost 42% the pre-prohibition peak of 0.67 gallons in 1911. On the other hand, beer per capita consumption by 1930, 6.9 gallons, had fallen by two thirds from its 1911 peak of 20.69 gallons. A dramatic shift took place from lower proof alcoholic beverages (beer) to higher proof ones (spirits and wine) during prohibition. As a clandestine enterprise it was more rewarding to engage in higher-proof higher-value beverages than in the opposite. Hence, America began to drink beverages with higher alcohol content effectively defeating one of the primary objectives of prohibition, the reduction — the elimination rather — of alcohol consumption by Americans. Events did not unfold as expected by the proponents of prohibition and in return a new atmosphere of lawlessness was created.

Table 6.2 Alcohol Consumption Patterns before and during Prohibition*
Gallons per Capita

Year	Spirits	Wine	Beer	Pure Alcohol
1910	1.42	0.65	19.77	1.64
1911	1.46	0.67	20.69	1.70
1912	1.45	0.58	20.02	1.66
1913	1.51	0.56	20.72	1.71
1914	1.44	0.53	20.69	1.67
1915	1.26	0.33	18.40	1.46
1916	1.37	0.47	17.78	1.51
1917	1.62	0.41	18.17	1.64
1918	0.85	0.49	14.87	1.13
1919	0.77	0.51	8.00	0.80
1920	0.26	0.12	2.45	0.25
1921	0.30	0.44	1.26	0.26
1922	1.54	0.57	1.71	0.90
1923	1.96	0.95	2.24	1.17
1924	1.75	0.90	2.84	1.08
1925	1.80	0.86	3.46	1.13
1926	1.91	1.05	4.21	1.24
1927	1.53	1.08	5.03	1.08
1928	1.75	1.07	6.05	1.23
1929	1.86	0.89	7.11	1.31
1930	1.33	0.87	6.90	1.03

* Extracted from The Economic Results of Prohibition by Clark Warburton: Table 1 (page 24), Table 29 (page 71), and Table 30 (page 72).

Warburton's work delivers invaluable lessons from alcohol prohibition for the current drug prohibition policy. They are:

- There was a significant drop in the consumption of alcohol during the first years of prohibition. During those years the clandestine producers had not developed their operating methods well enough to supply the market needs, once they did, the level of alcohol consumption went up. There is a clear parallel to current illicit-drug operations, where illicit-drug production and distribution organizations, after so many years, are very resilient and adaptable to new operating conditions and able to amply satisfy the needs of the consumer.

- There was a substantial shift in the alcohol consumption patterns from the pre-prohibition years to the peak years of prohibition. Less beer (low alcohol content) and more wine and spirits (higher alcohol content) were consumed. There was more value, liter for liter, in wine and spirits than in beer. A similar situation occurs today with cannabis versus other drugs, there is more value to the DTOs, ounce per ounce, in cocaine and heroin than in cannabis. Hence, it is more profitable to concentrate the illicit activities on the former rather than on the latter, as was the case during alcohol prohibition.

- The similarity of per capita consumption levels of alcohol during the war years, with high taxation and restricted production and sale, with the consumption levels during prohibition suggests there may be other ways to control the consumption of today's illicit drugs besides outright prohibition.

Overall consumer spending did not vary significantly with alcohol prohibition and the expenditure on alcoholic beverages prior and during prohibition also carry some lessons to more effectively face today's drug challenges. They are:

- There was only a temporary reduction of expenditure on alcoholic beverages at the beginning of prohibition, resulting from transitory deficiencies in the supply chain as commented on above. Warburton estimated that alcohol consumption would have been the same under a high taxation and restricted production and sale environment as they were during prohibition. This again speaks to the potential virtues of some alternative ways of dealing with today's illicit drugs.

- No major impact was identified by Warburton on other consumer spending and investment items resulting from prohibition versus pre-prohibition years. Hence, it is very likely that there would be no significant economic impact — consumer and investment patterns would not be altered — by alternative ways of dealing with today's illicit drugs differently from the current prohibition policy.

In summary, drug prohibition has not significantly reduced the consumption of illicit drugs in recent decades and has introduced other issues negatively impacting the stability and security of the U.S. and much of the world; in other words:

- It is more profitable for DTOs to produce and distribute high potency drugs such as cocaine and heroin than lower potency ones like cannabis. Hence increasing their availability in the market and the higher health risks associated with them.
- Alcohol prohibition created an atmosphere of lawlessness in America and the same has happened, but on a global scale, with the outright prohibition of today's illicit drugs.
- Similar to alcohol prohibition but on a much larger scale, current drug policy insures the flow of huge sums of money into criminal enterprises. It is not just the potential tax revenues which are forfeited, but the transfer of economic and political power into the hands of DTOs and their stealth business partners.
- The global nature of the DTOs and their relationship with known terrorist groups provide a potentially nurturing environment for the DTOs' and/or their business partners to build alliances with terrorist organizations. This potential threat goes beyond anything that could have been imagined during alcohol prohibition.

How did the U.S. escape from the alcohol prohibition trap? Is the repeal of alcohol prohibition a valid blueprint in the search for an alternative to current drug policy? The answer to these questions reveals the lessons history has in store for us.

6.3 The Repeal of Alcohol Prohibition

"It is my earnest conviction that total abstinence is the wisest, best, and safest position for both the individual and society. But the regrettable failure of the Eighteenth Amendment has demonstrated the fact that the majority of the people of this country are not yet ready for total abstinence, at least when it is attempted through legal coercion. The best next thing — many people think it a better thing — is temperance. Therefore, as I thought to support total abstinence when its achievement seemed possible, so now, and with equal vigor, I would support temperance." [4]

Those are the words of John D. Rockefeller, Jr. in the foreword of the book *Toward Liquor Control*, by Raymond B. Fosdick and Albert L. Scott, published in 1933. Rockefeller played a crucial role financing the work of Fosdick and Scott, but he did not get involved with the research or the conclusions presented in the book. Later on, in the foreword, Rockefeller points out: "Rightly, the first objective is the abolition of lawlessness. Any program offered in lieu of the Eighteenth Amendment must make that its chief aim, even if — and I weigh carefully what I say — the immediate result is temporarily away from temperance." And he goes on to say: "The second objective is the focusing of all the forces of society upon the development of self-control and temperance as regards the use of alcoholic beverages." Towards the end of the foreword he stated: "Another principle which the report (meaning the book) develops is that only as the profit motive is eliminated is there any hope of controlling the liquor traffic in the interest of a decent society. To approach the problem from any other angle is only to tinker with it and to insure failure. This point cannot be too heavily stressed."

Rockefeller had a vision shared by many at the time. Fosdick and Scott included, that by criminalizing the consumption of alcohol society had introduced greater evils, and that it was in the best interest of society and of individuals to first address the evils created by prohibition, and then proceed with new ways of addressing the perceived evils of alcohol

197

consumption itself. However, a transition was called for and this is where the work of Fosdick and Scott came in.

Background of the problem. Fosdick and Scott, after a thorough review and research of the background of the alcohol problem set down a few definite principles behind which they believed there was a substantial degree of public support. They adopted these principles as their own guide to writing the book and preparing the recommendations. These principles follow [5]:

1. "At all cost — even if it means a temporary increase in consumption of alcohol — bootlegging, racketeering and the whole wretched nexus of crime that developed while the Eighteenth Amendment was in force must be wiped out. The defiance of law that has grown up in the last fourteen years, the hypocrisy, the breakdown of government machinery, the demoralization in public and private life, is a stain on America that can no longer be tolerated. The American people are definitely aroused in a determination to clean up this source of corruption and to reestablish the integrity and dignity of the law.

2. "Wide areas of the public are unconvinced that the use of alcoholic beverages is in itself reprehensible. That there is grave peril of immoderate use is unanimously conceded. In respect to every human desire, intemperance has always been the chief frailty of humankind. But while hundreds of thousands of people are by preference and practice teetotalers, public opinion will not support the thesis that the temperate use of alcohol is inconsistent with sobriety, self-control, good citizenship and social responsibility. More than that, many people believe that such moderate use can be made an agreeable phase of a civilized mode of living.

3. "The saloon, as it existed in pre-prohibition days, was a menace to society and must never be allowed to return. Behind its blinds degradation and crime were fostered, and under its principle of stimulated sales poverty and drunkenness, big profits and political graft, found a secure foothold. Public opinion has not forgotten

the evils symbolized by this disreputable institution and it does not intend that it shall worm its way back into our social life.

4. "Despite the reaction from the Eighteenth Amendment, America is in no mood to stand any aggressiveness on the part of the brewers, the distillers and the liquor trade generally. The memory of their campaigns against temperance, of their corrupt legislative activities and of their insolent intrusion into our political life in the days before prohibition, is still alive. Any indication that they are once more pushing their business in violation of decent social standards will bring the pendulum swinging back.

5. "Public opinion is gratified by the record of sobriety that has attended the return of beer. It is distinctly apprehensive over the prospective legalized return of spirits. For America aspires to be a temperate nation. It has a passionate desire that its young people shall be protected against the greedy commercialization of the liquor trade and the pitfalls of intemperance. It dreads the hazards and inefficiencies that attend immoderation. It is fully prepared to take drastic steps if, as a result of the present attitude of toleration, conditions should once more get out of control.

6. "America is inclined to believe that there is some definite solution for the liquor problem — some method other than bone-dry prohibition — that will allow a sane and moderate use of alcohol to those who desire it, and at the same time minimize the evils of excess. There is no unanimity of opinion as to what that solution shall be, but the people at the moment are in an adventurous mood. A new philosophy of change is in the air, and political ideas are now being put into effect, which were unthinkable even a decade ago. The question is asked: Why should we follow the old pre-prohibition route? Why is it not possible to strike out on a fresh trail? If in relation to every other business new social and political controls are daily being devised, why in relation to this liquor business should we not create a new technique, a new

method, by which it can be brought within the compass of what the public really desires?"

Endowed with the above principles to address the issues raised by prohibition, Fosdick and Scott arrived at the conclusions of their report. The report became the foundation for most state legislations to follow suit upon the repeal of national prohibition. Their conclusions were as follows: [6]

1. "State-wide, bone-dry prohibition will prove unsuccessful in controlling the problem of alcohol, unless such a system has behind it overwhelming public support. Even then it will tend to carry in its trail the hypocrisy and lawlessness which marked the national experiment.

2. "The experience of every country supports the idea that light wines and beers do not constitute a serious social problem.

3. "While many states will doubtless follow the license method in the control of beverages of higher alcoholic content, this method contains a fundamental flaw in that it retains the private profit motive which makes inevitable the stimulation of sales.

4. "Wide experience in many countries indicates that the best approach to the problem of heavier alcoholic beverages is through state control. By state control we mean specifically a system by which the state, through a central authority, maintains an exclusive monopoly of retail sale for off-premises consumption. This authority determines prices, fixes the location of the stores, controls advertising, and in general manages the trade in such a way as to meet a minimum, un-stimulated demand within conditions established solely in the interest of society.

5. "The primary objective of taxation should be social control, not revenue. Taxes should be levied not with the idea of filling the public treasury at whatever cost to public morality and efficiency, but as a method of reducing the consumption of alcohol.

6. "Education in its broadest sense has a greater part to play in creating a sober nation than has legislative enactment. Temperance lies in the character, standards and self-discipline of individual men and women. Education is a slow process, but it carries a heavier share of the burden of social control than does legal coercion."

The work of Fosdick and Scott carries valuable insights into how today's illicit-drug challenge could be faced. The study spelled out the importance of having differentiated treatment for different types of alcoholic beverages based on degree of alcoholic content. The belief that greater alcohol content would lead to greater intemperance led them to differentiate how to treat beers, wines and spirits in the upcoming state legislations to follow the repeal of prohibition. Their approach to facing long-held beliefs by the temperance movement, which treated all alcoholic beverages the same, suggests that there may be different ways to deal with today's illicit drugs under a more innovative policy. Paraphrasing Fosdick and Scott, 21st century society may very well ask itself similar questions: Why should we follow the old drug criminalization route? Why is it not possible to strike out on a fresh trail? If in relation to every other business, new social and political controls and technologies are daily being devised, why in relation to this drug business should we not create a new technique, a new method, by which it can be brought within the compass of what the public really desires?

The legacy of prohibition. As Fosdick and Scott were writing the results of their investigation and America was getting ready to repeal prohibition, it became clear to them that many states had legislation in place, dating from pre-prohibition days, that in fact would still impose strict alcohol controls in some states (dry states) which would be neighboring states with no or little controls (wet states). "In spite of the adoption of the Twenty-first Amendment, prohibition will continue to operate in half the states, thirty in number." [7] Hence, and following on the steps of Fosdick and Scott, a new drug policy in America cannot be established in isolation from the rest of the world. *Toward Liquor Control* became the

201

blueprint used by most states in America between 1933 and 1934 to draft specific alcohol control state legislations. Today the world needs a blueprint for the implementation of a new drug policy across all nations.

Light wines and beers vs. spirits. President Roosevelt's decision to ask Congress to modify the Volstead Act and legalize 3.2% alcohol (essentially beer) on March 13, 1933 provided a real-life laboratory in which to measure the effects of moderate alcohol consumption prior to the repeal of prohibition in December 1933. Fosdick and Scott had the opportunity to examine the behavior of beer consumers during a few months prior to the repeal of prohibition. Pre-prohibition regulations had led to beer and spirits to be served at the same facilities and this induced the "beer saloons" serving both kinds of beverages to promote the sale of the more profitable hard liquors. With the liberalization of 3.2% beer, it became obvious that the stigma associated with all liquors was not true for beer. Hence, the myth which had labeled all alcoholic beverages as equally dangerous came to an end. Fosdick and Scott summarized that part of history as follows: "An overwhelming weight of medical and scientific testimony to the contrary was brushed aside by Congress. Facts were not wanted when they were in conflict with the fervently held belief that alcohol in a concentration of one-half of one percent, or more, makes a drink unfit for human consumption." [8] A widely held popular belief had led to the birth of the myth that beer was as inappropriate for human consumption as hard liquor, hence they were treated the same and the country was immersed for fourteen years in the lawlessness driven by prohibition. The death of the myth led Fosdick and Scott to present a liquor control proposal which differentiated the fermented drinks, mainly beers and wines, with an alcoholic content of not more than 12%, from distilled liquors, including whiskey and gin, which usually contained from 35% to 45% alcohol. It also became obvious to them that there was no supporting evidence to back up a second myth which expounded that beer consumption invariably led to a craving for whiskey.

Fosdick and Scott were convinced that wines naturally fermented — with alcohol content not to exceed 10 to 12% — should also be sold

202

by the bottle for consumption off-premises in the same fashion 3.2% beer was already being sold. Regarding consumption on-premises, they recommended some additional control. In summary, they suggested the following classification of permits for the sale of 3.2% beer and wines:

- "**A-Permits** to sell 3.2% beer and naturally fermented wines not in excess of 10 to 12% by the bottle for off-premise consumption.
- "**B-Permits** to sell 3.2% beer for on-premises consumption with or without meals."
- "**C-Permits** for sale of 3.2% beer and natural wines at hotels, restaurants or clubs for consumption on the premises with meals." [9]

They reserved the treatment of heavier beers, fortified wines and spirits to a more elaborate system of controls, which will be discussed later on in this presentation.

"To many people this liberal policy in relation to the control of beers and wines may seem a betrayal of the cause of temperance. With them no compromise with liquor in any form is possible, and the world they desire is a world in which alcoholic beverages are not consumed at all. We have no wish to argue with this point of view. Those who hold it have every right to their conviction and have every right to promulgate their conviction by persuasion and education in the interest of total abstinence, personally chosen and practiced. To write this conviction upon our statute books, however, as an affair of legal coercion, is another matter altogether. Today we are confronted with practical realities. It is not a question of the kind of world we might prefer; it is a question of what we can achieve in the kind of world we have. It is a question of human tastes and appetites which, as we have discovered, cannot be eliminated by statute. In our opinion there is but one major proposition to be faced in relation to alcohol. Granting that millions of our people will not drink at all, how can the cause of temperance best be served among those who choose to drink? It is because we believe that the whole temperance movement will be materially helped if the sale of beverages of low alcoholic content is liberalized that we have been led to the recommendations contained in this chapter." [9] With these words, Fosdick and Scott laid the foundation of their alcohol control proposal.

Regulation by license. As it related to the treatment of spirits or hard liquors, Fosdick and Scott saw the need to implement a different system of controls. They saw this category of alcoholic beverages as the core of the alcohol problem and bringing to it more complexity and stress. Recognizing the impracticality of prohibition as bold statutory abolition, they brought forward two options for governmental control: the license method and the public monopoly method. After exploring the effectiveness of the license method in a number of countries and pre-prohibition states in the U.S., they concluded: "The licensing system has a good name in the UK, but in most sections of this country (the U.S.) prior to 1920 it had a bad name. Before national prohibition, the saloon achieved an evil notoriety. Politicians were often bought by the liquor interests; vice and gambling came to be regarded as normal accompaniments of the liquor trade; and the abuse of drink, fostered by the drive for profits, produced its share of poverty and misery. All these evils were bred under the licensing system, and it was the complete breakdown of this system that gave momentum to the national prohibition movement." [10] At the same time their research unveiled that the licensing system had operated successfully in the UK and this led them to conclude that "The UK has a tradition of public order and respect for law that is sadly lacking in this country. The bootlegger and the gangster are not known there, and the speakeasy has not developed. The British are inclined to accept with good-humored tolerance the increasingly rigid restrictions of the licensing system. Certainly there are no organized attempts to defeat it." [11] They were convinced that the background of social habit in the UK made the difference as compared to the U.S. They actually believed that in pre-prohibition times, no state legislature had taken full advantage of the possibilities of the licensing method to pursue liquor control. "The licensing system of pre-prohibition days did not deserve the name of 'system'. Ordinarily 'system' was wholly lacking. The law was a hodge-podge of enactment and amendment. It was not an expression of a carefully thought-out plan

204

for social control of the liquor problems, but was usually an ill-conceived patchwork resulting from the conflict of interest between liquor dealers and reformers. Seldom was any attempt made to discriminate the handling of beer and of hard liquor. License administration was frequently in the hands of those who had a personal interest in making control ineffectual." [11] Liquor control during pre-prohibition days was a good example of a truly broken system resulting from the absence of an integral approach, and often generating amendments to regulations in order to address perceived symptoms while overlooking the root causes of the problem. In short, very similar to how today's drug problem is being addressed. Current drug policy focuses on legislation and initiatives to solve an apparent problem — drug use and availability — which are symptoms or the outcome of other events — genetic propensity, weak family structures, and a highly profitable illicit-drug business — which are truly the root causes, but which happen to be ignored.

Fosdick and Scott did not hide their preference for the public monopoly system and "recommended the frank abandonment of further legislative tinkering with licenses and the acceptance of an altogether different method of control." [12] Nevertheless, they recognized that some states would want to follow the licensing route after the repeal of prohibition; hence, they put forward specific guidelines for implementing a licensing method. What they called "the soundest possible licensing system" [13] would consider:

"**First:** The outstanding prerequisite of a licensing system is the creation of a single licensing board, with state-wide authority and responsibility, appointed by the governor and working through a well-paid, full-time managing director. The administration personnel of the board should be appointed on a merit basis, free from politics and with a permanent tenure. The board should have an appropriation commensurate with its responsibilities." Fosdick and Scott were trying to reduce the risks associated with multiple entities regulating the alcohol trade within a given state; this increased the risk of corruption of the officials in charge of regulations. They believed that, "experience has proved that a licensing

205

board with state-wide powers is more efficient, more responsive to broad public opinion and freer from political influence than autonomous county or municipal bodies can possibly be." They believed the board should be given the widest possible discretion in regard to the issuance of regulations within broad limits of policy determined by the state legislature.

"**Second:** The intelligence, character and integrity of the members of this board are considerations of the first importance. Unless these qualities are conspicuously present, the licensing system will be defeated before it starts. The members should be given long terms in office and should be eligible for reappointment. Their security of tenure will help to make them independent of political pressure. Salaries should be substantial. To attract the best brains obtainable. Under no circumstances should appointments to the board be made on the basis of partisan political considerations." Fosdick and Scott proposed the creation of a highly professional body to regulate the alcohol trade within the state with members free from the temptations of extra money or partisan allegiances.

"**Third:** The 'tied house,' and every device calculated to place the retail establishment under obligation to a particular distiller or brewer, should be prevented by all available means. 'Tied houses,' that is, establishments under contract to sell exclusively the product of one manufacturer, were, in many cases, responsible for the bad name of the saloon. The 'tied house' system had all the vices of absentee ownership. The manufacturer knew nothing and cared nothing about the community." Fosdick and Scott believed that the 'tied house' arrangement would lead to greater competition amongst brewers and distillers, which in turn would lead to greater promotions and an increase in alcohol consumption. Therein, their wide-open opposition to 'tied houses'.

"**Fourth:** Suitable restrictions should be established by the license law or the administrative regulation with respect to the number and character of places where liquor may be sold. This is regarded as of the highest significance in the UK, where great effort is being made to reduce the number of licenses from year to year and to improve the appearance and character of licensed places. The number of licenses may be limited on a

206

population basis as is done in Massachusetts and Rhode Island under the new law." This particular consideration reflected their desire to provide a respectable façade to the licensees, one that would not be contaminated by other activities associated with vice and low living. They also preferred specific restrictions to come from the regulating authority and not from the legislation.

"**Fifth:** Licenses should be classified to recognize the inherent differences between beer, wine and spirits as problems of control. One of the most satisfactory license classifications in this country before prohibition was in Massachusetts where seven kinds of licenses were provided. Somewhat on the line of this precedent a classification like the following might be desirable:

    a. For Off-Premises Consumption—
        Class I Beer to 3.2%.
        II Natural wines up to 10 or 12%.
        III Spirits and all other alcoholic beverages.
        IV Medicinal beverages and tonics, containing spirits.
        V Undenatured, industrial alcohol.
    For On-Premise Consumption—
        VI Beer to 3.2%.
        VII Natural wines up to 10 or 12%.
        VIII Spirits and all other alcoholic beverages.
    b. For Manufacture and processing—
        Divided as under (a).
    c. For Commercial Transportation—
        Divided as under (a), but distinguishing between shipments within the state and across state lines."

Though this was a general framework proposed by Fosdick and Scott, they reminded their audience that, as presented in the section on "light wines and beers vs. spirits" above, because of the nature of light wines and spirits they should be placed under a more tolerant system of control. At the same time they warned against the Class VIII license, as they saw great risks coming from an environment where light wines and beer were sold in the same premises as hard liquor. They believed this environment would induce the consumption of hard liquors on consumers who would otherwise be perfectly satisfied with the consumption of light wines or beer. Their guidelines continued:

"**Sixth:** The hours of sale of liquor, particularly for on-premises consumption (Classes VI, VII and VIII), should be carefully regulated. The British plan of stopping such sale and closing places of sale for two hours during the afternoon appeals to us as desirable. A closed period in the afternoon is of no inconvenience to normal consumption, but is extremely useful in preventing 'soaking' and the excessive use of alcohol. The hours for Sundays, holidays, etc, will require still further restriction. It must be remembered, however, that a too stringent limitation of hours will play into the hands of the bootleggers. This is to be avoided, particularly in the immediate future, while the organized bootlegging system is being stamped out." Fosdick and Scott were no alcohol promoters, they were actually interested in reducing the lawlessness that had been brought about by prohibition and in making sure that as many as possible of the practices that surfaced during prohibition, like bootlegging, were stamped out through appropriate and reasonable alcohol control regulations.

"**Seventh:** Licenses issued for the retail sale of liquor should run not only to the person who sells, but to the premises where the liquor is sold. Revocation of a premise license is a far more effective weapon of control than is the revocation of an individual license." The emphasis was on control and on making sure that the license holders strictly abided by the rules.

"**Eighth:** The license law should prohibit, as far as possible, all sales practices which encourage consumption. This would include treating on the house, sales on credit or IOU's, bargain days, and reduced prices previous to elections. Rules are also necessary forbidding sale to minors, habitual alcoholics, paupers, mental defectives and anyone who is drunk." Again, this guideline revealed their emphasis on regulation and control and on staying away from promotional schemes.

"**Ninth:** Advertising should, where possible, be rigidly restricted or forbidden. Six states have already passed such laws." Fosdick and Scott went as far as providing specific suggestions as to how to control advertising, but here again and recognizing the fact that the country believed in free enterprise, they recommended that the advertising code to be established "will be sufficiently elastic to meet the legitimate demand of the trade and at the same time to permit enforcement."

"**Tenth:** In addition to the foregoing possibilities, an effort may be made under the licensing system to control prices and profits." Fosdick and Scott cited the Rhode Island experience, where legislation of this type had already been passed, extending the price control provisions to the wholesale rather than to the retail trade.

With the above ten guidelines Fosdick and Scott believed that the license system could, if carefully managed, deliver the temperance society required. However, they saw great risks associated with the profit motive still present in the license system and the sale of hard liquor. They closed this segment of their presentation with the following words:

"Perhaps by a Herculean effort we could temporarily hold in check the instinct of business to increase its profits, but we would be gratuitously assuming a task that in the long run promises nothing but disappointment and defeat. The profit motive is the core of the problem. Unless that motive is divorced from the retail sale of spirituous liquor, unless society as a whole can take this business in the protection of its citizens, the future, at least in America, holds out only the prospect of endless guerrilla warfare between a nation fighting for temperance and a traffic that thrives on excess." [14] It was the profit motive, or in other words the inviolable law of supply and demand in concert with prohibition, which created an atmosphere of lawlessness during alcohol prohibition. Fosdick and Scott believed that if not properly controlled, the same profit motive would render the license system of control inoperative and ineffectual. This observation could prove useful when leveraging the alcohol prohibition and repeal experience in the search for a new drug policy.

The Authority plan or state alcohol monopoly. [15] The work of Fosdick and Scott revealed a clear preference for the control of alcohol through a state liquor monopoly, "a system by which the state government takes over, as a public monopoly, the retail sale, through its own stores, of the heavier alcoholic beverages for off-premises consumption." They believed such a system would make it possible "to meet an unstimulated demand within the limits of conditions established solely in the interest of society." They suggested that the state organization in charge could be called "State Alcohol Control Authority" and referred to such an organization as the Authority. In their work they highlighted the scope of the Authority's task and the powers of the Authority. They believed the following powers would be necessary for the discharge of the Authority's responsibilities:

1. "The exclusive right within a state to sell or control the sale of all alcoholic beverages which contain spirits; all wines known as fortified wines, the alcoholic content of which exceeds that produced by the natural fermentation process; and all fermented products, such as beers and ciders, containing more than 3.2% of alcohol by weight.

2. "The right to lease or own and to operate retail shops for the sale of those beverages by the package to the ultimate consumer for off-premises consumption, except that the Authority should be bound to abide by the decision of communities which vote to exclude the retail sale of any or all alcoholic beverages under local option provisions.

3. "The right to lease or acquire by purchase or condemnation, and to operate warehouses, blending and processing plants, and other facilities as may be required.

4. "The right to fix prices on its goods and to change prices at will.

5. "The right to establish in its discretion a system of personal identification of purchasers.

6. "The right to establish regulations and to issue permits to owners or occupants of establishments to sell beer and naturally fer-

mented wine or cider in sealed bottles or containers for off-premises consumption.

7. "The right to establish regulations and to issue permits to hotels, restaurants, clubs, railway dining cars, and passenger boats, for the sale of beer, with or without meals, and for the sale of naturally fermented wine or cider to be consumed with meals on the premises.

8. "The right to require private business concerns to certify the quantities of alcohol and alcoholic beverages manufactured in the state, and the amounts shipped into, within, and from the state, regardless of the purposes for which used; this to be worked out in cooperation with the federal government.

9. "The power to hold hearings on complaints about matters in dispute, including the power to subpoena witnesses and records and to make binding decisions."

In the Authority proposal they omitted any reference to the sale of heavier alcoholic beverages by the glass for on-premises consumption. They hoped that "a generous provision for the on-premises sale of beer and natural wines, together with sale of stronger beverages by the package in the Authority's shops, would be accepted as adequate in most jurisdictions by the preponderant majority of people." Their work put forward the possibility of a new set of rules and regulations that would be acceptable to a large majority of people. This consensus approval was crucial in a society which had lived under prohibition for close to fourteen years and which had for many decades been struggling with the issue of alcohol consumption and its perceived social ills.

Fosdick and Scott went as far as proposing how to organize the Authority, with a board of directors and a managing director heading the organization and made specific recommendations for its internal structure, its need for flexibility, the relationship between the Authority and the state government and the disposition of the Authority's profit by the state. It was clear to them that the methods of the Authority should not in any way stimulate the consumption of alcohol and that profits generated by its operation should go directly into the State Treasury and not be ear-marked for any activity linked with treating the ills of alcohol consumption. They believed such activities must be carried out by the state from specific budgets independent of the Authority's business activity. Their proposal was stepping into uncharted territory, hence the need to build flexibility into the operation of the Authority; learning and the gathering of experience was to take place as the implementation of the new system went into effect. The new alcohol control system was to benefit from live experience, whether it was the State Authority or the License System chosen by a particular state. In the end Fosdick and Scott were strong proponents of the state monopoly as reflected in their Authority proposal. They believed it was way superior to the license system and dedicated a full section of a chapter to highlighting the virtues of the Authority system over the license system.

In closing their argument in favor of the Authority plan, they stated: "On the basis of past experience in the United States and abroad, and the practical considerations we have just reviewed, we have come to the conclusion that the most satisfactory solution of the problem of alcohol requires elimination of the private profit motive in the retail sale of liquor. This cannot conceivably be accomplished under a license system, however rigid and well enforced. If we sincerely wish to meet only an un-stimulated demand for alcohol, we can no longer leave to any individual a private stake in its retail sale. There is in the licensing of the private selling of liquor an irreconcilable and permanent conflict with social control." They summarized the merits of the State Alcohol Control Authority plan as:

- It would effectively stifle the profit motive for enlarging liquor sales beyond a minimum demand.
- It would facilitate the control of advertising.
- It would provide freedom of action in regulating prices and conditions of sale, both as a means of checking the illicit dealer and as a method of curtailing the use of spirits.
- It would eliminate the saloon.

212

- It would minimize opportunities for the encroachment of political interference.
- It would keep clear the road for temperance education.

Fosdick and Scott strongly believed that the adoption of the Authority plan with an honest and competent administration would yield a maximum degree of protection against any potential revival of age-old abuses known to licensed regulation. And above all "against the more recent evils of a traffic unregulated by government and managed by law violators."

The Authority plan with adaptations. [16] Thirty-six states had to be ready for the upcoming repeal of prohibition when Fosdick and Scott presented their proposal *Toward Liquor Control*. The states did not have a uniform tradition on how to manage their affairs; as a matter of fact, there were almost as many different ways to conduct state business as there were states. There were different attitudes toward government ownership; different experiences in dealing with the liquor trade in the past, different problems relating to liquor control to be solved today and different levels of competence in governmental administration. Fosdick and Scott foresaw the importance of being open to modifications of the Authority plan in order to adapt to the prevailing conditions in each state. Their proposal recognized the variety of problems to be faced and the reality that uniform solutions are not always applicable across different social groups — a conclusion still valid in current times. They highlighted three possible modifications, as follows:

- The elimination of direct retail sales by the Authority.
- A plan for the establishment of agencies for the sale of spirits for on-premises consumption.
- A plan for the establishment of personal purchase permits.

To accommodate those states where sentiment was in favor of a State Alcohol Authority, but against direct government ownership and sale of alcoholic beverages, the sale function would be transferred from the Authority into a semi-private sales corporation. This corporation would be given monopoly rights over all commercial activity associated with the sale of all types of alcoholic beverages. The Authority would still govern the location of all retail shops and all retail prices. In effect this hybrid setup would split the responsibilities surrounding the control and sale of alcoholic beverages between the sales corporation and the Authority. Because it was acknowledged that established custom cannot be brushed aside at a stroke, it was believed necessary, at least in some places, to provide for the closely regulated sale of spirits by the glass for consumption with meals. By doing so there was no place left for the bootlegger to operate, and the demand for alcohol was not stimulated. Fosdick and Scott believed that "the legitimate need must be measured in terms of insistence of demand; it cannot be measured by what we might hope would be satisfactory". So they agreed on the need for some liberalization of the Authority plan to designate a "rigidly limited number of restaurants and hotels as its agents in selling by the glass beverages of higher alcohol content". All through the development and adaptation of the Authority plan their objective was always stated as developing a system by which alcohol consumption was not stimulated, but which allowed for the proper fulfillment of existing demand, without inducing lawlessness or the resurgence of the saloon; which they loosely defined as "the pre-prohibition barroom and its prohibition equivalent, the speakeasy". The issuance of personal alcohol purchase permits was a practice followed in Sweden and in five Canadian provinces. Such a scheme would require that the alcohol monopoly sell only to persons who obtain a permit to purchase alcoholic beverages. "Where the permit scheme is in force it applies only to liquors sold by the package at monopoly stores for off-premises consumption. Usually a limit is placed on the quantity of liquor a permit holder may buy at any one time, and sometimes a maximum amount is fixed which may be purchased within a month." Such a scheme was thought to carry many pros and cons and it was believed that "experiment alone will reveal the value of such a permit system in our states." Fosdick and Scott were fully convinced of the evil results of prohibition and recognized that there was not enough experience with a system of alcohol control for post-prohibition implementation. For this reason they were very much in favor of flexibility and experimentation in order for society to arrive at an effective method of alcohol control after the repeal of prohibition. They believed the Authority plan to be elastic and adaptable to divergent conditions; "it lends itself to adaptation to meet the peculiar conditions of individual states as well as the regional differences within each state".

Taxation. [17] Taxation of alcoholic beverages was an issue demanding the attention of the authorities as the country prepared to repeal prohibition. Historically, taxes had been imposed upon alcoholic beverages to provide revenue for the government and to reduce consumption. Though these objectives may seem contradictory, they had been present in most countries simultaneously. In the U.S. a third objective was present in the days before prohibition; it was a punitive objective. Because those who manufactured, sold or used alcoholic beverages were believed to be conniving with evil, it was thought fitting to punish them with special high taxes. Fosdick and Scott stated that "the fundamental objective should be not revenue but rational and effective social control". They also dismissed the punishment objective arguing that "if the moderate use of alcohol by those who desire it is generally accepted as legal, and as a matter of individual conscience, then such consumption cannot consistently be punished by high taxes". Focusing on the limitation of consumption as the key objective of taxation, they saw the need to strike the right level of taxation to achieve this primary objective, and at the same time not create incentives for bootleggers to continue their illicit business. Taxation "should not be applied to beer and light wines, since the consumption of light alcoholic beverages is least harmful and beer in particular is used by the lower income groups who cannot in justice be called upon to pay heavy taxes." Besides focusing their tax proposal on spirits, they advocated that "high taxes should be cautiously applied to spirits; such a policy increases the margin of profit for illicit manufacturers and stimulates the sale of spirits by the moonshiners and bootleggers who have become so well established and organized under prohibition." It was their belief that if taxes on spirits were too low, it would induce the consumption of spirits by a larger number of people because of the low prices. On the other hand if taxes were too high, the high price of spirits would encourage the illegal production and sale of spirits, defeating one of the major objectives of the 21st Amendment, the elimination of the lawlessness surrounding the alcohol trade.

Fosdick and Scott made a liquor tax program recommendation in the form of a general outline in order to illustrate where the emphasis of such a program should be placed. They believed that a manufacturing tax should be levied by the federal government and that it should apply higher tax rates to spirits than to wines and beers. Retail tax rates were believed to be unnecessary in states opting for the Authority plan or monopoly system, as the revenues to the states would already be included in the price. In states opting for the licensing system or any other system of private sale of liquor, a retail tax was considered necessary. This tax would take the form of a small flat license fee and some sort of excess profits tax. These taxes were to be levied by the state government and not by any other entity within the state, though revenues may be shared with other local units of government. The disposition of alcohol tax revenues was of great concern to them, as they believed that "no beneficial interests in liquor revenues should be created." They proposed that all revenue should go into the general fund of the State Treasury and should not be earmarked or designated for charities, hospitals, or any other specific purpose. They believed that "when particular governmental activities are made dependent upon particular revenues, changes in the tax rates, and therefore in the yield, which might be extremely desirable as social measures, can be made only with the greatest difficulty, if at all, because of the effect of such changes on wholly unrelated enterprises." They firmly believed that "the appropriate application of taxation would have a crucial impact on the successful handling of the new problems created by the repeal of the Eighteenth Amendment."

216

An important lesson across *Toward Liquor Control* is the recognition that new problems would result from the repeal of the 18th Amendment. It was not assumed that repeal was in itself a cure-all or magical solution to the problems brought about by prohibition; it was recognized that new problems would show up and those would have to be addressed effectively. And effectiveness was highly dependent on taking into consideration the realities of society. They conceived an ideal good to society, the situation in which nobody had the need to consume alcoholic beverages, and hence there was no need for alcohol or for alcohol control. However, they recognized, by the facts brought to the naked eye, that this had nothing to do with reality and they saw the benefit of striving for the lesser evil. A society free of the lawlessness brought about by prohibition and with the right controls to induce temperance on those who chose to consume alcoholic beverages.

Education. [18] "We have too often been blind to the prosaic necessities and slower processes involved in the word education". This is what Fosdick and Scott would go on to say after expounding on the limitations of legislation to solve the problem of alcoholic indulgence so deeply rooted in human nature. Education, even to this day, is thought of by many as a process taking place only in our schools. This is a narrow and inadequate conception, the schools by themselves can accomplish very little in the molding of the habits of the individual. There are other factors, by far more potent, which are involved in the process of education. "First and foremost comes the general social situation in which a child grows up....This vague but indisputable social pressure upon the growing individual is well-nigh irresistible." Secondly, they pointed to "the influence of the immediate environment in which a child grows up....The standards and manners of the circle in which he moves, his intimate associations — social, religious or otherwise: these factors sway and shape his thinking and conduct." They pointed towards a third influence "of wider, varying potency, but of tremendous importance, namely, that smaller but intensely interested group, the family....The standards and ideals of this unit, its capacity to lead and persuade, constitute, therefore, a third contributing factor to the education of the growing human being." Back in 1933, and it remains true today, Fosdick and Scott saw education as a complex and effective method, albeit slow, which involved the school attended by the child, the general social situation in which a child grows up, the influence of the immediate environment in which the child is growing up, and the family. It was also pointed out that the greater influence in the education of a child is that of the family, and from there the potency of the influence goes down as the steps are traced back to the school. This great insight ought not to be overlooked in the 21st century as society addresses the inadequacies of the current drug policy.

Fosdick and Scott believed that "temperance education, like all education, has been impeded not only by lack of aim, but by lack of knowledge....Indeed, one of the discouraging aspects of the liquor debate of the last decade has been the use of scientific and pseudo-scientific terminology as a weapon of war....In the heat of the controversy any kind of fact has served as a weapon, and these 'facts' have been fed out far too indiscriminately to the children in the school system." This is how they evaluated the reliability of school education as it pertained to temperance. They went further to propose that "just as in America the public schools are forbidden to take a biased attitude in respect to politics or religion, so they ought to refrain from taking a biased or prejudiced attitude toward any other subject related to personal conduct or manners." They were proponents of a new approach to temperance education and to do so emphasize the following principles:

"The need for research is paramount. We must have the facts about the effects of alcohol on the human system, facts which scientists of accepted standing can support. It is to be hoped that with the passing of the Eighteenth Amendment the heated spirit of controversy will subside, and objective consideration will take its place. There are many gaps in our knowledge at the present moment, and medicine and physiology have much to learn. In the meantime efforts should be made to bring together in tangible form the facts which have thus far been ascertained, and nothing should be taught upon which the leading authorities in medical science are in disagreement. Controversial issues, such as the effect of alcohol on heredity, can be explained and presented from the different points of view now held by various authorities. School textbooks should have constant and searching revision in these matters as in all others that require change through new gains in knowledge. Wherever exaggerated statements regarding the effects of alcohol are found, they should be eliminated in order to make possible the objective teaching of what is known to be true."

"Not only do we need research so that facts can displace opinion and superstition, but we need clear, unprejudiced dissemination of facts. This requires a tolerant spirit, and tolerance in education, free from the bias of preconceived objectives, is perhaps difficult to achieve. But it is distinctly within the range of possibilities to promote understanding of facts to a point where common knowledge supports a steadily improving national ideal."

"Whatever line temperance instruction may take, its chief emphasis, if it is to capture this younger generation, should be on life and health and not on disease and death. It should be constructive and not negative. The necessity of keeping fit for work and sport is a far more effective appeal than moral homilies. Our young people cannot be browbeaten into righteousness or frightened into good behavior. They are alert to detect exaggeration, and they are not moved by sanctimonious exhortation. It is this kind of approach which has too often made temperance teaching in the past what one well-known educator called a 'pedagogical monstrosity.' The only effective appeal today is an appeal not to fear or prejudice but to intelligence."

These principles applied within the school system were to be complemented with adult education programs fostered by civic organizations — our modern day NGOs. It was their belief that in the atmosphere of tolerance provided by the repeal of the 18th Amendment temperance education had a better chance to succeed than anything that could have been expected from the continuation of prohibition. It is highly notable how some of the ideas of Fosdick and Scott continue to be valid and take new life and relevance with the drug problem of the 21st century; they can easily and effectively be transposed into our day and age.

Toward control. [19] In their quest for alcohol control, Fosdick and Scott emphasized that "Law and education are twin pillars of the social order. In respect to most human problems, the hope of the future lies in laws soundly conceived and well administered and in an educational process rooted in self-discipline and self-control." For them it was crucial that effective legislation be in place in every state in order to face up to the new challenge of tolerance brought about by the 21st Amendment. Otherwise, they feared the return to the vices of the pre-prohibition era and the possibility that the pendulum would swing back again in favor of prohibitionist measures. Even if the increase in tolerance scared many people, they firmly believed such increase in tolerance was important in order to enter a new era in which the additional liberalization would bring to an end the activity of the bootleggers and provide a better chance for the success of real temperance. They also believed that no system was final, there was much to be learned and that was the fundamental reason for proposing an Authority plan with a great deal of flexibility, so that those in charge of alcohol control could adapt to new developments and incorporate new knowledge into their control program.

6.4 Lessons for the Illicit-Drug Problem of the 21st Century

"We are convinced that someday, as Edward Brecher [20] predicted, most Americans will look back on drug prohibition and judge it to have been (like alcohol prohibition) repressive, unjust, expensive and ineffective — a failure. In the twentieth century, a dozen major scientific commissions in the UK, Canada, and the United States have recommended alternatives to punitive drug policies. The United States is the only nation where these recommendations have been so consistently ignored. For starters, these recommendations should be more widely discussed and better understood in the United States. The experiences of

220

other nations, regions and cities also provide living examples of decriminalization and harm reduction programs *within* global drug prohibition. The full range of alternatives to current U.S. drug policy should be studied and debated — from futuristic visions to pragmatic reforms that could be implemented immediately. For drug policy, as was the case with alcohol policy, discussion of alternatives is an essential part of the transition from prohibition to regulation."[2] It is with these final words that Levine and Reinarman close their essay on Alcohol Prohibition and Drug Prohibition. Their research, supported by the works of Warburton, Fosdick and Scott, and many others, suggests that there are substantive lessons in the history of alcohol prohibition that can be applied to the current drug prohibition policy.

Parallel scenarios: alcohol and drugs. It may rub some people the wrong way that a parallel be drawn between the problems of alcohol in the early 20th century including the ensuing Alcohol Prohibition Era, and the current situation of drug prohibition in America that has acquired high intensity since the early 1970s. Perhaps it is because today we are used to having alcohol around us in different forms and society has come to grips with whatever problems may be brought about by extreme alcohol consumption. Driving a motor vehicle under the influence of alcohol (DUI) is severely punished by law, as is the selling of alcoholic beverages to minors. American society grabbed that bull by the horns and developed ways to regulate it and bring it under control. This does not mean that alcohol is necessarily a healthy substance to be widely and indiscriminately consumed by humans; it does not mean either that it is a dangerous substance that when introduced into the human body causes irreparable damage. It is neither. There are some people who do not consume alcohol because they do not like it, others choose not to consume it because of religious beliefs, and others have made a difficult decision to stay away from it because it does serious damage to their health. The latter are probably members of Alcoholic Anonymous (AA). AA is a support group that helps its members — recovering alcoholics — to build a life for themselves away from the ravages of alcohol. But there are still millions of

221

Americans who are able to consume alcohol without generating any kind of dependency and who are able to conduct perfectly normal personal, professional, and family lives. They are able to do so in the exercise of their right to choose what substances to introduce into their bodies. Since the ratification of the 21st Amendment on December 5, 1933 they are allowed to do so legally. Legislation and education (in a broad sense) are behind today's successful coexistence of people with differing views regarding alcohol; there is no group of people trying to impose their particular views on alcohol consumption through legislation. There is adequate legislation though to control and even punish those who in the exercise of their rights to consume alcohol imperil the safety or the rights of others.

In establishing parallels between the Alcohol Prohibition Era and the current drug prohibition policies in effect in the U.S. and in the whole world, it must be kept in mind that there is a gap of almost a century separating these events. A lot has happened during this time. The world economy is much bigger than it used to be, the world population has had a manifold increase, communications have revolutionized human contact, and technology overall has become a great facilitator of things that were only in the realm of science fiction a few decades ago. In short, the world has turned into a village; face-to-face communication takes place across the world today in far less time than it took to travel from the East Coast to the West Coast back in 1933. It is in this context of globalization that the following parallels between alcohol prohibition and drug prohibition should be viewed:

- **The rise of prohibition related organized crime and lawlessness**. When referring to the need to repeal prohibition back in 1933, John D. Rockefeller, Jr. highlighted as the first objective of repeal "the abolition of lawlessness". There was widespread disregard for the law as far as alcohol consumption was concerned and organized crime stepped in to fulfill the market demands. This resulted in an atmosphere of lawlessness in America, which many concerned citizens believed was a greater evil to society than the consumption of alcohol. In today's illicit-drug environment there is a huge apparatus operating outside the law and generating in the order of $322 billion of yearly revenue on a worldwide scale. Are the DTOs that form this organized crime network less dangerous, equally dangerous, or more dangerous to society than the organized crime running the alcohol business during alcohol prohibition? It took organized crime in the early 1920s about three years to develop the methodology to successfully operate the illegal alcohol business. After that initial period they were operating at full capacity for the next eleven years. Our present-day DTOs have had over thirty years of increasingly intensified experience in supplying the illicit-drug market; they have demonstrated their resiliency, and because of the incentives provided by drug prohibition, there is no end in sight to their business opportunities. Alcohol prohibition gave rise to the lawlessness brought about by organized crime getting into the illegal alcohol trade; drug prohibition has given rise, strengthened, and perpetuated the multiple DTOs supplying an ever-present drug market in very sophisticated ways. Current drug policy has become a business driver rather than a deterrent of the drug trade. This thirty-year-plus experiment ought not to pass in vain.

- **The rise in consumption of higher potency substances.** During alcohol prohibition there was an important shift from the consumption of low alcohol content beers (less than 3.2% alcohol) toward the consumption of wines (10-12% alcohol content) and spirits (35-45% alcohol content). Gallon per gallon it was more profitable for the illegal traders to sell the higher priced and higher alcohol content beverages as the risk was the same because all of them were equally illegal. In today's illicit-drug environment cannabis, cocaine and heroin are equally illicit, but their narcotic effects are not identical. It is recognized that heroin is a more powerful substance in terms of its impact on the human body than cocaine, and cocaine more than cannabis. However, the

223

commercial value of these drugs gram per gram is greater for heroin and cocaine than it is for cannabis. Hence there is a built-in incentive for the DTOs to engage in the distribution and sale of heroin and cocaine rather than cannabis as the distribution risks are essentially the same. In both scenarios, alcohol and drugs, the non-differentiated treatment of substances with varying degrees of potency led organized crime to promote more those substances with higher prices but which happen to pose higher potential damage to humans. The prohibition of alcohol in the past and the prohibition of drugs today, rather than becoming a deterrent, turned into a business driver defeating its own primary objective: the elimination from the market of substances with the potential to damage human health.

- **The impact of policy on neighboring states**. As alcohol prohibition approached repeal in America, it became a national priority to bring about legislation for the control of alcohol in all the states of the Union. The problems that would have arisen from the existence of bordering "dry" and "wet" states had to be addressed expeditiously in order to avoid the continuation of prohibition related conflicts. This is where the work of Fosdick and Scott became the basic document used by most states to draft their own particular alcohol control legislation. In today's illicit-drug environment a similar situation would occur — with respect to the rest of the world — if the U.S. decided to modify its current drug policy. As mentioned earlier, there are international treaties governing the prohibition of narcotics and OMAS all over the world and each individual country has its own legislation prohibiting their use. The U.S. was instrumental in writing and promoting these treaties and it ought to lead the way in their modification to reflect drug prohibition repeal. The U.S. should also be in a position to cooperate with other nations to provide guidance in the drafting of new drug control legislation in a non-prohibition environment.

- **From legal coercion to preventive programs**. The negative experiences of alcohol prohibition led many Americans to support its repeal. Many citizens who believed it was not good to consume alcohol came to the realization that education and persuasion were better tools to promote the cause of temperance or even abstinence. After repeal, legal coercion was to disappear from the land, and education and persuasion provided a far more effective instrument in building a deeply rooted society. There are many reasons to believe that a similar situation may apply to the use of narcotic substances in a scenario of repeal of current drug prohibition in favor of a more rational drug control policy.

The above parallels are invaluable lessons for reviewing America's current drug policy, but there are other lessons that can be learned from alcohol prohibition and repeal in America. Many of these lessons can be extracted from the works of Warburton, and Fosdick and Scott.

Additional lessons from alcohol prohibition. The works of Warburton, and Fosdick and Scott documented valuable conclusions from their research on alcohol prohibition. Wisdom leads to reflect on these conclusions and their potential relevance in a drug policy review initiative. They are:

- Prohibition is not the only path to substance control.
- Prohibition does not reduce expenditure on illegal substances.
- Prohibition does not deliver a healthier nation.
- Taxation of illegal substances can generate the government significant additional revenue and reduce consumption.
- Risking greater consumption in exchange for an end to lawlessness may turn out to be a lesser evil.
- Temperance instead of coerced abstinence is not so bad after all.
- There is no need to sympathize with producers.
- The preponderance of beliefs over facts led to prohibition of alcohol and drugs.

- A rational policy under an effective system of supervision and control can be a better instrument of social control than prohibition.

The parallels and lessons from alcohol prohibition and repeal in the early 20th century carry a strong message for policymakers in a position to review current drug policy in favor of a more rational and effective one. Society does not need a quest for a "free for all" drug liberalization program, it must be a quest that brings together the key components of the drug problem: drug use and abuse, the drug trade, the war on drugs, and drug money laundering. These four elements, as mentioned before in this presentation, are intimately intertwined and cannot be addressed independently of each other. This fact together with the global nature of the problem makes the drug problem much more complex than the alcohol problem was a century ago. The solution requires creativity and innovation to design a new policy and the political will to craft the legislation and the institutions to implement the drug controls called for by American and global society in the 21st century. During the past century technology has revolutionized the way society works, and technology can assist in the implementation of a new drug policy.

Understanding the alcohol prohibition and repeal experience of the early 20th century is a wake up call from the nightmare of drug prohibition in the early 21st century. There is no room for the myths surrounding the drug problem to prevail as facts and condemn the true drug facts to eternal silence. This lesson of history brings hope of waking up from this silent American nightmare and opens new possibilities for a refreshing, rational, and effective drug policy.

7

THE SOLUTION SPECTRUM

The full range of alternatives to the current U.S. drug policy should be studied and debated, as was the case with alcohol policy in the early 20th Century, discussion of alternatives is an essential part of the transition from drug prohibition to regulation in the 21st Century.

7.1 Exploring the Potential Drug Policy Spectrum

Three enduring myths have kept the current drug policy alive for too long, while three crucial root causes of the drug problem have not received proper attention. In addition, a number of relevant events continue to shape the landscape of the four intertwined issues — the prevailing drug use and abuse, the thriving illicit-drug trade, the un-winnable war on drugs, and the stealth drug money laundering — which day in and day out nurture this complex American nightmare. Complex, because there is more than meets the eye; some events are broadly acknowledged, others are blatantly ignored, and some even pass unnoticed. Those passing unnoticed or ignored are kept silent and contribute to the ever-increasing threat to the health — physical and spiritual — of American society. America has proven its ability and competence to grow out of complex social situations throughout history: slavery in the 19th century, legal racial discrimination in the 20th century, and alcohol prohibition almost a century ago. It was the American conscience in motion, rooted in the groundwork laid by the founding fathers: the right of every American to life, liberty and the pursuit of happiness. The drug problem in the U.S. today requires the active participation of every American, in particular of the seventy million parents of children and young adults. Without their involvement there will be no change of course; most politicians are too afraid of losing the next election to take up any cause without the active support of their constituency. And without a change of course — a change of policy — drugs will continue to flow in the streets of America, the DTOs will become evermore rich and powerful, the war on drugs will continue to drag on and without victory, and the stealth business associates of the drug lords will pose an increasing threat to U.S. allies and to the U.S. itself; this they will do by climbing positions of power within the social structure of countries allied with the U.S. and within strategic U.S. industries.

A thorough analysis will undoubtedly lead to an abundance of drug policy options. This chapter presents four fundamental alternatives, or policy guidelines, which cover the full spectrum. Elements are provided with every one of the options for the reader to reflect upon; they deserve proper consideration by civil society. Policymakers — politicians in particular — will do well to acquaint themselves with the options and, with confidence, enrich them in the process of democratic exploration and debate. The four policy guidelines are:

- Zero tolerance
- Consumption tolerance
- Laissez faire legalization
- Legalization and control

The assessment of each of these policy guidelines is done against the backdrop of drug-related events under the current policy, the myths, and the root causes as summarized in Chapter V and the enhanced understanding provided by the alcohol prohibition and repeal as illustrated in Chapter VI.

7.2 Zero Tolerance

A zero tolerance drug policy sits at one end of the spectrum. Zero means nothing is tolerated: no drug use, no trade is allowed to happen, drug trading is vigorously persecuted and the "war on drugs" is carried to the limit; a dragnet is put in place to prevent any kind of money launder-ing. An airtight strategy is implemented to eliminate drugs from the mar-ketplace and do away with the DTOs and their partners in crime. A zero tolerance policy will result in the hardening of the current drug policy to the extreme; can it work? It did in China in the late 1940s and early 1950s, after Mao Tse-tung and the communists took over the government. What were the underlying social, political, and law enforcement consid-erations in effect in China that allowed for a zero tolerance policy with respect to the opium trade and use to succeed?

A review of the history of opium use and abuse and the historical trade patterns helps understand how China became the largest opium con-suming country in the mid-20th century. Professor Alfred W. McCoy [1] of the University of Wisconsin, Madison, an expert in Southeast Asian his-tory, has written a number of books and essays on the subject. In his essay *Opium History Up To 1958 A.D.* [2], he documents how opium use and addiction grew in Asia and many countries around the world. The colo-nial powers of the 18th and 19th centuries, among them the British Empire, France and Holland, played an active role in the promotion and distribu-tion of opium throughout Asia. According to McCoy, in the colonial Asia of the late 18th century and during the first half of the 19th century, the successful European economies were involved in the commercialization of caffeine, nicotine, and opiates. It was during the 18th century that these drugs were transformed from luxury goods into commodities for the con-sumption of the general population; this event turned them into an inte-gral component of the economies and lifestyles of Asian and Atlantic na-tions. The colonial powers saw in the opium trade a tool for colonial domination in more than one way. Opium addiction weakened the local populations, but strengthened the finances of colonial governments. In the early 20th century opium sales provided 16% of taxes for French Indo-china, 16% for the Netherlands Indies, 20% for Siam, and 53% for British Malaya according to McCoy. Opium use spread worldwide and opium came to play an economic and political role and soon became the target of prohibition campaigns led by Protestant churches. The most profound and

229

lasting legacy of the American prohibition movement turned out to be the underlying concept of applying the force of law and police to regulate what individuals were allowed to do to with their own bodies. The intrusion of the state into a realm previously thought personal and private marked a small but still significant turning point in modern political history. With the passage of the Harrison Narcotics Act in 1914, the U.S. imposed the force of law over the right to use or abuse the body as the individual saw fit. Nevertheless, opium use continued to flourish in many countries, legally in some and illegally in others. The illicit trade also became a source of corruption of government authorities everywhere, including China. China, however, did find a way to end the use of opium; they implemented a zero tolerance policy in the late 1940s and early 1950s. During World War II and after the war in China, it was demonstrated that perfect coercion could have an influence, direct and dramatic, on the international heroin trade. Pervasive wartime security over ports, impossible in peacetime, prevented drug smuggling to the United States. It can be deduced that, less than perfect coercion would have little impact on the global narcotics traffic and would, under most circumstances, produce minor seizures that operate as a surcharge to be passed on to consumers. The Chinese Communist regime used a mix of unrestrained repression and social reform to eradicate the world's largest opium market. By the mid 1950s, opium areas had converted to new crops, dealers had been executed, and the ten million estimated Chinese addicts had been forced into compulsory treatment.

Perfect coercion during World War II prevented opium from arriving to the U.S. and reduced the population of opium addicts in the country. In addition, perfect coercion, as implemented by a totalitarian regime like the one led by Mao Tse-tung, can succeed in the eradication of drug addiction and use. The compelling arguments of the firing squads drove Chinese dealers into their graves and compulsory treatment convinced the ten million opium addicts to part with their addiction. History unveils that, even if rooted in a 200-year-plus government driven tradition, addiction can be wiped out from a whole nation; it only takes unrestricted force to achieve it. This is what a zero tolerance drug policy is all about; as it sits at one end of the spectrum of alternative policy opportunities. Zero tolerance is not about tightening the screws of the current drug policy a bit more. Between zero tolerance and current policy there are an infinite number of possibilities, all of them are very likely to vary the outcome to some extent, but none is very likely to deliver the results of zero tolerance. All of them will just produce minor seizures that will serve as a surcharge that will be passed on to consumers; these options will continue to drive drug prices up and make the drug business more attractive, similar to what current policy does today. How can drug-related events be expected to change from an intermediate policy option — a policy sitting between zero tolerance and current drug policy, a policy approaching zero tolerance but not quite there?

A policy approaching zero tolerance does not acknowledge the myths identified in Chapter V, and either ignores the root causes or nurtures them. It does nothing to address the needs for medical and psychological research free from the coercive force of prohibition. HIV/AIDS and hepatitis C infections are not likely to see a reprieve. The multiple demand drivers — e.g., genetic considerations, proactive parenting, and others — do not come into the picture; neither do other drug-use prevention approaches. As they do under current policy, the drug trade will continue to find in prohibition an excellent business driver and the business of fighting the war on drugs will thrive in the face of resilient DTOs. The new environment will do nothing to deter the DTOs from channeling resources to terrorist groups in detriment of the security of U.S. allies and the U.S. itself. Mexican DTOs will continue to gain strength south of the U.S. border and further challenge U.S. national security, besides threatening the stability of Mexico and the development of its democratic institutions. Corruption will continue to have a field day everywhere the DTOs operate — producing, transshipment or consuming countries. Our global village will not escape the socio-political-economic impact of the new policy. American prisons will have to make room for an increasing number of residents because of drug-related offences, unless the new policy comes together with the death penalty. The Bill of Rights will experience even greater attacks than under current policy, which will help us remember that Mao Tse-Tung could implement a zero tolerance policy because he did not have the same concerns for human rights and freedom as did Thomas Jefferson. However, on approaching zero tolerance, the business of illicit drugs will continue to thrive and fill the coffers of DTOs and their business partners. Drug money —— properly laundered —— will continue to transfer power from truly legitimate businessmen into the hands of drug lords and their partners, while they build economic empires with abundant inexpensive cash. As this newly acquired power will, in crescendo, cross borders unhindered in today's global village, it should surprise nobody to discover down the road that the "businessman" sitting at the board of directors' meeting of an otherwise legitimate business is a DTO partner. And to finalize, the true legitimate businessmen will find it ever more difficult to compete with "businessmen" who have very deep pockets, but who do not need to focus on customer service, or business productivity to deliver outstanding financial statements.

A halfcocked zero tolerance policy will lead nowhere; it will only make the business juicier for the DTOs and their partners in crime. However, can a true blood zero tolerance policy work in America as it did in Communist China a half century ago? Such a policy exacts a very high price from society; is America willing to pay the price? Our democratic principles and the respect for individual freedoms will be cancelled and the rule by coercion will take their place. Is a zero tolerance policy capable of delivering a lesser evil than the current policy? Is there not some other policy capable of delivering more benefits or a lesser evil than the current policy and zero tolerance? These two questions beg for answers in the process of searching for a better drug policy. The task must be addressed if America's current drug problem is going to find a well-grounded solution.

7.3 Consumption Tolerance

A policy of consumption tolerance aims at decriminalizing the use of drugs; it does not have to be all drugs, decriminalization can be implemented on a selective basis. There are countries that have decriminalized or tolerated the use of certain drugs and/or their usage within specific locations; therefore there is experience available that can be relied upon to evaluate the merits of a consumption tolerance policy. Decriminalizing consumption is not the same as trading the drugs legally. Even if the user is not penalized for consuming it, the drug remains an illicit substance and the production, importation and distribution remain a criminal activity, though retailing is tolerated under a given set of rules. In the Netherlands the use of cannabis has been decriminalized since the early 1980s. According to Levine and Reinarman, "national policy in the Netherlands allows over 800 cafes and snack bars to sell small quantities of cannabis to adults for personal use, on premises and off. These "coffee shops" are permitted to operate as long as they are orderly and stay within well-defined limits that are monitored and enforced by the police. Unlike legal businesses, cannabis sales are not taxed and coffee shops cannot advertise cannabis." [3] The non-taxable component of the policy speaks to the illegal nature of the activity itself. The retail sale and the consumption of cannabis are tolerated, but it is still considered an illicit activity, hence it cannot be taxed. The supply of cannabis to the coffee shops is done through the "back door", as the Dutch say. "This is still formally drug prohibition and the Netherlands prosecutes importers, dealers and commercial growers who handle large quantities of cannabis — as required by the UN anti-drug treaties. In short, for over two decades, the Netherlands has sustained a unique system of regulated, open, quasi-legal cannabis sales supplied by illegal importers and growers. This is as far as any country has been able to go within the current structures of global drug prohibition." [3]

Also, there has been an active harm reduction movement associated with drug use since the mid 1980s. For over two decades this movement has sought to provide drug users and addicts with a range of ser-

233

vices geared towards reducing the harmful effects of drug use. According to Levine and Reinarman, "Harm reduction encourages policymakers to shift drug policies away from punishment, coercion, and repression, and toward tolerance, regulation and public health. Harm reduction is not inherently an enemy of drug prohibition. However, in the course of pursuing public health goals, harm reduction necessarily seeks policies that also reduce the punitive effects of drug prohibition." [3] Levine and Reinarman go on to suggest that "implicitly and sometimes explicitly the harm reductionist stance toward drug prohibition is exactly the same as its stance toward drug use. Harm reduction groups seek to reduce the harmful effects of drug use without requiring users to be drug-free. Harm reduction groups also seek to reduce the harmful effects of drug prohibition without requiring governments to be prohibition-free. Harm reduction's message to drug users is: *we are not asking you to give up drug use; we just ask you to do some things (like use clean syringes) to reduce the harmfulness of drug use (including the spread of AIDS) to you and the people close to you.* In precisely the same way, harm reduction's message to governments is: *we are not asking you to give up drug prohibition; we just ask you to do some things (like make clean syringes and methadone available) to reduce the harmfulness of drug prohibition.*" So, harm reduction is a form of consumption tolerance advocating better facilities for the drug user to improve health conditions without being penalized on account of the illegality brought about by prohibition while making these facilities available. However, consumption, as illustrated throughout this presentation is only one component of the drug problem, one of four key issues. It deals with drug use and abuse, but ignores the other three issues: the drug trade, the war on drugs, and drug money laundering.

By implementing the consumption tolerant model, the Netherlands has taken the lead amongst European countries for drug use tolerance. Detractors of the model, including the DEA, claim that such a model opens the way for increased drug addiction, not just of the tolerated drug, but also of other more harmful substances. According to a DEA document, "the Netherlands has led Europe in the liberalization of drug policy. *Coffee shops* began to emerge throughout the Netherlands in 1976, offering marijuana products for sale. Possession and sale of marijuana are not legal, but coffee shops are permitted to operate and sell marijuana under certain restrictions, including a limit of no more than 5 grams sold to a person at any one time, no alcohol or hard drugs, no minors, and no advertising. In the Netherlands, it is illegal to sell or possess marijuana products. So, coffee shop operators must purchase their marijuana products from illegal drug trafficking organizations. Furthermore, drug abuse has increased in the Netherlands. From 1984 to 1996, marijuana use among 18-25-year-olds in Holland increased twofold. Since legalization of marijuana, heroin addiction levels in Holland have tripled and perhaps even quadrupled by some estimates."[4] The Netherlands experience brings out the sort of things that can happen when the issues associated with the illicit drugs are addressed independent of each other. By trying to obviate the criminalization component of cannabis (marijuana) use and not address the illicit-drug trade, the war on drugs, and money-laundering issues in unison, the Netherlands introduced a drug business multiplier. The DTOs were still in business as cannabis distribution remained illicit. This situation kept prices up and the economic incentives for the DTOs to stay in the cannabis distribution business prevailed. Besides, the tolerated consumption of cannabis and the supporting trade became a pivot for the commercialization of stronger drugs like heroin and cocaine, perhaps using the same distribution channels.

A consumption tolerant policy, whether implemented for practical or sanitary reasons, is bound to expand the use of drugs in the population as it ignores three of the four key issues sustaining the drug problem. It chooses to overlook the myths surrounding the drug problem and ignores its root causes. Besides, it is so focused on tolerance to consumers that it does not necessarily call for medical and psychological research to get at the scientific facts linked to each type of drug. Its major contribution is providing better sanitary conditions which will help thwart the spread of HIV/AIDS and hepatitis C infections. Nothing in the policy addresses demand-related issues — e.g., genetic considerations, proactive parenting, and others, the policy does not show any concern with the thriving narcotics business or with the business of fighting the DTOs — both are ignored. There is no reason to believe the policy will alter in any way the resiliency of the DTOs to carry on their illicit business, and whatever links DTOs may have with terrorist organizations will continue to exist under this policy. Mexican DTOs, at the U.S. doorstep, will continue to thrive under the policy in the same way they have been under current policy. Corruption will continue to be an ally and a powerful tool of the DTOs to assist in the expediting of their business needs. Given the policy does not provide an integral global solution, the global village will continue to be subject to the global drug trade business and the global war on drugs. Because the policy tolerates consumption, it is very likely less people will serve prison sentences than under the current policy — a minor but important contribution of the policy. The individual rights of Americans will be better protected with respect to certain drug uses, but as drugs remain illicit and law enforcement will continue to act — the war on drugs will continue — the zeal of law enforcement may continue to infringe on the rights of certain individuals pretty much in the same way it happens under current policy. Hence, is a consumption tolerance policy capable of delivering a significant lesser evil to society than the current policy? Is there some other policy capable of delivering a lesser evil than current policy and a consumption tolerance policy? Again, these questions must be answered if the drug problem is going to meet with an effective solution.

7.4 Laissez Faire Legalization

A policy of laissez faire legalization sits at the other extreme of the spectrum of policy options; it would be in direct opposition to a zero tolerance policy. Under such policy the laws of economics will be unrestricted and supply and demand will rule with whatever imperfections the drug market may carry. This section explores approaching laissez faire legalization, as a true laissez faire policy will be more like free-for-all chaos. Though in economic theory the law of supply and demand is supposed to rule unrestricted, in real life it faces many circumstantial constraints. One such constraint is that minors are not allowed by law to consume certain substances like alcohol and tobacco; hence, it is to be expected that under any policy approaching laissez faire, minors will not be allowed to consume drugs of any nature either. History illustrates situations where conditions approaching laissez faire have occurred. The history of opium during the 18th, 19th and early 20th centuries is a good example of approaching laissez faire. Opium did not enjoy a perfect market condition, but it was not considered an illicit substance worldwide. Hence, the major colonial powers were directly involved in the opium trade. Though the British were using monopolistic practices in the promotion and control of opium, they were not restricting the consumption of opium, but rather promoting its use and profiting from it. At the time, production quotas drove prices up, a direct result of the market laws at play, and unsatisfied demand was quickly met by new suppliers attracted by a profitable market. Later on, as the British lost the monopoly in the early 19th century and China's opium imports increased many fold, opium addiction grew rapidly.

Later, in the second half of the 19th century, Britain lost the near monopoly over the Asian opium trade and the drug became, for the first time in its history, a free-market commodity. Traded in mass volume through unrestricted trade, opium gained new markets in the West and expanded its trade in Asia. During this timeframe opium sale controls remained within the colonies, but its international trade was unrestricted. Once fully commoditized, opium spread beyond its Asian trade axis to become, through the modern pharmaceutical industry, a major item of mass consumption in the West. Driven by global commerce, world opium production reached an historic peak of 41,000 tons in 1907; this was ten times the production level in 1993, according to McCoy. This is a good illustration of what a policy approaching laissez faire can achieve for the market expansion of narcotic substances. What kind of social, economic, and political impact can be expected from such policy?

If the opium experience so vividly described in McCoy's work is a good reference point, and there is no reason to suggest it should not be, a policy approaching laissez faire legalization of drugs in today's world would unquestionably lead to increased drug consumption. The licit-drug business, in replacement of the illicit-drug trade, is likely to increase significantly as prices drop in the face of legalization; the opium experience of the 18th, 19th and early 20th centuries is a good illustration of what can happen when today's illicit drugs become licit under this policy. The big difference is that the licit-drug business would be taxed and would generate revenues for the government treasury. Given the laissez faire nature of the policy, there need not be much interest placed on medical and psychological research to expand the knowledge of drugs' impact on the human body, except to further the promotion of drug consumption. Under the legalized environment provided by this policy there would be a marked reduction of HIV/AIDS and hepatitis C infections as the unsanitary use of needles would no longer be necessary — sanitary needles could be readily available. The demand related issues would not be part of the policy. Afghanistan, Colombia and Mexico would not necessarily continue to be the most important suppliers of drugs. For one, Mexico need not be used as a transshipment country for Colombian cocaine; Colombia may share production with other Andean countries like Peru and Bolivia, and even Ecuador. Afghanistan need not continue to be the main grower of the opium poppy, as other countries in Asia and in Latin America could get into this business. Local U.S. growers of cannabis can look forward to increasing their share of the U.S. cannabis market. Cannabis consumption would be likely to increase in the U.S. and all over the world, keeping its place as the most popular narcotic drug. The illicit-narcotics trade would disappear from the face of the Earth, and hence, the need to fight it. DTOs will disappear into oblivion — the market would no longer have any use for them. Terrorists will run out of the financial resources provided by the DTOs under current policy. Under a free-market operation it is very likely that the Taliban and al-Qaeda would not benefit much from the opium poppy. If extraordinary levies were imposed by these two groups in Afghanistan on opium poppy growers, it would be very likely that drug manufacturers would buy their raw materials from cheaper countries where extraordinary levies were not imposed at the farm gate. A similar situation would take place in Colombia if the FARC and the AUC insisted on imposing levies on coca bush growers; production would be displaced to other regions of Colombia or to Ecuador, Peru, and Bolivia. Hence, terrorist groups' financing through extraordinary levies imposed on peasant growers would disappear or be significantly reduced. Mexico would stop being a transshipment country for Colombian cocaine, but could continue the legal production of heroin and cannabis, the latter in direct competition with U.S. producers. However, Mexico's stability would be greatly enhanced as the omnipresent corrupting power of illicit drugs disappeared, and Mexico would have a better chance to build its democratic institutions and consolidate the rule of law. Corruption would no longer have the illicit-drug trade as a partner in crime — there would not be any illicit-drug trade. The drug trade — legal under this policy — would continue to be global, but there would not be any illicit global drug trade or a global war on drugs. No longer would drugs be a criminal offense, thus drug-related crimes would not exist and the prison population would ease. Thousands of young people in America would not be graduating in crime in U.S. prisons because of drug-related sentences. The Bill of Rights need not come under attack under this policy as it does under current policy because of the war on drugs — there would be no war on drugs. The rivers of cash filling the coffers of DTOs and their business partners under current policy would dry up, and there would not be a power transfer from truly legitimate businessmen into the hands of drug lords and their business associates. No economic empires would thrive with the nourishment provided by illicit-drug revenues, and there would not be any stealth businessmen financed by drug money sitting on the boards of directors of strategic industries. Finally, truly legitimate businessmen would not have to face unfair competition derived from easy cash in the hands of competitors in partnership with drug lords, as there would be no drug money laundering going on, and businesses would focus on customer service and productivity in a wholesome free market economy not tainted by drug money-laundering operations.

Current myths surrounding the drug problem would pass on to history, they would cease to be relevant under a policy of laissez faire legalization and no attention would be paid to the root causes feeding the once-prevalent prohibition environment. Under the policy, drugs would become a commodity to be traded by legal enterprises; the profit margins in a legal environment would not be attractive enough for organized crime to step into the business.

A drug policy approaching laissez faire legalization addresses three of the four key issues driving the drug problem in America and in other countries. However, it does not address the issue of drug abuse in any way or form. Judging by McCoy's account regarding the opium trade, it is conceivable that drug use and abuse would become rampant under this policy and that there would be a substantial increase in the number of addicts. It is logical that the other key issues driving the drug problem under the current policy would no longer be operational; there would be no illicit-drug trade and no organized crime to deal with regarding drugs; therefore the need to fight a "war" would no longer exist, and there would be no illicit-drug money to be laundered and hence no power being accumulated in the hands of groups and individuals who might in time pose a security threat to the U.S. However, the issue of drug abuse may overwhelm society and exact a steep price. In summary, under this policy three of the four fundamental issues would cease to exist and the fourth — drug use and abuse — would be exacerbated; drug use and addiction would reach new heights carrying grave consequences for human health derived from the increased probability of precocious use leading to significant damage to the human nervous system

7.5 Legalization and Control

A policy of legalization and control draws sustenance from the alcohol prohibition and repeal experience of the early 20th century in the U.S. It recognizes non-desirable effects on human health from the use of drugs. As with the repeal of alcohol prohibition, when it was recognized that not all alcohol had the same impact on humans, a policy of drug legalization and control incorporates the need for un-coerced medical and psychological research to properly determine the human health impact of different drugs. The policy strives for fact-based decisions versus the belief-based — myth-based — decisions and practices prevalent under the current policy. Scientific research has a crucial role to play under this policy, and it goes hand in hand with the end of lawlessness. The latter was the primary goal of those furthering the cause of alcohol prohibition repeal and it is the focus point and a cornerstone of this policy. The words of John D. Rockefeller, Jr. [5] back in 1933, "Rightly, the first objective is the abolition of lawlessness" find echo in the 21st century. The atmosphere of lawlessness brought about by the illicit-drug trade is by far a bigger threat to society than the health problems associated with the consumption of today's illicit drugs. The lawlessness referred to by Rockefeller was very much focused on the U.S. and on the operation of organized crime on a much more limited scale than today's operation of DTOs with illicit drugs on a global scale. The world has turned into a global village, the impact of technology, for better or for worse, has radically transformed modern society. The DTOs, their stealth business partners, and the many government officials attracted to their entourage by the sheer corrupting appeal of drug money, in the U.S. and many other countries, are amassing huge power capable of shaking the very foundations of free and democratic societies. In the face of this modern-day threat of lawlessness, not always visible to the naked eye, a policy of legalization and control provides an integral approach to address the four key issues prolonging the illicit-drug problem: drug use and abuse, the illicit-drug trade, the war on drugs, and drug money laundering.

Pricing the drugs. The illicit-drug trade is driven by the profit motive amplified by the illegality of drugs. Illegality drives drug prices up to compensate for additional risks in delivering the drug to the consumer. Making drugs illegal does not abolish the law of supply and demand. Thus, a policy of legalization and control must make drugs legally avail-

241

able to users under some predetermined set of simple rules — perhaps different rules for different drugs — that would fashion the drug business unattractive for organized crime. This was actually a key point made by Fosdick and Scott in *Toward Liquor Control* [5]; they proposed a "State Alcohol Control Authority" as the best mechanism to manage and control alcohol distribution after prohibition. The Authority would have to strike a balance between "the prospective consumer desires for low price", and the prohibitionist "on the side of high prices, for he believes that if liquor is expensive, it will be placed out of the reach of many persons". Fosdick and Scott saw the price of liquor as "a central factor regulating both legal and illegal consumption". They were "equally concerned with defeating the bootlegger and with avoiding the stimulation of consumption which might follow too low a level of prices". As presented earlier, under a policy approaching laissez faire legalization, market forces are likely to drive prices down and stimulate consumption. Hence, a legalization and control policy must design the mechanisms to keep organized crime out of the illicit-drug business through the lack of economic incentives resulting from low enough prices which would render the business unattractive to organized crime. At the same time, prices ought to be high enough to stem the consumption of drugs. A neat balancing act needs to be put in place, one that would rely on a flexible control environment capable of feeding sound data to the policymaking body to allow for a dynamic adjustment of regulations.

Prevention and rehabilitation strategy. A broad educational strategy was, in Fosdick and Scott's minds, the best foundation upon which to build a solid non-alcohol consuming culture. They also thought education to be a much-abused term believed by some to deliver miraculous results. In their view, education went beyond the formal and systematic instruction used for developing temperate habits with respect to alcohol; they believed this to be a narrow and inadequate concept. "As a matter of fact, the schools alone can accomplish little in modifying or stabilizing the habits of the individual." They were convinced that schools alone could not "compete with the influences nor successfully oppose the tendencies of other stronger agencies of social control." They believed such agencies to be stronger than the conventional educational process. In their view the agencies included, first and foremost, "the general social situation in which a child grows up....This vague but undisputable social pressure upon the growing individual is well-nigh irresistible." Next in importance, they placed "the influence of the immediate environment in which the child grows up....The standards and manners of the circle in which he (child and adult) moves, his intimate associations — social, religious or otherwise: these factors sway and shape his thinking and conduct." In third place they identified the family as an influence of wider, varying potency, but of tremendous importance, and a highly interested group. "The standards and ideals of this unit, its capacity to lead and persuade, constitute, therefore, a third contributing factor to the education of the growing human being." These three factors integrated over and above the formal educational process were highly valued by Fosdick and Scott. "Far more important in the development of rational and balanced living are those subtle and intangible factors which constitute the tone and quality of the nation, the community and the home." There is much to learn from their research and writings in the early 20th century to effectively address today's illicit-drug problem.

A prevention and rehabilitation strategy must focus on demand-driven issues as part of any effective drug policy. However, as mentioned earlier, the focus of this presentation is not on the demand-driven issues which merit a study of their own, they ought to be contemplated in any drug policy with the aspiration to succeed. Fosdick and Scott were talking about society, community, and family values as a critical component of an effective temperance education process. This has little to do with an education process supported by coercion through law enforcement and the sowing of fear in American youth. It is a process that requires hard work, perseverance, and commitment; the process focuses on building a culture of abstinence from drugs which is supported by strong national, community, and family values. Americans must recognize that arduous commitment and perseverance are required from them to build and consolidate a foundation of values in American society; nevertheless, this is a more robust path towards building an America capable of successfully facing the drug challenge. Intimidation and fear are more likely to generate rebellion and push some children to look for ways to counter the message — like experimenting with drugs to prove the authority figures wrong. Therefore a broad prevention strategy must start with the family, this approach requires parents to assume a leading role in the education of their children — active parenting. Schools are no substitute for parents in the building of strong family values. Schools do come in as reinforcement in the children's education; as part of the community, they have a complementary role to play in the development of a child's character and values. What the child sees and hears in the classroom and the availability of sport facilities in schools and in the community at large — including churches — would go a long way toward building a child's character and values. It is imperative that children be exposed to the positive elements of life like sports, and cultural and outdoor activities in order to build a strong generation of healthy drug free Americans. Coercion and intimidation would not do the required work from the ground up. On the national level there is much to be done, society must assume its responsibility to promote and reward patterns of behavior and role models that would encourage healthy living in American youth. Movies and television have a critical role to play in this context. It does not mean that censorship is called for, but it does mean that parents should reward those who provide healthy value building messages and punish — with their purchasing dollars — those that do otherwise.

Perhaps there are some parents who would question this long and arduous path toward the building of a drug-free community of American youth; they might prefer the state to take care of that responsibility, it would be easier on them, maybe they are too busy with their professional or social occupations to take time for value building in their children. They are wrong; the state is no substitute for proactive parenting. And, proactive parenting, which is important under current policy, remains as important under a policy of legalization and control. Drugs would remain illegal for minors under this new policy — in the same way that alcohol and tobacco are illegal for them today — and this is one more reason to promote the development of values through schools, churches, community groups and the family.

Drug distribution, use, and abuse. Drug abuse and addiction are facts of life in America today and a new legalization and control policy must address the issue. As previously mentioned, the policy promotes unhindered medical and psychological research to effectively identify the impact on human health of different drugs. Research results may lead to a differential treatment for different drugs, pretty much along a similar path suggested by Fosdick and Scott for differentiating beer, wines and spirits back in the early 1930s. It would not be appropriate to suggest in this presentation a specific breakdown for today's illicit drugs in the absence of sound research findings, but it is imperative that the absence of such findings not be allowed to justify the continuation of current policy. The primary objective of a legalization and control policy is "the abolition of lawlessness"; hence society must define a flexible and dynamic process for the implementation of such policy so that the wheels of change can be set in motion. Such implementation strategy may require preliminary definitions subject to modification along the way as experience and research data are gathered. It may be expedient for milder drugs to be placed initially under constraints similar to those imposed on alcohol and tobacco today; they would not be legal for minors, and would also be subject to similar restrictions and controls, including warning labels and restrictions on advertising. Later on, if medical research identifies health hazards warranting more stringent regulations, these drugs could be placed under a more strict system of control. Cannabis might be a drug qualifying for such preliminary treatment, though this is not in any way a statement of fact; expert knowledge must be called upon to render judgment. For drugs deemed to have a large population of addicts to begin with, the policy must provide an effective way of dealing with them. To begin with, a regulated but straightforward system must be in place to legally provide these drugs to users. Whether this is done through a cen-

245

tral government Authority, like the one proposed by Fosdick and Scott back in 1933, or some other mechanism managed by the private sector, the system should provide for a strict control of drug production and distribution on a worldwide scale. This may have not been possible during alcohol prohibition back in the early 1930s, but technology has come a long way and it is possible to effectively monitor drug production, distribution, and consumption with today's satellite, telecommunication, and information technologies.

The control of the cultivation-production-distribution cycle can be effectively achieved using readily available technology. Cannabis, heroin and other opium based drugs, and cocaine have their origin in crops. All of them, except for cannabis, are solely cultivated in the open air. Cannabis can be cultivated in covered facilities with artificial lighting. Current satellite surveillance technology is accurate enough to identify, on a worldwide scale, the location of the cultivation fields and to project crop yields. Because under a legalization and control policy these crops would be legal, it is just a matter of accounting for the drugs produced and making sure they enter the legal distribution channels. The pricing policy itself should be powerful enough to encourage the use of the legal channels and prevent the diversion of drugs into illegal markets. Information and telecommunications technologies should facilitate the tracking of the drugs all the way from the fields to the hands of the consumers. Of course, a worldwide system of monitoring and control would be required, but there is no technological impediment to building such a system. The technology required is readily available and the problem is a global problem to begin with; hence, the cooperation of all nations involved in the cultivation-production-distribution cycle should not be difficult to obtain under a global policy of legalization and control. Thus, a system of satellite crop monitoring together with an expeditious system of production and distribution control could effectively account for the supply side of the licit-drug business. Accounting for the demand side of the business does not face any impediments; the same information and telecommunication technologies used to monitor and control the supply side can be

246

used to monitor and control consumption. For those drugs requiring strict monitoring and control, beyond the controls provided by the basic regulations — labeling, advertising and age requirements — a National Registry of Drug Users (NRDU) could be established. There is no technological impediment to sharing information amongst various registries of drug users from different countries or even to building a single international registry if deemed necessary. Any individual drug user will be allowed to purchase enough drugs to satisfy his needs — given prior NRDU registration; each purchase would be authorized against the national registry, and each user's consumption history and pattern would be updated online. Individual history of use would be kept online and tracked to prevent extraordinary purchases and the potential diversion of drugs into the illegal market. The effective and ethical management of the NRDU becomes a crucial component of the legalization and control policy. Some people may express concern about privacy issues surrounding the NRDU; while others will see in it a great opportunity to launch well orchestrated campaigns to promote the treatment of drug addicts — non-compulsory treatment it ought to be. The specifics of how the NRDU should work would require the contribution of experts from a variety of fields, but the concept brings forward a mechanism to facilitate the implementation of a policy of legalization and control.

It remains open how to address the issue of drug addicts who do not have the resources to pay for their addiction, even if prices are not as steep as they are under current policy. The specifics on how to deal with this group of people should come out of expert opinions from different fields. Are these individuals to be classified as sick and entitled to special treatment? If so, what kind of special treatment? Would they just get their daily drugs at some special clinic and go home every day to wait for next day's shot? Would they be required to enter a compulsory drug treatment program in exchange for a smooth transition away from their drug addiction? This is a segment of the population requiring special attention and, for the sake of the overall health and security of society, it would be crucial to provide it under a legalization and control policy.

The destinies of the illicit-drug trade, the war on drugs, and drug money laundering. As stated earlier, the primary objective of the legalization and control policy is to purge the atmosphere of the lawlessness prevalent under the current policy. It is through a combination of the laws of economics, offering drugs to the adult consumer on the legal market at prices low enough not to lure organized crime and high enough to discourage consumption, and the implementation of some prudent and focused control mechanisms supported by off the shelf technologies, that the illicit-drug trade can be brought to a standstill. Still the question remains as to what would happen to minors in this environment. All drugs, like alcohol and tobacco today, would be off limits to minors, anybody wishing to consume drugs legally would have to be an adult. The logical question to follow is: How to prevent minors from accessing licit drugs in the same way they access alcohol and tobacco today? This will remain the responsibility of law enforcement and the judicial system; not to punish the minor but to punish those adults who make drugs available to them. Anyway, except for the "soft" drugs, there will be a much stricter control on the supply of "hard" drugs — those qualifying for strict controls through the NRDU. Hence, it would be more difficult for a drug-dealer-in-the-making to gain access to hard drugs. In addition, in this environment, the huge profit incentives associated with illicit drugs today would not be there. In today's illicit-drug market there is a huge incentive to make drugs available to kids, not just because the profit margins are very attractive, but because by introducing them to drugs the DTOs are expanding the business even further, all the way up to turning them into addicts of hard drugs as they grow up. By eliminating or drastically reducing the profit incentive to organized crime, the probability of having drug dealers roaming the schools in search of their prey would be dramatically reduced. This illustrates how by leveraging the laws of economics rather than ignoring them, society can move closer to a generation of young Americans less involved with drugs. Of course, a generation of young American with a lower incidence of drug use does not travel alone; it

248

needs the company of the broad prevention efforts described earlier in this chapter.

A policy of legalization and control leads towards an environment free of the illicit-drug trade or with an illicit-drug trade very much limited to independent freelance neighborhood drug dealers feeding from the cracks of the legal market. Hence, there is not much need for the so-called war on drugs to continue. The bulk of resources allocated today to the war on drugs can be reassigned to drug prevention in the broadest sense, to addict treatment, and to monitoring and controlling the cultivation-production-distribution cycle to keep it operating within the rules. There would no longer be a need for laundering drug money, the pipeline supplying illicit revenues of $322 billion a year to DTOs would dry up, and the need to launder this money would evaporate. The once stealth business associates of DTOs would find themselves short of cash. A sudden jolt would shake up their business structures from the foundations; in the absence of easy cash they would have to figure out how to manage their businesses in a competitive environment. Some may succeed, some others are likely to go under, and all would see their business empires significantly reduced and their formerly acquired powers — economic and political — greatly diminished. In the end, America would be a lot safer because the potential threat of alliances between these individuals and groups with terrorist organizations would cease to exist.

The balance of legalization and control. It probably never crossed the minds of Fosdick and Scott that their work on alcohol control could have an even greater impact on America almost a century later. Nevertheless, a review of their alcohol policy recommendations as applied to today's illicit drugs is bound to have an overwhelming effect on the myths and facts surrounding illicit drugs today. This would be the net result of addressing the root causes of a problem and of society turning away from tinkering with the symptoms. Drug consumption would not disappear overnight from the face of the Earth, but in time, with the sound development of drug free values, it can be greatly diminished. Community safety because of DUI of drugs would be better controlled by providing access to the NRDU to law enforcement in case of accidents. Broad-based drug education grounded on values and not on intimidation and fear, together with reduced availability of drugs in schools, would reduce experimentation with drugs amongst the children of America. These children would be less exposed to drugs, as the profit incentive to promote drugs amongst minors would be significantly reduced. Drug addicts would be properly identified and provided treatment and assistance under a health focus and not a criminal one. HIV/AIDS and hepatitis C cases resulting from the use of unsanitary syringes would disappear. Preventive programs, being at the core of the legalization and control policy, will take their rightful place at the center of a society striving to become freer from drugs. The U.S. cannabis producers will be in a position to enter the legal market and provide assurances about the quality of their products. By the same token these producers would have to assume the legal responsibilities derived from the potentially ill effects of their products, very much as today tobacco companies are facing huge legal claims from smokers. It is quite likely that cannabis would continue to be the most popular drug amongst users, but the users would be better protected by better quality assurance and the threat of legal actions against manufacturers under the law. There would not be any significant illicit-drug trade or the need to allocate massive resources to fight it, as there would not be any DTOs to speak of, just some aspiring drug peddlers trying to feed from cracks in the legal drug distribution system. Terrorist groups would not have DTOs to feed from. The terrorist organizations, the FARC and AUC, operating in Colombia and from there in many countries of the hemisphere would run out of the resources provided to them by the illicit-drug trade; hence, their threat to the security of the U.S. and its allies in Latin America would be greatly diminished. Afghanistan would be able to trade its opium and heroin in the open market; hence, the risk of drug resources falling into the hands of terrorist groups like the Taliban and al-Qaeda would be immensely reduced. Mexico would still share a 2,000-mile border with the U.S., but in the absence of DTOs, it would have a better opportunity to build strong democratic institutions for its own good and the good of the U.S. It would no longer be a transshipment country for Colombian cocaine, its local production of cannabis and heroin would be legally introduced into the market. America would be safer as a direct result. Colombia would deal with the production of cocaine, heroin and cannabis in the legal market and away from the influences of organized crime. Corruption would lose a powerful ally with the disappearance of DTOs. The world would continue to be a global village, but a safer and healthier one in the absence of DTOs. U.S. prisons would be relieved of providing accommodations to individuals serving drug-related sentences — there would be very few. Moreover, more young Americans would be replacing with a college education the once inevitable prison education in crime. The Bill of Rights and American democratic values would breathe more easily. The $322 billion of illicit-drug proceeds once filling the coffers of DTOs and requiring the laundering services of their business partners would disappear under the policy and no economic empires would be built with the rivers of easy and inexpensive cash — they would dry up. Therefore, the border crossing of powerful groups nurtured by drug money would cease. Finally, the business community would enjoy a level playing field in the absence of unfair competition fueled by drug money, and customer service and productivity would once again be at the forefront of business enterprises focus of attention.

In the end, a policy of legalization and control on a global scale would do away with the myths surrounding illicit drugs today. The licit use of soft drugs is very likely to keep many people away from hard drugs; the supplier of soft and hard drugs would be different, hence the incentive to push the higher profit margin drugs (hard drugs) on the user would not be present. Drug addiction is very likely to decrease significantly in time. The new system would provide the mechanism for preventing crime by those with a compulsive need for drugs and no money; the addict would be presented with opportunities to kick the habit. In addition, the war on drugs would be over; there would no longer be a need to fight a war that cannot be won; society would have implemented a better solution at a much lower economic and social cost. Those with a genetic propensity to become addicts but not experimenting with drugs because they are not so readily available, would never find out they had this genetic inclination. Those, who did experiment, would be better equipped to handle their addiction in the open as alcohol addicts handle their problem today. There would be no need to go into crime to pay for drug addiction, the drugs would be cheaper, and if not cheap enough for some the system would provide a mechanism to keep the registered addict away from crime and hopefully from his addiction too. Drugs would cease to be an attractive business; the price would be low enough to keep organized crime away from the illicit-drug business.

7.6 Policy Tradeoffs

For a long time America has listened to the evils of illicit drugs and the need to fight the war on drugs as the only way to get rid of these ills. However, it has been over three decades since President Nixon declared the war on drugs, and the bottom line is quite discouraging. Drug use and abuse prevail in America, the trade has generated trillions of dollars in revenue for the DTOs and their stealth business associates, the actions of law enforcement, rather than deterring the expansion of illicit drugs, drive prices up and sustain the economic incentive to get into the business. DTOs have an unending supply of replacements for drug lords who end up in prison. And power has been shifting from truly legitimate hard-working businessmen all over the world and into the hands of the DTOs' stealth business associates who pose a potential security threat to U.S. allies and to the U.S. A policy of legalization and control of today's illicit drugs within the guidelines presented above — on a global scale — provides the best hope of coming to grips with the problem of illicit drugs. The advocates of the status quo — under a mythical cloud — would like America to believe that all that is needed is an additional push, more resources, and a bigger budget; they would like to approach zero tolerance because they know that pure zero tolerance would not be tolerated in a democratic society. However, a policy approaching zero tolerance cannot address the crucial issue of lawlessness undermining the security of America — some of it silent and out of sight. Consumption tolerance would address some of the collateral damage resulting from current policy, but does not get to the core of the drug problem. On the other hand, laissez faire legalization, or a policy approaching it, can effectively deal with the issues of the illicit-drug trade, the war on drugs, and drug money laundering, but would place America dangerously at risk of massive drug use and addiction as happened in many countries in the 18th, 19th and early 20th centuries with opium — too high a social cost. A promising solution is at hand — a lesser evil and a huge improvement over the current policy — and it requires resolve from policymakers and support from the American public. As Levine and Reinarman concluded in their essay: "The full range of alternatives to current U.S. drug policy should be studied and debated — from futuristic visions to pragmatic reforms that could be implemented immediately. For drug policy, as was the case with alcohol policy, discussion of alternatives is an essential part of the transition from prohibition to regulation." This author understands that such policy exploration exercise ought to take place within the framework provided by a policy of legalization and control on a global scale as presented in this chapter. This is the only way to address the four key issues surrounding the problem of illicit drugs: drug use and abuse, the illicit-drug trade, the war on drugs, and drug money laundering. Only by addressing these four issues as a unit, with an integral approach, can America expect to come to grips with the scourge of today's illicit drugs.

Diagrams 7.1, 7.2, and 7.3 illustrate the expected behavior of some key parameters — key performance indicators or KPIs — as they are observed under the drug policy spectrum from a zero tolerance policy at the extreme left of the x-axis, passing through a consumption tolerance policy, a legalization and control policy, and ending in a laissez faire legalization policy at the extreme right. Current policy is located somewhere between zero tolerance and consumption tolerance. Diagram 7.1 shows:

- **HIV/AIDS and hepatitis C infection** peaking as there is a move toward a policy approaching zero tolerance, and then it drops to zero at the point of full implementation of zero tolerance. It decreases significantly as we move from the current policy towards laissez faire legalization, passing through consumption tolerance and legalization and control.

- **Addiction and drug use** can be expected to increase somewhat as we move from the current policy towards a policy of consumption tolerance, but it drops significantly under a policy of legalization and control. It peaks though under the implementation of a laissez faire legalization and it increases as this state is approached. It remains fairly high as we move from current policy towards a zero tolerance policy and drops dramatically under a policy of zero tolerance.

DIAGRAM 7.1 HEALTH PERFORMANCE INDICATORS ACROSS DRUG POLICY SPECTRUM

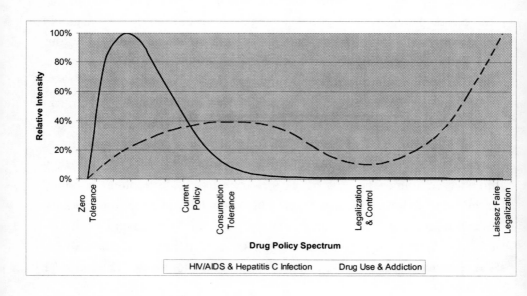

Diagram 7.2 reveals:

• **The prison population and the drug law enforcement budget** both peaking as zero tolerance is approached and coming down all the way to zero as laissez faire legalization policy is approached.

• **The protection of civil liberties** has the lowest point at zero tolerance and increases steadily until it peaks at laissez faire legalization.

• **The strength of Mexican democratic institutions** behaves in a similar way to the protection of civil liberties curve.

DIAGRAM 7.2 LAWLESSNESS PERFORMANCE INDICATORS ACROSS DRUG POLICY SPECTRUM

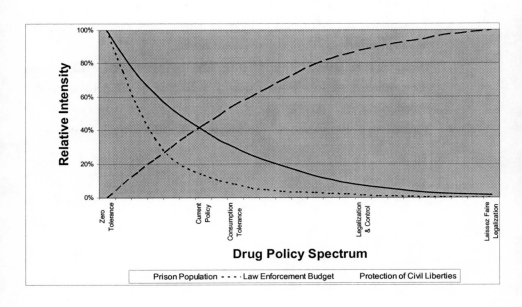

Diagram 7.3 illustrates:

- **Illicit-drug revenue** peaking as a zero tolerance policy is approached, but it drops to zero under the full implementation of the policy. As we move from current policy towards consumption tolerance illicit-drug revenue decreases slightly, comes close to zero under a legalization and control policy and hits zero at a laissez faire liberalization policy.

- **Drugs will reach more children** under a laissez faire legalization policy, but they reach a significant number of children under a policy approaching zero tolerance, though the number comes to zero at full zero tolerance. It is lower under a legalization and control policy than under current policy.

- **The transfer of drug money to terrorist groups** behaves similarly to the illicit-drug revenue curve.

- **The power of Mexican DTOs in their own country** also behaves similarly to the drug revenue curve.

- **Drug driven corruption within law enforcement and among government officials** also has a behavior similar to the drug revenue curve.

- **Laundered drug money** also behaves like the drug money curve.

DIAGRAM 7.3 CIVIL LIBERTIES AND FINANCIAL PERFORMANCE INDICATORS ACROSS DRUG POLICY SPECTRUM

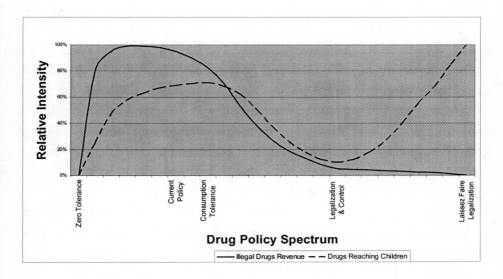

Leadership is called for to carry forward the design and implementation of a new drug policy. American political and social leaders must stand up and be counted, nothing less is expected by the parents of young Americans. These parents are eager to meet face to face with a leadership strong enough to come to grips with the scourge of drugs hovering over the towns and cities of this country. It is also important for these parents to understand the implications of current policy, see the myths for what they really are, and assimilate the root causes driving the drug problem in America today; without their support, no politician would dare propose a change in policy — they do not wish to lose an election. Nothing short of an innovative policy will do the job, tinkering with current policy, treating symptoms as if they were the real cause of the problem has only clouded the landscape and made the problem even more complex than it need be. In coming to grips with the drug problem, these leaders will encounter great opposition from the advocates of the

257

status quo; the same people who for decades preferred to act based on beliefs rather than make an effort to understand the facts and proceed based on them. Leadership will be in high demand to effectively face the many special interest groups linked to current policy. These interest groups include the DTOs, their stealth and very powerful business associates, and the law enforcement industry that keeps the war on drugs alive; also, the unethical politicians and government officials, who directly or indirectly benefit from the policy. They are strange bedfellows, but all of them are benefiting from the current policy at the expense of the nation's health, the future of American youth, and even national security. Asking those responsible for America's law enforcement activities to remake themselves, to change gears, and play a different role in monitoring the drug cultivation-production-distribution cycle under a new policy, instead of organizing raids and sting operations to demonstrate their effectiveness, requires strong leadership. The task requires grabbing the bull by the horns, but it is indeed the best path to deliver, perhaps not a drug free America, but an America where the use of drugs is greatly diminished and where the collateral damage resulting from the current policy disappears. Opting for a policy of drug legalization and control is equivalent to choosing the lesser evil — in lieu of an impossible dream — as the most effective and expedient way to improve the lot of Americans; it is also the option offering the greatest rewards and opportunities within the drug policy spectrum. Besides, American leadership is called upon to drive a new global drug paradigm based on a universal policy of legalization and control.

APPENDIX A - THE STOCK TRANSACTION MODEL ILLUSTRATION

The stock-transaction model is a compelling payback mechanism involving a private and public stock transaction combination of the stock of the company laundering money. This illustration uses the terms of beneficiary and business as explained in Chapter IV and is reflected in Tables A1, A2, A3 and A4. The operation is designed as a medium to a long-term payback vehicle. This particular example illustrates how $275 million of drug money introduced into a laundering process can yield $220.55 million of clean money to the beneficiary company controlled by the drug lord, a conversion factor of 80% — not a bad feat. Through the process the legitimate business associate increases the value of his company, thanks to the drug money being laundered, by $236.7 million — a nice reward for the stealth operation. The conversion factor is 86% in the case of the legitimate business associate. And finally, the government tax collector gets $100 million just for fulfilling its responsibilities, a conversion factor of 36%; not bad for standing on the sidelines. Following is the detailed illustration of how the stock-transaction model works. To set the stage, the operation begins with the private sale of a block of stock of the business to the beneficiary of 42.5 million shares at $1.00 per share, a transaction valued at $42.5 million and paid for with clean money; the business retains 100 million shares worth $100 million to begin with; this operation is illustrated in Table A2 in the sections of Ownership Structure and Capital Structure. Next, fictitious sales with drug money are registered in the business and the money delivered to the business, this is shown under Fictitious Sales (DTO) in the Income Statement in Table A1. A total of $250 million is introduced over a five-year period plus the corresponding sales tax of $25 million (a 10% tax rate is assumed); the sales tax is shown in Table A4 under Sales Tax, this is the table reflecting the government revenue from the laundering operation. A total of $275 million of drug money is introduced by the DTO into the business. These sales inflate the business performance and this sets the stage for a public offering of the company stock at a healthy P/E ratio. In the example, in Table A2 under the section Company Valuation the price/earnings ratio (P/E) is shown to increase from 10 in Year 1 to 18 in Year 5, prior to the initial public offering of the stock or IPO; this reflects the improved performance of the company, as reflected in the Income Statement, over the five years of the exercise. In Year 5 the company goes public through a combined package of new and existing stock; the package includes the 42.5 million shares of the beneficiary and a new stock issue of 57.5 million shares, making the total offering of 100 million shares. This operation is reflected in Table A2 under the "At IPO" column in the Ownership Structure, Capital Structure, and Capital Account sections. When the IPO is executed at the market price of $6.19 per share, the beneficiary obtains $263.05 million from the IPO, recovering the original investment of $42.5 million of clean money and obtaining a capital gain of $220.55 million, coming from a legitimate stock market transaction. There is no capital gains tax in the example, which is the case for this kind of transaction in Mexico and other countries. The new public stock holders buy 50% of the business shares with the expectation of the continued growth of the stock, while the original owners of the business retain control with their 50%. In the transaction the business obtains additional capital of $355.89 million from the public stockholders. Therefore the business has a new capital account or book value of $673.39 million (including the retained earnings of the previous five years); this capital is 50% owned by the original stockholders and 50% by the new public stockholders, each group owns 100 million shares of stock after the IPO and the beneficiary no longer owns any shares. The net result of this five-year laundering operation is that the DTO, through the beneficiary, converted $275 million of drug money into $220.55 million of legitimate capital gains — clean and legitimate money for all practical purposes: a conversion factor of 80%. In the process, the legitimate business associate increased the value of his holding in the company from $100 million to $336.7 million an increase of 237 % through the help of the $275 million from the DTO: a conversion factor relative to the laundered money of 86%. The government does not stay behind in the operation; it collects $100 million in sales and income taxes over the five-year period: a conversion factor of 36% over the $275 million supplied by the DTO to the laundering process. This model is a powerful tool in the hands of the DTO/beneficiary-legitimate business partnership to launder drug money away from the inquisitive sight of law enforcement.

Table A1.- Stock-transaction Model Involving Legitimate
Business, Beneficiary Business and DTO
Income Statement **(Million $)**

	Year 0	Year 1	Year 2	Year 3	Year 4	Year 5	Total 1-5
Legit Sales	400.00	400.00	400.00	400.00	400.00	400.00	2000.00
Fictitious Sales (DTO)	0.00	30.00	40.00	50.00	60.00	70.00	250.00
Total Sales	400.00	430.00	440.00	450.00	460.00	470.00	2250.00
CG&SS	300.00	300.00	300.00	300.00	300.00	300.00	1500.00
Gross Profit	100.00	130.00	140.00	150.00	160.00	170.00	750.00
Admin Costs	100.00	100.00	100.00	100.00	100.00	100.00	500.00
EBT	0.00	30.00	40.00	50.00	60.00	70.00	250.00
Income Taxes (30%)	0.00	9.00	12.00	15.00	18.00	21.00	75.00
Net Profit	0.00	21.00	28.00	35.00	42.00	49.00	175.00

Table A2. - Stock-transaction Model Involving Legitimate Business, Beneficiary Business and DTO — Ownership, Capital Structure, Company Valuation, and Capital Account

	Year 0	Year 1	Year 2	Year 3	Year 4	Year 5	At IPO
Ownership Structure (Shares in Millions)							
Legitimate Owners	100.00	100.00	100.00	100.00	100.00	100.00	100.00
Beneficiary Owners [1]	0.00	42.50	42.50	42.50	42.50	42.50	0.00
Public Owners	0.00	0.00	0.00	0.00	0.00	0.00	100.00
Total Ownership	100.00	142.50	142.50	142.50	142.50	142.50	200.00
Capital Structure (Million $)							
Legitimate Owners	100.00	100.00	100.00	100.00	100.00	100.00	100.00
Beneficiary Owners	0.00	42.50	42.50	42.50	42.50	42.50	0.00
Public Owners	0.00	0.00	0.00	0.00	0.00	0.00	100.00
Retained Earnings	0.00	21.00	49.00	84.00	126.00	175.00	175.00
Add Public Capital	0.00	0.00	0.00	0.00	0.00	0.00	298.39
Total Capital Account	100.00	163.50	191.50	226.50	268.50	317.50	673.39
Company Valuation							
EPS ($)	0.00	0.15	0.20	0.25	0.29	0.34	0.25
P/E	N/A	10.00	12.00	14.00	16.00	18.00	18.00
Mkt Value (Million $)	100.00	142.50	336.00	490.00	672.00	882.00	882.00
Price per Share [2] ($)	1.00	1.00	2.36	3.44	4.72	6.19	4.41
Capital Account (Million $)							
Paid Capital	100.00	142.50	142.50	142.50	142.50	142.50	200.00
Retained Earnings	0.00	21.00	49.00	84.00	126.00	175.00	175.00
Paid In Excess Cap [3]	0.00	0.00	0.00	0.00	0.00	0.00	298.39
Total Capital	100.00	163.50	191.50	226.50	268.50	317.50	673.39
Conversion Factor	0.86						236.7/27!

Note 1   Beneficiary owners buy with clean money shares of the business doing the laundering in Year
Note 2   IPO at end of Year 5 at Year 5 price per share. Afterwards IPO EPS are diluted and price drop:
Note 3   Business retains capital paid in excess at IPO time, increasing value to original shareholders.

Table A3. - Stock-transaction Model Involving Legitimate Business, Beneficiary Business and DTO — Cash Flow In and Out of Beneficiary Business and DTO (Million $)

	Year 0	Year 1	Year 2	Year 3	Year 4	Year 5	At IPO
ney Movements between DTO and Beneficiary							
o Laundry from DTO							
titious Sales		30.00	40.00	50.00	60.00	70.00	
% Sales Tax		3.00	4.00	5.00	6.00	7.00	
mulative Entering		33.00	77.00	132.00	198.00	275.00	275.00
t Laundry-Capital Gain							
t to Beneficiary [4]							220.55
nversion Factor: 0.80							220/275

te 4   Beneficiary capital gain at IPO time after recovering investment in business stock.

Table A4. - Stock-transaction Model Involving Legitimate Business, Beneficiary Business and DTO — Government Revenue from Laundering Operation (Million $)

	Year 0	Year 1	Year 2	Year 3	Year 4	Year 5	Totals
Sales Tax		3.00	4.00	5.00	6.00	7.00	25.00
Income Tax		9.00	12.00	15.00	18.00	21.00	75.00
Cumulative Govt Revenue [5]		12.00	28.00	48.00	72.00	100.00	100.00
Conversion Factor: 0.36							100/275

Note 5   Taxes collected over 5 years.

263

APPENDIX B - BUILDING ECONOMIC EMPIRES WITH DRUG MONEY — ILLUSTRATION

This Appendix illustrates the results of a hypothetical laundering operation over a twenty-year period. The model was developed on a yearly basis, but the results are presented in a compacted format — five-year blocks — for clarity. The assumptions behind this laundering operation are the following:

- Fifty percent of the money is laundered through a fees-paid model and 50% through a stock-transaction model. Two billion dollars are laundered every year for each of the twenty years.
- The fees-paid model yields a payback with a pre-income tax conversion factor of 70% for the beneficiary and 30% for the business on the same year the money is introduced into the business. This assumption is derived from the example in Table 4.2 of Chapter IV.
- The stock-transaction model yields a net conversion factor of 80% for the beneficiary and also 86% for the business. This payback is received in a five-year cycle at the end of every fifth year. These conversion factors are the ones illustrated in Appendix A.
- The benefit accrued to the government tax collector in both models is 36% of the total drug money delivered for laundering. Some is derived from the sales tax (10%) and the rest from the income tax (30%) in both models.
- It is assumed that both the business and the beneficiary invest the clean proceeds derived from the laundry at a 5% compounded annual rate of return.
- Over the twenty-year period, $40 billion in drug money is introduced into the laundering operation.

The results obtained from the twenty-year laundering operation illustrated in Table B are as follows:

- The business obtains net benefits of $32 billion, of this money $11 billion result from reinvesting in legitimate businesses or monetary instruments, at a compounded annual rate of return of 5%, their share of the laundered money received. The beneficiary gets $38.7 billion, of which $13.8 billion result from reinvesting in legitimate businesses or monetary instruments, at a compounded annual rate of return of 5%, the laundered money received by the beneficiary. The tax collector, just by standing on the sidelines, gets $14.5 billion.
- The net direct losers are the unsuspecting investors who bought stock in the various laundering companies' IPOs and may experience a temporary or permanent drop in the value of the stock.

The model illustrates the transfer of wealth amongst the different players, some as active participants made out like "bandits", others as passive players register substantial benefits — the government tax collector. The other set of players — the unsuspecting stock market investors — end up footing the bill. It may be argued that the model is somewhat simplistic, and it is so in a certain way. Nevertheless, the overall laundering mechanism is valid and there is no reason why it cannot be currently in use. It is very likely that there are some additional costs associated with keeping the legal business structure of the beneficiary which are not included in the model. Also, not all the profits shown may materialize, as the beneficiary may choose to use some of the money to pay salaries and/or bonuses to its employees and/or associates of the DTO or the beneficiary organization instead of reinvesting it. On the other hand, the model would be completely valid if it reflected a complementary drug laundering operation on top of an existing legitimate business structure. In reality such a laundering machine can be built and it would be very difficult to discover by law enforcement, as it operates within the rules of the legitimate business world in the formal economy.

Table B. - Money Laundering Setup over Twenty Years
(Million dollars)

| | YEARS OF OPERATION | | | | TOTAL |
	1-5	6-10	11-15	16-20	20 Years
DTO's Contributions to Laundry Operation					
To Fees Paid Model	5000	5000	5000	5000	20000
To Stock Transaction Model	5000	5000	5000	5000	20000
Total Yearly DTO Contribution	10000	10000	10000	10000	40000
Business Returns from Laundry Operation					
Benefits from Fees Paid Model	955	955	955	955	3818
Benefits from Stock Transaction Model	4300	4300	4300	4300	17200
Benefits from Investing Laundered Benefits	100	1580	3468	5878	11026
Total Benefits to Business	5355	6834	8723	11132	32044
Beneficiary Returns from Laundry Operation					
Benefits from Fees Paid Model	2227	2227	2227	2227	8909
Benefits from Stock Transaction Model	4000	4000	4000	4000	16000
Benefits from Investing Laundering Benefits	234	2019	4298	7206	13757
Total Benefits to Beneficiary	6461	8247	10525	13433	38666
Government Income from Laundry Operation					
Sales Tax from:					
Fees Paid Model	455	455	455	455	1818
Stock Transaction Model	455	455	455	455	1818
Total Sales Tax	909	909	909	909	3636
Income Tax-Fees Paid Model	2727	2727	2727	2727	10909
Total Government Income from Laundry Operation	3636	3636	3636	3636	14545
Conversion Factors in Laundering Model					
Sales Tax Rate	10%	10%	10%	10%	10%
% Fees Paid Model to Legal Business (1)	30%	30%	30%	30%	30%
%Fees Paid Model to Beneficiary Business (1)	70%	70%	70%	70%	70%
% Stock Transaction Model to Legal Business (2)	86%	86%	86%	86%	86%
% Stock Transaction Model to Beneficiary Bus (2)	80%	80%	80%	80%	80%
Growth Factor for Additional Legal Businesses	5%	5%	5%	5%	5%
Growth Factor for Additional Beneficiary Bus	5%	5%	5%	5%	5%
Corporate Income Tax Rate	30%	30%	30%	30%	30%

(1) Transferred in same year.
(2) Benefits accruing with a five-year delay.

FOOTNOTES

Chapter 1

1. 2005 World Drug Report. United Nations Office on Drugs and Crime (UNODC). ISBN 92-1-148200-3 Volume 1 and ISBN 92-1-148201-1 Volume 2.

2. See National Institute on Drug Abuse web site at http://www.nida.nih.gov./

3. The figures reported in the 2006 World Drug Report do not change significantly from the 2005 Report suggesting a rather stable world market. UNODC ISBN 92-1-148214-3 Volume 1 and ISBN 92-1-148215-1 Volume 2.

4. 2004 National Survey on Drug Use and Health (NSDUH). Department of Health and Human Services, Substance Abuse and Mental Health Services Administration, Office of Applied Studies, September 2005. www.oas.samhsa.gov. Table 1.1A.

5. What America's Users Spend on Illegal Drugs 1988-1998. Office of National Drug Control Policy, December 2000.

6. What America's Users Spend on Illegal Drugs 1988-1998. Office of National Drug Control Policy, December 2000, pp 21-23.

7. Binge alcohol use is defined as drinking five or more drinks on the same occasion (i.e., at the same time or within a couple of hours of each other) on at least one day in the past thirty days. Heavy alcohol use is defined as drinking five or more drinks on the same occasion on each of five or more days in the past thirty days; all heavy alcohol users are also binge alcohol users.

8. Table A below illustrates drug use during the **past month, and abuse plus dependency, as a percentage of lifetime use**. It complements the results shown in Table 1.2 and goes a long way to suggest that drug use does not necessarily lead to drug addiction. The data is a compendium of data extracted from Table 1.1A of the 2004 National Survey on Drug Use and Health and from the ONDCP report What America's Users Spend on Illegal Drugs 1988-1998. The data suggest that some of these drugs are more

addictive than others, though all of them are deemed by U.S. health authorities as damaging to humans.

Table A - 2004 Selected U.S. Illicit-Drug Use in Lifetime, and Past Month Users, and Abusers plus Dependents among Persons Aged Twelve and Older
(Figures in thousands)

Drug Type	Lifetime Use	Past Month Use		Abusers & Dependents	
Heroin	3,145	977	31.1%	977	31.1%
Cocaine	34,153	2,021	5.9%	1,571	4.6%
Cannabis	96,772	14,576	15.1%	4,469	4.6%
Ecstasy & ATS	34,333	929	4.0%	450	1.3%

NOTE: % of sometime in lifetime users shown for "past month users" and "abusers and dependents".

Chapter 2

1. This chapter relies on information provided by the United Nations and U.S. government agencies. These sources are used to illustrate the nature of the illicit-drug industry as well as to validate the figures associated with the business. The reader will get a real-world feeling through the validation of the size of the drug business. The cultivation-production-distribution cycle by which illicit drugs are produced and finally sold to the consumer is illustrated. Further along, the evolution of the drug trade from the 1980s through to the present day is reviewed. Three decades of critical history, a period of time during which the industry grew beyond anybody's wildest imagination, are covered. The history of three drug supplying countries, Afghanistan, Colombia, and Mexico, is covered in sufficient detail for the uninitiated reader to become acquainted with the points of origin of some of the drugs. In recent years, and particularly after September 11, 2001, the issue of international terrorism has taken center stage in the United States and all over the world. The exploration of the links of terrorists with drug traffickers is included because of the implications this relationship may have for U.S. national security. Finally, the collateral damage inflicted by the drug trade upon American society is examined.

2. What America's Users Spend on Illegal Drugs 1988-1998. Office of National Drug Control Policy, December 2000. The ONDCP publication presents the data in 1998 dollars; we have converted it to current dollars. Hence, the figures reflect the actual or current dollars of the years in which they were spent.

3. 2005 World Drug Report. United Nations Office on Drugs and Crime (UNODC). ISBN 92-1-148201-1 Volume 2, Sections 7.1 and 7.2.

4. 2005 World Drug Report. United Nations Office on Drugs and Crime (UNODC). ISBN 92-1-148200-3, Volume 1, Chapter 2.

5. The UN exercise used a conservative approach; a more liberal approach would yield a global retail revenue estimate around $400 billion.

6. The UN 2005 World Drug Report shows, in Chapter 2, the 2003 estimates by region and the U.S. are included in North America. Because, North America includes Mexico and Canada besides the U.S., our analysis disaggregated the North American figures by taking into consideration the percentages of users in each country provided in Chapter 8 of the UN report and each country's population. The analysis assumes the per capita consumption was identical in all countries of the region. This methodology may introduce a margin of error not greater than 10%, given that the U.S. accounts for about 90% of the North American market. The resulting share of consumption by each country is shown in the table below for each drug.

Distribution of Illicit-Drug Consumption in Countries in North America (% of consumption in North America)

Drug Type	United States	Canada	Mexico
Heroin	88.1	6.8	5.1
Cocaine	89.3	6.6	4.1
Cannabis	87.6	11.0	1.4
ATS	93.1	4.6	2.3
Ecstasy	91.1	8.6	0.3

As illustrated in the table above, the U.S. accounts for most of the illicit-drug consumption in North America, hovering around 90% for all drugs. To estimate the quantity of each illicit drug consumed in the U.S., the retail prices in Chapter 7 of the 2005 UN report were used. It should be noted that Chapter 2 of the 2005 UN World Drug Report provided valuable insights into the composition of the global drug market. This chapter was eliminated from the 2006 Report.

7. As stated by Dick Lamargo, DEA Chief for Financial Investigations in the   Caribbean and Southern Latin America at a Sympo-

sium in Florida International University in November 2005. Reported in El Nuevo Herald, November 24, 2005. Lamargo reported a $65 billion U.S. illicit-drug trade. Our analysis supported by UN reports yields a U.S. trade volume of $125 billion.

8. Calculated from Chapter 2 - Table 7 and the U.S. price for cannabis reported in   Table 7.3 of the 2005 World Drug Report UNODC using U.S. percentage from table in footnote 6 above. These numbers have a margin of error no bigger than 10% because Chapter 2 of the UN document reports figures for North America and the assumptions reflected in footnote 6 are incorporated.

9. Calculated from Chapter 2-Table 10 & 11 of the 2005 World Drug Report UNODC using U.S. percentage from table in footnote 6 above.

10. Calculated from Chapter 2-Table 12 & 13 of the 2005 World Drug Report UNODC using U.S. percentage from table in footnote 6 above.

11. The UN estimated that 31.5% of the ecstasy consumed in 2003 in North America was produced in North America; the balance was imported from Central and Western Europe.

12. Drug Intelligence Brief. The Evolution of the Drug Threat: The 1980s through 2002. Prepared by the DEA Intelligence Division, Office of Domestic Intelligence, Domestic Strategic Unit, in May 2002. DEA-02046.

13. UNODC 2005 World Drug Report, Section 5.1. Heroin production for 2003 in Mexico was 8.4 MT and in Colombia 7.6 MT.

14. Mexican political analyst Jorge Fernández-Menéndez, author of El Otro Poder (The Other Power). Nuevo Siglo Aguilar, 2001. Fernandez-Menendez raises the suspicion that U.S. authorities look the other way when U.S. domestic cannabis production is involved.

15. The Drug Trade in Colombia: A Threat Assessment. March 2002. Prepared by the South America/Caribbean Strategic Intelligence

Unit (NIBC) of the Office of International Intelligence. The report reflects information through December 2001. DEA-02006.

16. Drug Intelligence Brief. Mexico-Country Brief. January 2001. DEA-01002. Prepared by the Mexico/Central America Unit of the Office of International Enforcement Support.

17. Idem, page 1.

18. 2005 World Drug Report. United Nations Office on Drugs and Crime (UNODC). ISBN 92-1-148201-1 Volume 2, Section 7.2.

19. Drug Intelligence Brief. Mexico-Country Brief. January 2001. DEA-01002. Page 4.

20. Mexico Country Profile for 2003. Drug Intelligence report. November 2003, DEA-03047. Page 13.

21. Harrison, Lana D., Michael Backenheimer and James A. Inciardi (1995), Cannabis use in the United States: Implications for policy. In: Peter Cohen & Arjan Sas (Eds)(1996), *Cannabisbeleid in Duitsland, Frankrijk en de Verenigde Staten*. Amsterdam, Centrum voor Drugsonderzoek, Universiteit van Amsterdam. pp. 231-236.

22. Speech by Errol J. Chavez, Special Agent in Charge, DEA Phoenix Division. April 30, 2003

23. Drug Intelligence Brief. Drugs and Terrorism: A New Perspective. Prepared by the DEA Intelligence Division, International Strategic Support Section, Europe/Asia/Africa Unit. The report reflects information received prior to June 2002. DEA-02039.

24. ILLICIT: How smugglers, traffickers, and copycats are hijacking the global economy. Moises Naim, October 2005. Doubleday.

Chapter 3

1. Certain drugs have been illicit in the U.S. since Congress passed the Harrison Narcotics Act in 1914. This Act imposed the force of law over the right to use or abuse the body as the individual saw fit. What President Nixon did, by declaring the "war on drugs",

was to place additional emphasis, focus and resources on the persecution of those in violation of drug prohibition legislation.

2. Drugs: Cash Flow for Organized Crime. The Economic Addiction to Illegal Drugs. Remarks, by Antonio Maria Costa, Executive Director, United Nations Office on Drugs and Crime, to the Diplomatic Academy, Warsaw, Poland, February 1, 2005. Page 5.

3. Drug Intelligence Brief. The Evolution of the Drug Threat: The 1980s through 2002. Prepared by the DEA Intelligence Division, Office of Domestic Intelligence, Domestic Strategic Unit, in May 2002. DEA-02046.

4. This yield relationship was true in 2003; it became twelve times larger in 2004 with the drop in the price of opium. Quote from page 2 of speech referenced in footnote 2 of this chapter.

5. Karsai Rejects U.S. Criticism on Opium, the New York Times, May 22, 2005.

6. The Drug Trade in Colombia: A Threat Assessment. DEA Intelligence Division. Prepared by the South America/ Caribbean Strategic Intelligence Unit (NIBC) of the Office of International Intelligence. Published March 2002 with reflecting information through December 2001. Code DEA-02006.

7. Las FARC se vuelcan sobre América Latina. (The FARC turn on Latin America) Gerardo Reyes, El Nuevo Herald. March 27. 2005.

8. United Self-Defense Forces of Colombia (AUC) Indictment. John Ashcroft, Attorney General. Remarks at AUC Indictment Press Conference. Washington, DC, September 24, 2002.

9. Drug Enforcement Administration. Mexico: Country Profile for 2003. Drug Intelligence Report. Prepared by the Mexico/Central America Strategic Intelligence Unit with information received prior to September 2003. Code DEA-03047.

10. The number of drug-related murders in Mexico in 2005 was reported by the Mexican newspaper Reforma to be 1,261 and the

year to date figure for early September 2006 suggested a trend leading to close to 2,500 murders in 2006.

11. HEAVY TRAFFIC: 30 years of headlines and major ops from the case files of the DEA. By David Robbins. Published by CHAMBERLAIN BROS. a member of Penguin Group (USA) Inc. 2005.

12. Reporter Steven T. Jones of New Times published in June 24, 1999 and available in http://www.mapinc.org/drugnews/v99/n667/a01. From the Media Awareness Project (MAP) of DrugSense a non-profit organization.

13. Bureau of Justice Statistics, www.ojp.usdoj.gov/bjs/.

14. www.usdoj.gov/dea/deamuseum/dea_history_book/1985_1990.

15. Ex-Officer Admits to Robberies, Los Angeles Times. Reported by Matt Lait and Scott Writers, Times Staff Writers. October 20, 2004.

16. Temptation Stalks Officers in Drug Cases, by Michael Kranish. Boston Globe, August 19, 1989.

17. General Gutierrez to Head Up Mexico's War Against Drugs, by Mark Fineman from Mexico City. The Los Angeles Times. December 6, 1996.

18. Ernesto Zedillo was President of Mexico from 1994 to 2000.

19. U.S.-Mexican Drug Collaboration Fails When Lives Are on the Line, by Molly Moore and John Ward Anderson. The Washington Post, November 5, 1997.

20. Operation Millennium was a multi-jurisdictional, multi-agency investigation that tied drug trafficking activity within the United States to the highest levels of the international cocaine trade. Operation Millennium, a one-year investigation, concluded in October 1999 with the arrest of thirty-one individuals, including Fabio Ochoa-Vasquez and Alejandro Bernal-Madrigal, former members of the original Medellín cartel. At the time of their arrest, they were considered two of the most powerful international traffickers of cocaine in the world.

21. Incarcerated America. Human Rights Watch Backgrounder. April 2003.

22. Why Our Drug Laws Have Failed and What We Can Do About It, Judge James P. Gray. Temple University Press. Judge James P. Gray is a veteran Judge of the Superior Court in Orange County in Southern California, former federal prosecutor in Los Angeles, and criminal defense Attorney in the Navy JAG Corps. Judge Gray has fought for a change of U.S. drug policy.

Chapter 4

1. ILLICIT: How smugglers, traffickers, and copycats are hijacking the global economy. Moises Naim, October 2005. Doubleday.

2. From FinCEN Strategic Plan for Fiscal Years 2003-2008. http://www.fincen.gov/strategicplan2003_2008.pdf

3. Data obtained directly by the author during a field visit to Mexico.

4. As stated by Dick Lamargo, DEA Chief for Financial Investigations in the Caribbean and Southern Latin America at a Symposium in Florida International University in November 2005. Reported in El Nuevo Herald, November 24, 2005. Lamargo reported lees than 1.5% of the $65 billion trade was intercepted. Our analysis yields a trade volume of $125 billion; hence less than 1% is intercepted every year.

5. United States Department of State, Money Laundering and Financial Crimes Report, March 1, 2000. Published in the Web at http://www.state.gov/

6. Mexico Country Profile for 2003. DEA Drug intelligence Report November 2003. Code DEA-03047.

7. Corruption Hampers Mexican Police in Border Drug War, by Ginger Thompson. Published in NYT on July 5, 2005.

Chapter 5

1. 2004 National Survey on Drug Use and Health. Department of Health and Human Services, Substance Abuse and Mental Health Services Administration, Office of Applied Studies, September 2005. www.oas.samhsa.gov.
2. El Otro Poder: Las Redes del Narcotráfico, la Política y la Violencia en Mexico. (The Other Power: The drug trafficking networks, politics, and violence in Mexico.) Published by Nuevo Siglo Aguilar, Mexico. September 2001.
3. Why Our Drug Laws Have Failed and What We Can Do About It, Judge James P. Gray. Temple University Press. Judge James P. Gray is a veteran Judge of the Superior Court in Orange County in Southern California, former federal prosecutor in Los Angeles, and criminal defense Attorney in the Navy JAG Corps. Judge Gray has fought for a change of U.S. drug policy.

Chapter 6

1. Professor Harry G. Levine, Department of Sociology, Queens College, Flushing, New York, and Professor Craig Reinarman, Department of Sociology, University of California At Santa Cruz, Santa Cruz, California.
2. Harry G. Levine and Craig Reinarman. "Alcohol Prohibition and Drug Prohibition: Lessons From Alcohol Policy for Drug Policy." pp. 43 to 76 in Jefferson M. Fish (ed) Drugs *and Society: US Public Policy.* Roman and Littlefield, 2006. Also available at CEDRO. http://www.cedro-uva.org/lib/levine.alcohol.html.
3. The Economic Results of Prohibition by Clark Warburton. 1932 Columbia University Press. The book was reprinted by AMS PRESS, INC. in 1968, but is currently out of print.
4. Toward Liquor Control by Raymond B. Fosdick and Albert L. Scott, Harper and Brothers Publishers, New York and London 1933.
5. Idem, pp 15-18.

6. Idem, pp 18-19.

7. Idem, p 21.

8. Idem, p 29.

9. Idem, p 33.

10. Idem, p 39.

11. Idem, p 40.

12. Idem, p 41.

13. Idem, pp 41-52.

14. Idem, p 61.

15. Idem, Chapter Five, pp 63-93.

16. Idem, Chapter Six, pp 94-106.

17. Idem, Chapter Seven, pp 107-130.

18. Idem, Chapter Eight, pp 131-146.

19. Idem, Chapter Nine, pp 147-152.

20. Brecher, E. M. 1972. *Licit and Illicit Drugs*. Boston: Little Brown.

Chapter 7

1. Alfred W. McCoy is professor of Southeast Asian History at the University of Wisconsin, Madison. Educated at Columbia and Yale, he has spent over thirty years writing about Southeast Asian history and politics.

2. Opium History Up To 1958 A.D. Essay published by Alfred W. McCoy in www.opioids.com/opium/history.

3. Harry G. Levine and Craig Reinarman. "Alcohol Prohibition and Drug Prohibition: Lessons From Alcohol Policy for Drug Policy." pp. 43 to 76 in Jefferson M. Fish (ed) Drugs *and Society: US Public Policy*. Roman and Littlefield, 2006. Also available at CEDRO. http://www.cedro-uva.org/lib/levine.alcohol.html.

4. Speaking Out Against Drug Legalization. DEA publication May 2003 in **www.dea.gov**.

5. Toward Liquor Control by Raymond B. Fosdick and Albert L Scott, Harper and Brothers Publishers, New York and London 1933.

INDEX OF TABLES,

CHARTS AND DIAGRAMS

DESCRIPTION OF ACRONYMS

AAPA: The Association Against the Prohibition Amendment. An organization during the 1920s which advocated the end of alcohol prohibition.

ATS: Amphetamine-type stimulants.

AUC: Autodefensas Unidas de Colombia (United Self-defense of Colombia), a right wing paramilitary group operating in Colombia, presumably against the FARC.

DEA: Drug Enforcement Administration. An agency of the U.S. Department of Justice.

DTO: Drug Trafficking Organization, a term used in the book to identify the multiple illegal organizations involved in drug trafficking.

FARC: Fuerzas Armadas Revolucionarias de Colombia (Armed Revolutionary Forces of Colombia), a leftwing guerrilla group fighting the government of Colombia.

FinCEN: Financial Crimes Enforcement Network, a Division of the U.S. Treasury Department.

FRB: Federal Reserve Board, a U.S. government banking regulatory agency.

GDP: Gross Domestic Product.

IPO: Initial public offer of a company stock to the general public. Subsequent to the IPO there can be other public offers usually referred to as secondary public offers. Subsequent to the IPO the company stock trades in the stock exchange. Prior to the IPO, the company stock can be bought and sold in private transactions.

LAPD: City of Los Angeles Police Department.

NGO: Non-governmental organization.

NIAAA: National Institute on Alcohol Abuse and Alcoholism. A dependency of the U.S. Department of Health and Human Services.

NIDA: National Institute on Drug Abuse. A dependency of the U.S. Department of Health and Human Services.

NRDU: National Registry of Drug Users. A term used in the book to describe a potential instrument of a new drug policy based on legalization and control of today's illicit drugs.

NSDUH: National Survey on Drug Use and Health. A survey done periodically by the U.S. government to identify patterns of illegal drug use in the U.S.

OCC: Office of the Comptroller of the Currency, a U.S. government banking regulatory agency.

OFAC: Office of Foreign Assets Control, a division of the U.S. Treasury Department.

OMAS: Other Mind Altering Substances. Substances different from narcotics (heroin, cocaine, cannabis) such as ATS and ecstasy.

ONDCP: Office of National Drug Control Policy. A dependency of the Executive Branch of the U.S. government in charge of coordinating drug policy and programs in the U.S.

UN: United Nations Organization.

UNODC: United Nations Office on Drugs and Crime. The agency of the United Nations in charge of monitoring illicit-drug use and trade worldwide.

U.S.: United States of America.

USG: United States Government.

BIBLIOGRAPHY

1. 2005 World Drug Report, United Nations Office on Drugs and Crime. Volume 1 ISBN 92-1-148200-3 and Volume 2 ISBN 92-1-148201-1.
2. 2006 World Drug Report, United Nations Office on Drugs and Crime. Volume 1 ISBN 92-1-148214-3 and Volume 2 ISBN 92-1-148215-1.
3. After Prohibition: An adult approach to drug policies in the 21st century. Edited by Timothy Lynch. Cato Institute, 2000.
4. Busted: Stone cowboys, narco-lords and Washington's war on drugs. Edited by Mike Gray. Thunder's Mouth Press/Nation Books, 2002.
5. Crime School: Money Laundering-True crime meets the world of business and finance. Chris Mathers. Firefly Books, 2004.
6. Drug Crazy: How we got into this mess and how we can get out. Mike Gray. Routledge, 2000.
7. Drugs and Narcotics in History. Edited by Roy Porter and Mikulas Teich. Cambridge University Press, 1995.
8. Drugs *and Society: US Public Policy.* Jefferson M. Fish (editor), Roman and Littlefield, 2006.
9. El Imperio de la Droga: Narcotráfico, economía y sociedad en Los Andes. Francisco E. Thoumi. Editorial Planeta Colombiana, 2002.
10. El Otro Poder: Las redes del narcotráfico, la política y la violencia en Mexico. Jorge Fernández Menéndez. Nuevo Siglo Aguilar, 2001.
11. Ending the War on Drugs: A solution for America. Dirk Chase Eldredge. Bridge Works Publishing Company, 2000.
12. Heavy Traffic: 30 years of headlines and major ops from the case files of the DEA. David Robbins. Chamberlain Bros., 2005.
13. ILLICIT: How smugglers, traffickers, and copycats are hijacking the global economy. Moises Naim. Doubleday, 2005.

14. The Art and Science of Money Laundering: Inside the commerce of the international narcotics traffickers. Brett F. Woods. Paladin Press, 1998.
15. The Economic Results of Prohibition by Clark Warburton. 1932 Columbia University Press. The book was reprinted by AMS PRESS, INC. in 1968.
16. The Money Launderers: Lessons from the drug wars – how billions of illegal dollars are washed through banks & businesses. Robert E. Powis. Probus Publishing Company, 1992.
17. Toward Liquor Control by Raymond B. Fosdick and Albert L Scott, Harper and Brothers Publishers, New York and London 1933.
18. Why Our Drug Laws have Failed and What We Can Do About It: A judicial indictment of the war on drugs. Judge James P. Gray. Temple University Press, 2001.

Printed in the United States
96252LV00002B/100/A